SITES UNSEEN

SITES UNSEEN

Edited by Dianne Harris and D. Fairchild Ruggles

LANDSCAPE AND VISION

UNIVERSITY OF PITTSBURGH PRESS

Published by the University of Pittsburgh Press, Pittsburgh PA 15260

Copyright © 2007, University of Pittsburgh Press

Manufactured in the United States of America

Printed on acid-free paper

10 9 8 7 6 5 4 3 2 1

Frontispiece: Markus Rätz, *Binocular View*, 2001. Color photogravure 22 $^1/_2$ x 27 $^1/_4$ in., edition 60.
Published by Crown Point Press. Reproduced courtesy of Markus Rätz and ProLitteris.

Library of Congress Cataloging-in-Publication Data

Sites unseen : landscape and vision / edited by Dianne Harris and D. Fairchild Ruggles.

   p. cm.

  Includes bibliographical references and index.

  ISBN-13: 978-0-8229-4308-2 (cloth : alk. paper)

  ISBN-10: 0-8229-4308-5 (cloth : alk. paper)

  ISBN-13: 978-0-8229-5959-5 (pbk.: alk. paper)

  ISBN-10: 0-8229-5959-3 (pbk. : alk. paper)

  1. Landscape architecture—History. 2. Landscape design—History. I. Harris, Dianne Suzette. II. Ruggles, D. Fairchild.

  SB470.5.S58 2007

  712.09—dc22

             2006039162

CONTENTS

ILLUSTRATIONS

PREFACE

IN RECENT YEARS, LANDSCAPE HISTORY HAS GAINED WIDE RECOGNITION FOR ITS many contributions to discussions of nature and the natural, now at the forefront of contemporary analysis. But it remains a discipline still in the process of defining its scope and aims. At this stage in its development, any attempt at a comprehensive volume on landscape and vision would be premature. Conspicuous in their absence from this volume are essays examining South America and Africa. These lacunae are regrettable but not surprising given the current state of the field: only a few landscape historians are at present studying those geographic areas. Thus, as a collection, the book presents a series of case studies linked, not by chronology or geography, but rather by a common investigation of the perception and reception of landscape.

Although advancing the literature on visual theory was not the primary goal for contributors, they inevitably shed new light on some imperative issues as they brought visual theory to bear on the three-dimensional spatial context, especially at the huge scale of landscape. There is, for example, a considerable difference between analyzing a spatial context where landscape is both the medium and the object of representation, and in mimetic representation in painting where "there is no *there* there." It is precisely the spatiality of the experience that separates these studies from those that focus on two-dimensional representations. Our goal in these chapters is not to revisit familiar ground with the same intellectual apparatus that has served us well in the past in which the landscape is a stable entity, but instead to explore and advance new ways of understanding the landscape as embodied experience in which the eye operates in collaboration with the other senses in a dynamic corporeal system.

The chapters in this book should be read not as a monographic argument, but rather as case studies that approach the landscape from a range of perspectives. Although each chapter can stand alone, as a group they offer a coherent set of lessons about the central importance of landscape as a precisely crafted means for understanding the world. The contribution by Martin Jay—an acclaimed scholar of visual theory as well as European intellectual history—shows how the control of vision leads to the control of landscape, and how both belong to the larger problematic project of modernity. Zygmunt Bauman's startling "condemnation of the gardening impulse as a motor of modern totalitarian violence" serves as Jay's point of departure for an incisive analysis of the production of "scenic wonders" through violence to the land or to those working on it. With these disturbing questions of power, Jay provides a framework for subsequent chapters that pursue questions about the control of landscape and vision for political and sometimes violent purposes (see Mitchell, Cosgrove, Harris, Kryder-Reid, and Ruggles). Such texts treat walls, gates, windows, churchyards, architectural drawings, and territorial maps as literal and metaphoric framing devices for personal and institutional ideologies absorbed through the visual perception of landscapes. Other chapters, in particular those by Favro, Isenstadt, and Treib, discuss vision's relationship to corporeal experience when both are mediated by gardens, houses, and city. These authors contend that as movement is framed and organized into sequences, it becomes central to the creation of a staged experience that may carry an aesthetic experience or a sociopolitical agenda.

If societies reveal their changing character most clearly in the ways that they address the "natural" world, then it behooves us to attend in ever more precise ways to the eye's share of that address. What we know—or believe that we know—about landscape is predicated upon certain physical, psychological, and cultural conditions that govern the eye and our knowledge systems. Our ability to observe or to represent any landscape is conditioned by a social contract in which we agree to participate in a mutually understood visual (and verbal) language of form and signs. This requires a sensitive negotiation of empirical and theoretical ways of thinking about landscape. We intend the chapters in this volume to serve as a roadmap pointing to such possible future avenues of research.

No book emerges at once, wholly formed. The seed for this volume was planted at the "Landscape and Vision" symposium held in 2002 at the University of Illinois, Urbana-Champaign. We would like to acknowledge the excellent contributions of all who participated in the presentations and discussions. The symposium, organized by Dianne Harris, was funded by the Brenton and Jean Wadsworth Endowment, the Graham Foundation for Advanced Studies in the Fine Arts, and supported by the Department of Landscape Architecture and the College of Fine and Applied Arts at the University of Illinois, Urbana-Champaign. We are thankful for their support, as well as that of the many individuals who made this publication possible. Although their papers do not appear here, we would like to acknowledge Mirka Beneš and Kathryn Gleason for their participation in the symposium. Robert Riley's contribution was a particularly important one, since he was among the authors of the documents that resulted in the eventual implementation of the doctoral program at the Department of Landscape Architecture at the University of Illinois, Urbana-Champaign, which the symposium celebrated. We are grateful for his inspiring efforts over the past thirty years.

We also wish to thank Gloria Kury formerly of the University of Pittsburgh Press. Her vision has made this printed discourse on vision possible. We also extend our gratitude to the anonymous readers for the press, as well as others who read and generously provided helpful comments on the manuscript, especially John Tagg.

As ever, our thanks to our families: Madeleine and Lawrence Hamlin; Isabel and Oscar Vázquez.

SITES UNSEEN

PART I

LANDSCAPE IN SIGHT

LANDSCAPE AND VISION

Dianne Harris and D. Fairchild Ruggles

LANDSCAPE HISTORIANS AND THEORISTS CAN BENEFIT FROM THE RICH
developments that the field of visual theory has experienced in recent decades. These
perspectives challenge existential beliefs about the world and our place within it, and
thus it is a difficult task—and ultimately an unfinished one. Some historians of the
built environment have been resistant to these new approaches, which they regard as
intellectually elitist because highly technical language is often employed in the questioning of basic philosophical assumptions about the nature of reality, subjectivity,
and authorship. The demand for meticulous and highly specialized reading in such
fields as psychoanalysis and semiotics can be alienating, and yet, these same perspectives can be immensely productive for those who choose to engage with them.

5

How do we know landscape? For most human beings, the primary way of knowing the material world is through vision, the simple act of opening the eyes and looking at an object, a scene, a horizon. The physiological processes engaged when the lid retracts from the eye are, when not impeded by pathologies, universal among humans. Because vision is an embodied experience, it is altered by the infinite range of the possibilities presented by corporeal performance. The body moves in space—quickly or slowly, the head still or moving side to side, up or down—the eyes view a scene, and a cognitive process begins in which particles of light are assembled by the brain to create an ordered image. As W. J. T. Mitchell points out, this dimension of vision as a sensory mechanism "operates in animal organisms all the way from the flea to the elephant."[1] But the act of looking is nevertheless far from simple. It results from a complex array of physical, psychological, and cultural conditions and is studied by scholars in an equally wide spectrum of disciplines. The landscape is similarly produced by physical and cultural conditions and exists on such a large scale that it can rarely be known or discerned through a single, simple glance but is instead perceived by an accumulation of observations in which not only optics but also memory come into play. These two complex phenomena—landscape and vision—are deeply connected since, as Denis Cosgrove has noted, "landscape is a way of seeing."[2]

The etymological link between landscape and vision is ancient; the second part of the word "landscape" derives from the Greek verb *skopein*, which means "to behold, contemplate, examine, or inspect."[3] Visual theory has ancient origins beginning at least as early as the fourth century BCE with Plato and his story of the cave, but in art and architectural history the interest in vision (as distinct from structure and form) is generally attributed to the fourteenth century when architects such as Brunelleschi (1377–1446) and Alberti (1404–1472) began to analyze three-dimensional space perspectivally. Later, in the sixteenth and seventeenth centuries, architects and stage designers constructed not only built form but also the spaces between and beyond the buildings, especially in theaters and piazzas. They worked to control and manipulate visual axes and perception through the use of the stage niche, the scenery, and the organization of seating of the audience, and questioned how spatial illusions could enhance the perception of space without actually changing its dimensions. Moreover, designers experimented with axes of vision to articulate the social relations of the members of the audience, so that the most elite patron knew that s/he enjoyed the most complete view of the stage and actors. In the built environment, the question of representation, in the sense of a picture that substitutes for or depicts a missing object, became less important than these articulations of positions in space and the perception of space by a human viewer.

The new emphasis on the object-viewer relationship occurred when art historians began to critique the term "art history" and to replace it with the more inclusive term "visual culture" in order to signal the shift in emphasis from the work of art to the humans that produced, received and interpreted it. But critical visual theory—like the "new art history"—is hardly new. The application of visual theory dates to classics like Erwin Panofsky's *Perspective as Symbolic Form* (1927) and Ernst Gombrich's *Art and Illusion* (1956). Even Norman Bryson's influential *Vision and Painting: The Logic of the Gaze* of 1983 is nearly a quarter of a century old; Martin Jay published his early works on visuality (such as "Scopic Regimes of Modernity") in the 1980s; and Hubert Damisch's *The Origin of Perspective* first appeared in France in 1987. These works dealt with pictorial space, mimetic representation, art objects, and viewers. But the role of actual three-dimensional space and its representation and perception has remained comparatively unexamined.

Scholars of visual culture interpreted the *meaning* of art differently too: it was understood not to reside uniquely in the work itself but rather to emerge from a complex range of cultural, political, and economic conditions. As a consequence, some historians rejected the producer/product model that had formerly kept the roles of artist, audience, and art distinct and asserted the autonomous existence of the object or image; they instead began to emphasize reception. Because the art object was no longer necessarily central to visual analysis, these scholars opened a door to admit many other kinds of received representations and objects, such as gardens, landscape, and space itself. Moreover when Derrida and others argued that there is no chronological or spatial causality between text and "context"—the very word is problematic —and that the frame that purportedly defines a field is as much a product of the field as of the space external to it, landscape and its attendant concepts of space suddenly became essential to the debate.[4] This kind of scholarship presented an important opportunity to reconsider landscape as neither an object nor a contextual field but as always simultaneously both.

During the last quarter of the twentieth century, art historians and scholars of visual culture and media developed the themes of vision and visuality to sophisticated levels. Studies in visual culture changed significantly when scholars began to read the philosophy, literary theory, and semiotic analysis of French theorists such as Merleau Ponty, Lefebvre, Barthes, Foucault, de Certeau, and Derrida. Such influences prompted visual culture scholars to establish and debate new terms that demanded the deconstruction of the visual field and the analysis of it as a discursive system.[5] According to the new theory, representation could not be regarded as a fixed and neutral relationship among artist, audience, and work of art: instead, those roles became defined as positions, all aspects of which were unstable, interdependent, and articulating political power. In the field of visual culture, the new theory primarily focused on representation and signage. However, to study the history of vision one must trace two paths: one in the pictorial field where representations and iconography are central, and the other in three-dimensional space where the distinction between fictive, created representations and real or natural entities can be hard to distinguish, even before one considers the deconstruction of those definitions and why they matter.

With the appearance of numerous texts during the 1980s and 1990s that focused on theories of vision and visuality, scholars in a range of fields began to question the notion that sight is simply a physiologically determined phenomenon and the world homogeneously perceived.[6] One group of visual culture scholars treated vision as a cultural construction in which perception and reception are configured by aspects of the world that are culturally privileged by specific social groups at moments in time. From this perspective, vision is not innately given or innocent but must be learned, based on the assimilation and use of what Elizabeth Kryder-Reid calls "a visual vocabulary of perception" that may be used as a tool for seeing in a specific manner. According to this assessment, vision is culturally determined and serves as a device for creating connections between sight, space, and social order.[7]

Scholars of poststructuralist theory, in contrast, did not rely on contextual explanations but rather pursued the structure of discourse itself, regarding vision as a discursive system (like language). They examined the ways that discursive systems could produce the positions of image and frame, object and subject, and text and author, all of which are pertinent to the framing of the visual field. They showed that the positions are not fixed, but rather mutually constitutive, emerging from the play of difference in discourse. Although these positions seem to emerge naturally, to be already in place, as the existence of a building implies the prior existence of its architect, poststructuralist theory posits that every element of the discursive field is produced by the discursive system itself. Hence, instead of a socially contextualized vision, we can identify a discourse of vision.

The immediate impact of both forms of this poststructuralist turn was more profound in the study of painting, prints, and photography than in the study of the built environment. Vision and representation became the subject of serious inquiry in fields such as art history, geography, cinema, feminist studies, psychology, and, to a lesser degree, architecture. As a means for apprehending space, visual theory should also serve as a productive tool of analysis within the field of landscape studies, and yet it has been virtually ignored.[8] This is surprising considering the existence of such well-known mediating devices for vision as the Claude Glass (a handheld framed glass, sometimes tinted) and the stereoscope. Dating from the eighteenth and nineteenth centuries, respectively, these devices were intended to manipulate vision in order to generate a specific experience for the viewer. The Claude Glass was produced for viewing landscape, creating both a frame and an atmosphere for particular landscape settings that could be manipulated by the individual holding the device. The stereoscope facilitated views of a range of subjects (including pornography, a practice which may have been responsible for the devaluation of the stereoscope) but made landscape views into arresting experiences for observers who would frequently jump back from the mechanism after a first glance revealed a startling depth of perspective. It blinded the viewer's peripheral vision and controlled perspective in order to create dramatic illusions of a landscape that appeared real.[9] Implicit in the use of both instruments was the assumption that landscapes require or are improved by mediation for visual comprehension. In each case, devices guide the eye to see in a culturally privileged manner. Much like the twentieth-century mirror projects of the environmental artist Robert Smithson, these devices made the viewer aware that visual experiences such as retinal fusion are the result of prior conditioning.[10] Mechanisms such as the Claude Glass and stereoscope can be understood to perform the task that W. J. T. Mitchell has called "showing seeing . . . they make seeing show itself, put it on display, and make it accessible to analysis."[11]

In vernacular landscape studies, there is a strong tradition of careful observation —the method advocated and most skillfully practiced by John Brinkerhoff Jackson. But historical research based on the use and application of critical visual theory remains scarce. Although reading the landscape is a useful analytical tool, it is an essentially descriptive technique that often reveals only partial and even misleading information.[12] Furthermore, such readings ignore the fact that all looking is motivated from the outset by intellectual or political investments. Just as the idea of the sightseer assumes that a location will be consumed in a uniform manner (by any viewer or tourist, since most tourism is predicated on this assumption), so too this method assumes that all readers will view and understand a landscape in the same way. But such readings are undermined by a fundamental flaw because both location and viewer are contingent upon each other. Vision is neither universal nor neutral in its motivations and operations.

Some scholars, such as Jay Appleton, have used studies of specific types of vision as a foundation for their research into environment and behavior. Appleton's prospect-refuge theory is based on the notion that landscape aesthetic preferences stem from universally held and evolutionarily determined desires for sites that provide an unobstructed view over surrounding territory (to search for prey or observe a predator's approach) while simultaneously fulfilling the desire to retreat into a protected realm.[13] More recently, landscape architects and environmental planners have used computer simulations and human focus groups in visual assessment studies that predict the aesthetic impact of environmental change in specific regions. Environmental psychophysiologists use landscape representations (paintings and photographs) to measure human physiological responses to images of specific settings. Both of these modes of scholarship link landscape and optics. But they treat landscapes as primarily a visual and therefore aesthetic entity, and they regard vision as a physiological and universal phenomenon. Their methods therefore turn a blind eye to cultural conditioning and political motivation.

Vision is a powerful sense. Humans have the ability to control vision and therefore feel empowered in ways that are less available with the other senses. Sounds and smells can, for example, pervade spaces in uncontrollable manners, crossing architectural boundaries in ways that images cannot. To avoid a scent or noise in a room, one leaves the space, but to avoid a view, one can simply close one's eyes.[14] Views can be created, controlled, manipulated, and even eliminated with the blink of an eye, and this ease privileges the eye as an organ for analysis since we "own" it more consciously than we do our other senses.

Vision remains an essential tool for understanding and analyzing the built environment, but it does not operate in isolation from the other senses. Sight, by virtue of its location in the body, is mobile and occurs in consonance with touch, hearing, and smell. The tradition that equates observation with scholarship, together with studies that privilege landscape as an aesthetic entity, occasionally have provoked claims that vision receives too much attention in scholarly publications. Indeed, some scholars complain that examinations of the haptic, auditory, and mobile aspects of landscape have received little scholarly attention.[15] The criticism is just, but the problem is not the privilege accorded to vision but rather the simplistic way in which the visual and the descriptive are conflated.

Because vision is understood as an embodied sense, the study of sight should be a study of bodily movement and sensation. Sunlight and shade are visual effects, felt in the body as heat and cold (not to mention their role in circadian rhythms, depression, and the production of vitamin D). In this volume, vision is explored in multifaceted and historical forms, because the complex relationship between landscape and vision demands extended critical inquiry. This does not entail removing vision from the other senses or denying their impact. The study of landscape may be, as some have claimed, ocularcentric; however, visual theory itself remains little explored and underutilized in the field. As Dell Upton has noted, "If vision is indeed so privileged, then scholars are lamentably incompetent in making use of it. Vision's great power to frame and to define seems to be lost between eye and pen. Consequently, scholarly analysis of visual evidence remains curiously descriptive and inarticulate."[16] Moreover, Kate Soper has argued that privileging the gaze does not detract from studying other sensory responses. Yet she also cautions that a more sensorially inclusive approach to landscape analysis is not necessarily more universal or democratic.[17]

In the studies of visuality and visual theory that emerged in the last quarter of the twentieth century, landscape was rarely the object of inquiry. Nonetheless, there is an abundance of theoretical material on vision relevant to scholars of landscape.

In return, landscape scholars can make a significant contribution to the field, for what they investigate is how vision occurs in environments so huge, enveloping, and elusive that they can be "seen" only as remembered images linked sequentially in time. The existing literature on vision is useful, but it should be understood only as a starting point for scholarship that will lead in new and fruitful directions. In particular, the interdisciplinary nature of the study of visual theory allows students of landscape to pose questions based, not on direct observation alone, but instead on apparatus that engenders more profound analysis.[18]

In mapping and representing the earth, geographers and historians have asked: Where do we situate ourselves in the perception and conceptualization of place and space? In defining a center and its margins (or infinity), what values are expressed, implicitly or explicitly? What are the political ramifications of such relationships? How are human perception or perceptual modes reflected in the built environment?[19] The fields of semiotics and psychoanalysis take a different approach, examining the positions of subject and object in the visual field and the way that each is constituted: How then does identity—in the elemental senses of self-consciousness and autonomy —emerge from the act of seeing?

Michel Foucault and Michel de Certeau have taught us to give great weight to the institutions that govern our modes of seeing and produce subjectivity.[20] How, they have asked, is the power entailed in vision institutionally regulated? How have individuals, political forces, and social groups controlled or attempted to shape the visual field? Can we identify moments of disruption or subversion in which power relations are altered by manipulating the positions of viewer and viewed within the visual field?[21] On one hand, these institutions are seen to be inscribed spatially in specific places, so that we can interrogate the relationship between vision and location. On the other hand, they are effective because of a *dislocation* that allows them to operate not as places but as spaces that are neither here nor there but everywhere.[22] Vision, too, is both precisely located and broadly spatial. It is in the eye but encompasses specific objects in the foreground and swathes of background too extensive to be captured by a single glance. More importantly, because vision engages knowledge and memory, it shifts rapidly, even imperceptibly, between specific moments and places, present and past experiences; the way one sees a landscape now is deeply affected by the memory of seeing it in the past or by prior knowledge brought by the viewer even before the first encounter with that landscape.

The question of nature, illusion, and "the real" should be at the center of landscape inquiry.[23] However, "the real" is particularly problematic. It entails far more than questioning the notion of objective reality as distinct from the viewer's own subjectivity. According to that understanding, "the real" is not visible in a pure sense because it is filtered through perception, comprehension, interpretation, and the viewer's own identity and desire. The world is knowable but only in terms negotiated by the subject.[24] However, visual theorists influenced by semiotics regard "the real" as beyond reach, not because of the vagaries of personal perspective but because the subject has no direct access to reality, only to the signs that represent it (themselves formed not as absolutes with resident meaning but rather as plays of difference and social coding). For theorists following the psychoanalytic work of Jacques Lacan, "the real" is utterly unknowable and inextricably tied to the question of subjectivity. Lacanians argue that the subject, ever separated from the world, only realizes the existence of that objective world, that thing which is not him/herself, through the act of vision. Vision does not unite subject with object so much as it discloses the eternal chasm between them. According to John Tagg:

> In relation to Lacan's discussion of vision . . . it is clear that the Real is what cannot be encountered. It is what the eye must shield itself against and, indeed, it is in the recoil from this unwelcome, scorching encounter that the split occurs from which the subject emerges, separated from the world as object, but hanging on its loss, for which the elusive object of the look's desire will henceforth stand. It is not, therefore, a matter of a filter through which the Real is subjectively known. The Real is radically unknowable and the product of this loss is the subject for whom the Real will only be traced in its interruptions, parapraxes and other returns of the repressed.[25]

The frame becomes an important element in this respect. It *appears* to make a distinction between "the real" (nature) and the representational (art), and thus appears to determine positions within the spatial field and to establish the very categories of "real" and representation. But what is the spatial location of the frame? Does the frame belong to the represented object (the view), or to its exterior (the outside that defines an inside), or to the viewer (shaping our ability to see)?[26] Derrida wrote that the frame, or "parergon," separates the object from the non-object (or in our case, between landscape and everything that is not the landscape). Yet inasmuch as it produces an object *qua* object (or work of art *qua* art), it also belongs properly to the object. The object could not exist without its frame.[27] How does the apparent naturalism of the frame, both defining the view and emerging from it, lend authority to these spatial relations?

Like the frame, authorship is often regarded as natural and as external to the work. Consideration of author and audience can be useful in investigations that examine the role of the designer and patron in shaping a landscape.[28] Does either the architect or patron produce the built landscape that then generates a receiving audience? Or, does the very category, "built landscape," generate the categories of both architect and audience so that the work itself precedes its supposed author? To what extent does the audience contribute to or control the construction of meaning? Is meaning already in place before the artist/author expresses him or herself? Barthes famously argued that writing is the absent author's trace and, once released in the form of written (alienated) marks, becomes an artifact external to the author's person. He argued that with the liberation of the text, authorial intention is lost so that the text depends entirely upon context and the reader for comprehension. However, the context and the reader are similarly dependent, unstable, and infinite.[29] According to Foucault, the text is not simply detached from author, but, rather, discourse constitutes text, author, and reader (for which we may substitute landscape, architect, and viewer).

Dell Upton has asserted that whatever meaning is ascribed to landscape is to be treated with caution: "Seeing is not always believing. . . . [B]ecause the meaning and experience of landscape are fragmented and debated, the political and economic processes that shape landscape are not the final word on its meaning."[30] Visual theory combined with deep archival and interdisciplinary historical research brings the seen and the unseen together to uncover a range of experiences that delve beyond the "landscape's pretenses" and aesthetic veil.[31] Much as with the question of nature and "the real," there is in the question of meaning an insistent tension between an empirical model of cause and effect on one hand, and on the other, the discursive model that posits a field in which each position is contingent, an effect of the internal and external rules of the discourse itself. Landscape may have an enduring physical presence independent of culture, but it is unlikely that human beings have access to it except through the mediation of signs. In other words, there is a philosophical quandary: Lacanian theory insists that the viewing subject is constituted by a discursive field in which neither the subject nor the object (world) precedes one another, yet like no other object, landscape seems always to already exist.

Most contemporary architectural theorists seem unaware that vision functions so as to establish the subject's position in a field of relations.[32] Perhaps the aggressive "thing-ness" of a building has distracted them from the debate that has raged among scholars of painting, prints, and film. Be that as it may, at various places and times, designers, patrons, and others have sought to direct the gaze and the visual experiences of known and imagined viewers in landscapes. In all such instances, vision is neither simply a phenomenon of the eye and the mind, nor is it a pictorial representation created to mimic or analyze visual experience. Vision is instead a three-part entity in which viewer, viewed, and space together constitute the visual field existing always in a state of tension. The principal tools for analyzing and interpreting the relationships among viewer, viewed, and space include examination of the science of optics, culturally produced habits of perception, scopic regimes, psychoanalysis, and iconographies.[33]

Although finding evidence of an audience's reception of the visual world is difficult, some aspects of intention and perception are clear.[34] Fundamentally, landscapes, like paintings, are subject to the discriminating eye of the beholder, which is to say, we see in them not only what we want to see, but also what we are trained and directed to see. The art historian Michael Baxandall addressed the latter with his concept of the "period eye," meaning that in particular historical moments and locales, the viewer's response to art reveals the "culturally relative pressures of perception" from which specific "cognitive styles" develop.[35] Conceived for Baxandall's study of *quattrocento* Florentine painting, the notion was adapted and applied again recently in Marvin Trachtenberg's study of medieval urban open space on the Italian peninsula.[36] Our own application of those concepts to landscape history therefore has an important precedent in architectural history. What is more, Denis Cosgrove asserted nearly twenty years ago that landscape is a learned way of seeing that is "visual ideology made hegemonic."[37] But it is not monolithically construed, and an important contribution of this volume is the exploration of variable modes of landscape seeing that have been learned or taught in specific cultural and physical contexts.

We may not be certain about the ways specific individuals or groups actually saw the landscape at a given moment in history, but examining various types of evidence and embracing a range of approaches allows us to reconstruct and imagine the practices for viewing implicit in both sites and artifacts. Although some aspects of the subject's experience as s/he looked through the frame, the screen, within the boundary, beyond the wall, or in the drawing must remain unknown, we can nonetheless make informed scholarly assertions about the intended subject and underlying rationales. Baxandall's models provided a means for drawing the particular toward an understanding of something more general—of linking the case study to a broader understanding of cultural history in particular places and times.

Pliny the Elder wrote that having rosemary in a garden "sharpens the eyesight." According to Indra Kagis McEwen, "sharp" eyesight in this case referred to the accuracy of remembered images.[38] Good memory conferred status and cultural authority to those who possessed it. Much like the members of the Lincean Academy of the seventeenth century (who called themselves "the sharp-sighted ones"), Pliny valued visual precision and equated scopic virtuosity—for example, the ability to see across long distances or microscopically—with intellectual authority.[39]

Contemporary environmental artists, such as Robert Smithson, Nancy Holt, Robert Irwin, and James Turrell, have approached landscape as a medium for experiments in modulating vision, by making some feature of landscape and/or its natural processes more visible.[40] Many landscape architects understand their task in parallel fashion. They manipulate landscape forms to induce ordered spatial and visual experiences of significance. For them, this process is an assumed aspect of their profession, and manipulation of the eye is taken for granted. Yet landscapes are often regarded by both scholars and the general public as transparent or even "invisible." The designed landscape seems common enough to go virtually unnoticed in everyday life. For example, on a typical architect's plan drawing, the buildings are figural while the landscape is "ground"; the architecture emerges as solid, material, and substantive, while landscape, if it appears as anything other than a white void, seems soft, formless.

Our tendency to regard landscape as neutral ground may be enhanced through architectural means to make the viewer adopt a preferred view. The result is what might be called "spaces of constructed visibility," in which forms are masked or revealed so as to render "things seeable in a specific way."[41] If design can enhance vision, it can also hinder it, making spaces of constructed invisibility. In the Islamic world, such invisibility historically maintained the divide between the sexes and between public and private space. In antebellum America, rows of trees separated the plantation manor from the slave quarters, hiding from view slaves whose sweat and toil produced the wealth that supported the owners.[42]

If landscape is less frequently noticed and harder to discern than architecture, it is by that very fact more persuasive. Landscape is "always already there" and thus seems not to have been created but simply to *be*, not a constructed form but rather a preexisting or even primordial one. It appears above all "natural" because it is composed of plants, soil, geological formations, sunlight, and water and because it seems to exist in the absence of human management or design. Even human interventions such as topographical leveling, deforestation, and drainage appear natural when landscape and nature are thus conflated. From an analytical perspective, this association is deeply problematic. Hiding human agency naturalizes cultural processes that are by no means spontaneous or innate. Even more importantly, ideologies and social constructs are rendered invisible, or at the very least, made to appear equally inherent. Scholars of the English landscape and its textual and visual representations have demonstrated that the rural and garden scenery of the eighteenth century masked the political, economic, and social hegemony of an elite landed class.[43] With verdant rolling hills, shade trees, serpentine waterways, and distant vistas, the so-called picturesque landscape gave the appearance *par excellence* of a benign Arcadia, justly given in disproportionate amounts to a powerful landed minority. The distribution thus seemed morally right, an inherent characteristic of the land itself, ordained by heavenly powers. The frequent presumption that landscapes are God-given and natural has led with equal frequency to the notion that what we believe we see in the landscape must be so. When one combines this premise with scientific assumptions about the physiology of vision ("seeing is believing"), it becomes easy to imagine nature, landscape, and vision as a powerful trio for conveying ideology.

Herein lies one of the perplexing ironies of landscape: it is regarded as natural and eternally present, and yet it is also ignored as if it did not matter. How then can the study of landscape and vision illuminate cultural discourses that are essentially spatial, yet normalized to the point of invisibility? How does one study such an elusive, unstable object? One strategy entails focusing on mechanisms that are not easily seen, such as the frame, the controlling perspective, illusionism, the lens or screen through which we are induced to look, and the wall or landform that intentionally conceals. Spatially determined, vision can support the construction of "difference" through what is revealed and what remains concealed—marking class, race, and gender. What we see, and the manner in which the built world directs our gaze, contributes to our daily instruction about insiders and outsiders, privilege and denial, domination, submission, and, in some cases, resistance.

In their studies of race, Owen Dwyer and John Paul Jones have pointed out that sociospatial epistemologies are largely visually determined.[44] Single-point perspective and its close corollary, the Cartesian mode of viewing, which is predicated on space that is at once infinite and centered,[45] assigns subjects to a specific social space. Moreover, the privileged vantage point assumed in surveillance typically belongs to a white male "secure in his position as a surveyor of the social terrain." Sociospatial boundaries of race, Dwyer and Jones contend, derive in part from the mode of vision now widely known as "the Western gaze."[46] In the United States, subjects are literally mapped into zones that imply hierarchies often related to racial privilege and exclusion. Belonging is understood through cues designed into and reinforced by the built world. The ghetto, the barrio, the reservation, and the suburb are defined by clear boundaries in which individuals are firmly placed through categories of difference. Although these can be breached, social identities too often depend on the observance of these boundaries.

The ability to "see race" and, vice versa, the inability to see individuals in another race, can demonstrate the way vision, as a cultural construction, becomes spatially embodied. In the antebellum South, for instance, fugitive slaves sometimes traveled between plantations at night without being discovered because plantation

DIANNE HARRIS AND D. FAIRCHILD RUGGLES

overseers could not distinguish one slave from another and believed that blacks actually bore few traits of individual distinction. Ironically, the fact that overseers literally could not see the differences among slaves provided an opportunity for resistance as slaves took advantage of white myopia in making their way toward freedom.[47]

The built environment is where we encounter the ironic simultaneity of both the visibility and invisibility of whiteness in the United States, where whites are everywhere presumed to be the dominant and majority culture. Whites are always portrayed as typical Americans, even as the authentic Americans. Similarly, persons are presumed male unless specifically marked as female, so that male forms neutral ground against which the female can be perceived only as different and other-than-male. Gender and race have many parallels. Just as blackness appears as a measure of racial difference from the perceived neutral ground of whiteness, when "woman" is produced as a generic category that supplements "man," her marginality is ensured. This strategy of addition leaves the initial structure (of patriarchy, of history, of architecture as a field) intact, homogenous, and replete with authority. Until the 1980s, for example, women were excluded from the canons affirmed in art history survey books, which then provided proof that they did not create art. If acknowledged as producers of art and architecture, women were treated as a monolithic category that existed only by virtue of a binary relationship to the dominant category "man." Even today in texts meant to be inclusive, the term "women" appears in the index, which has, of course, no listing for "men." The very selection of them as an object of study produces the effect of marginalization.[48] Continually reinforced by the sociopolitical and economic constructs of American life, white and male privilege and their correlated notions of race, gender, and minority status have become, like the landscape in which they appear, naturalized and impossible to see until they are revealed through social activism.[49] Race, gender, and vision are all social and cultural constructs. The special power of vision lies in its inherent ability to persuade (seeing is believing) and in its ongoing collusion with systems and practices of authority.

The apparent naturalness of vision makes it seem to occur without agency. Whether or not we want to see a landscape as created through human endeavor, or simply arising from climate, geography, and ecology, most humans retain an image of an Edenic world, "pure" and "natural." An ideal of a primordial world anchors the three major Western religions: Judaism, Christianity, and Islam. In all three, the earth, oceans, plants, and animals are created prior to the appearance of humankind, but the appearance of Adam and Eve initiates a declensionist narrative. Placed in a garden they are enjoined to use creation, to subdue nature.[50] The Bible gives humankind "dominion" over the fish, birds, and animals of the earth, as well as the plants and trees, with the directive to "be fruitful and multiply." The Islamic narrative is strikingly similar to that of the Old Testament. After creating nature, God appoints the human being as the trustee who controls it: and thus a Qur'anic verse (2:29) enjoins: "He made for you all that lies within the earth." The idea of the world as a manifestation of God is extended in the Qur'an so that natural phenomena such as lightning, rain, and the change from day to night are identified as "signs for those who believe" (30: 20–25).

In granting humankind the responsibility and power of possession, God gives the right—even the mandate—of domination, a dominance that always threatens danger because of the ease with which it accommodates violence. The violence may be explicit, as in the battles waged between communities over territory and resources. Alternatively it may occur through the subjugation of the laboring class (or sex), as in slavery and medieval serfdom. It may also take the less noticeable forms of a "tyranny of vision" and of a "violence to the land for aesthetic effect," as when pleasing vistas are produced through the violence of hard physical labor (as Martin Jay's essay in this volume proposes). In all these cases, power and authority operate not by persuasion, but by coercion. The troubling connection between aesthetic delight in landscape and the toil of producing that landscape has passed virtually without comment in the scholarly literature, perhaps because its mechanisms—like those of the landscape itself—have been hidden from view so as not to interrupt the experience of pleasure with harsh realities. The suppression of references to labor and production is not only a historical phenomenon: in gardens visited by tourists today, such as the missions of California and Mexico, the history of toil and oppression has been denied for the sake of modern delight in gardens bursting with colorful bloom.

Pleasure is as important as the issues of control, authority, and motivation in assessing the powers of vision. To look at a landscape, whether it is a garden, park, wilderness, or even an urban panorama, is to activate the visual senses. Color, motion, form, and light combine to create scenes that can be deeply moving in their aesthetic content and that provoke judgments of preference. Most obviously, preference can be a tool humans use to assess and "read" the landscape in order to survive. Recent work in the field of landscape perception explores human visual preferences and the sense of well-being that certain kinds of landscape can provide.[51] Vision and its pleasures then, present both cultural and environmental strategies for critically assessing the benefits provided by landscape.

Visual pleasure is deeply political. The feminist geographer Gillian Rose links the "pleasure of looking" with the gender politics of the development of the field of human geography. The geographer's gaze, she contends, is male; he sees the landscape as female, and therefore mysterious and elusive. Repressing the aesthetic pleasure of viewing landscape was central to the male geographer's mission since the emotive pleasure of that which was seen was not considered scientific. What Rose calls the "analytic look" has been essential for the discipline of landscape history, yet she claims it has become an ambivalent pleasure for those scholars in a range of disciplines devoted to understanding landscape beyond its aesthetic dimensions.[52] This insistence upon a quasi-scientific rigor received considerable reinforcement from the field's art historical heritage. The field, having grown largely from art history, has long employed its analyses of form, typology, iconography, and style.[53] Even today, as landscape historians adopt more interdisciplinary methodologies, they remain reluctant to engage visual desire and its attendant psychoanalytic questions.

The pleasurable aspects of looking at the landscape deserve greater attention. Landscapes are visually and intellectually compelling not just because they are complex and replete with visual subtleties, but also because they are in many cases quite beautiful. When not conventionally so, they are at least aesthetically intriguing, and there is pleasure to be gleaned in the visual examination of a complex setting or its representations. Historians are often drawn to the visual by the beauty of the subjects, whether drawings, paintings, maps, photographs, buildings, gardens, or landscapes. Arguably, without the pleasure of viewing, we might never have given our subjects a second look, let alone the prolonged scrutiny required by scholarly analysis. Yet, the very power of vision to provide pleasure is another dimension of its strength as a tool for enforcing dominant cultural constructs. Aesthetic beauty can seduce powerfully as it acts as a veil that masks other possible readings[54] and sometimes it is necessary to disregard questions of beauty to see how else a landscape matters. The pleasure of viewing can be acknowledged without allowing it to limit the analytical format and prevent alternative landscape narratives from emerging.

Scholars have seldom addressed the range of devices used to control or manipulate vision in space. These include perspectival manipulation, optical illusion, panopticism, screening, selective presentation, framing, masking, re-presentation, and positioning the viewer. In the case of the stupas of Buddhist religious precincts, the control is overt. The faithful follow a sacred path (*pradakshina patha*) where enclosing walls restrict vision in order to enhance prayer and inward spiritual experience. Similarly, the medieval labyrinth offered the pilgrim both a real and a symbolic path, leading forward and backward until reaching the goal. Many picturesque or irregular gardens of the eighteenth century, such as Stourhead (fig. 1.1), were carefully designed to provide a sequence of movement and vision, controlled through screens of plants and topographic variation, according to intricate iconographic programs. These are explicit examples of intentionality. By contrast, other landscapes, such as the quadrangle of a college campus with its paths that can be used or bypassed, guide the viewer through a sequence that shapes experience, yet may also be ignored or overlooked. The built environment is not rigidly deterministic: it usually suggests rather than controls, and patterns of use frequently depend on a range of unpredictable variables, including human volition.[55]

The most famed of such site engineering is found in the seventeenth-century gardens at Vaux-le-Vicomte and Versailles. F. Hamilton Hazelhurst's precise analysis of both sites reveals the existence of a series of optical illusions (fig. 1.2).[56] Garden axes might appear either foreshortened or longer than they actually are, and changes in grade are masked from specific viewpoints to first hide and then reveal the spectacular waterworks, terraces, and other landscape elements. The control of vision and perception through the manipulation of landforms allows revelation of the garden's features to occur in a specific sequence and enhances its drama and iconographic program. Similar techniques are evident in courtly, noble, and aristocratic gardens throughout Europe. The seventeenth and eighteenth centuries saw a veritable explosion of such formal gardens at the country seats of European aristocracy from

Figure 1.1. Henry Hoare, Stourhead, c. 1741–1765. Photo: D. Harris.

Great Britain to Russia. Directing the gaze became a form of staging; looking and performance were choreographed simultaneously. Estate boundaries are screened through tree plantations or the ha-ha fence (a wall sunken from view that kept grazing animals from entering the manicured grounds), which makes the grounds of the estate seem more extensive than they actually are. Manipulations of ground plane, terrace walls, and planting allows directed "views" of overt theatricality.[57] This garden culture is by no means an exclusively Western phenomenon of any specific age. Illusions of expansiveness also became a part of Japanese garden design. By masking middle-ground features with hedges and walls, a distant view, known as borrowed scenery, could be incorporated into the garden.

The all-seeing eye facilitated by the bird's-eye view, the elevated perspective or panorama, the map, or the axonometric drawing all overlook spatial boundaries. Studies of aerial views, such as those of airplane pilots, and axonometric drawings of

Figure 1.2. André Le Nôtre, garden, Vaux-le-Vicomte, c. 1658–1661. Photo: D. F. Ruggles.

garden views demonstrate the ideological power inherent in representational forms that allow the perception of visual control from above.[58] In panoptic vistas, the viewer brings a landscape into being but remains unseen, and therefore is imbued with a globalizing sense of totality and with an imperial and even divine power. Such techniques give the spectator the guise of neutrality, but, in fact, they serve as powerful tools for the conveyance of specific points of view and specific hierarchies of information. Consider the selective nature of maps, aerial views, and perspective drawings: certain features can be eliminated or downplayed, while others are highlighted or even exaggerated, a technique Raymond Williams referred to as "selective erasure."[59]

The link between vision and dominance is important. The role of power relations in space, representation, and performativity has been examined with keen interest not only by scholars but also artists and the public. In *Discipline and Punish* (1975), Foucault proposed panopticism as a system of coercion that is simultaneously particular and immense, and that serves as an instrument for a power structure that appears "natural" and therefore unassailable.[60] Foucault used the term "natural" not in the sense of an ideology, but in the sense of a set of internalized relations accepted by self-regulating subjects who do not fully perceive the system to which they submit. The force necessary to maintain the system is not exerted from outside through overt violence but emerges from within as a persuasive and pervasive system of coercion that is not seen because the system of power is indistinguishable from the objects that are regulated and subdued by it. Thus, it appears to be natural.[61] As John Tagg has shown, this regime of truth gains exceptional power in photographs used as evidence in courts of law.[62]

The concepts of "the real," "truth," and "the natural" are of crucial importance for landscape studies. The landscape is often perceived and represented as a natural and therefore unconstructed entity that is uninflected by relations of power. Contemporary artists such as Bill Brown, Denis Beaubois, and the Surveillance Camera Players reveal the links between vision and power in acts of seemingly innocent watching (fig. 1.3). The Surveillance Camera Players have staged performances in the public streets of New York, Sydney, and other cities in which they face one of the ubiquitous surveillance cameras on a street corner or shopping district, addressing it with placards that state "You are watching me" and "Who am I? What's my name?"[63] Instead of being everywhere and nowhere, the camera is suddenly engaged as a specifically located instrument whose purpose is to document and control human presence. In the garden, despite its claim to innocence, surveillance is no less present. As Martin Jay points out in this volume, supervision and surveillance are common activities for gardeners who maintain a vigilant eye for weeds, mildew, and pest invasions.

Screening and framing create powerful devices for the selective presentation of landscape elements. In the palaces of Islamic Spain, for example, *miradors* (literally viewing places) not only formalized the vista and drew attention to its pleasures, they also enhanced sovereign authority over the land.[64] Similarly, in Mughal palaces of South Asia, window frames called *jharokas* played an important role in producing the public image of the emperor, framing his figure as he appeared for view and providing a ceremonial locus similar to that of a throne or hall of audience (fig. 1.4). In the landscape itself, carefully placed vegetation affects the visual experience. Leaves and

Figure 1.3. Surveillance Camera Players and Denis Beaubois, *Amnesia,* c. 2002. Photo: Surveillance Camera Players.

Figure 1.4. *Jharoka* window, Fatehpur-Sikri, India, c. 1570s. Photo: D. F. Ruggles.

branches may partially occlude sight, and water can duplicate a view through reflection or serve as a device for veiling. The Taj Mahal famously has a setting in which the white marble memorial shimmers in bright sunlight or looms through a veil of "bright water," to borrow James Wescoat's apt phrase.[65]

As windows between architecture and the landscape, frames frequently serve the pragmatics of lighting and thermal modification. But they also "capture" a piece of space, ordering the gaze with a degree of precision rarely found with other viewing devices. The frame conjures a positioned observer who complies within specific constraints (looking up, down, left, and right) with its imperatives. From royal thrones that allowed a specific, authoritative view over the court and its territories, to baroque churches with their perspectival ceiling frescos intended to be viewed from a specific location demarcated on the floor below, controlled vision depends on the location of the eye. In the expanded scale of landscape where the viewer is usually mobile, control of vision is always difficult, and the frame plays a crucial role in helping the viewer to read and interpret what s/he sees.

If some walls reveal landscape elements, others can hide them. At Monticello the framing is so selective, it might be better termed a masking. A colonial technique, masking can be seen as another form of the selective erasure mentioned above. Thomas Jefferson located the service wings of his compound at Monticello below grade so that they would be hidden from the primary facades and gardens of the house. Moreover, the hilltop location of the house provided Jefferson with a commanding, nearly panoptic view over the surrounding countryside, while the rural and elevated location simultaneously allowed him a refuge from the prying eyes of outsiders. Monticello was an ideal setting for both prospect and refuge: the president could see without being seen, the apparent master of all he surveyed.[66] Similarly, the enclosing walls of nineteenth-century California mission complexes served to control the vision of Native Americans, directing their gazes inward toward a landscape designed to inculcate them with the teachings of the Catholic Church. Isolated from the California landscape they knew and had inhabited, they were coerced day by day to find refuge in the mission landscape that taught European notions of piety and citizenship.

Vision is a prism for understanding (and misunderstanding) space. Study of the ways people see is as important as studying the objects of the view. Historians have long approached architecture and landscape as entities apprehended with eyes endowed with perfect clarity, objectivity, and control. But sight is not autonomous; nor is it universal. Like the built environment that is viewed, vision is itself a construction. Thus it can be analyzed as having its own mode, style, or habit in which framing, occlusion, illusion, and the place of the viewer play as important a role in perception as the object itself. The intense interest in visual theory among art historians and scholars of "visual culture" in recent decades may inspire historians of architecture and landscape to make similar theoretical inquiries, although the scale and dimensionality of such spatial studies will surely lead to different conclusions. If landscape studies are to move forward, scholars must begin to explore the variously mediated modes of embodied experience that continuously shape and reshape our understanding of the spaces we inhabit. Such investigations can be politically provocative, disturbing, and even angering, but they ultimately lead us outside the confines of a field long constrained by connoisseurship and devotion to "the beautiful."

Wayne Thiebaud, *Dark Glasses*, 1994.

PART II

CHARTING VISION

LANDSCAPE AND INVISIBILITY

W. J. T. Mitchell

Gilo's Wall and Christo's *Gates*

BEFORE WE TALK ABOUT LANDSCAPE, ABOUT PLACES, SPACES, VISTAS, views, etc., we have to reckon with the blind spots built into vision itself. Every interesting theory of vision since Descartes has grounded its model of the visual process on the figure of the blind man. Seeing, as Bishop Berkeley noted long ago, is grounded in touching, and without the learned coordination of optical and tactile impressions, we would not be able to see the world at all.[1] "The innocent eye is blind," remarks Ernst Gombrich, and this is true at every level, from the physiological to the ethical-political to the aesthetic.[2] The physical eye, trapped in a body that has never moved in space, that has never walked upright, or reached out to touch objects, sees nothing but a blurry chaos of light and color. Relations of figure and ground, the occlusion

33

of objects, estimations of distance, and the relation of colors and objects are all elements of the basic vocabulary of vision, a vocabulary that has to be learned as part of what Berkeley called a "visible language." Seeing, even the most fundamental and transparent acts of taking in objects, is a kind of reading—the kind of reading we experience when we are absorbed in a "page-turner" novel, and the words seem to disappear as we immerse ourselves in the fictional world of the narrative.

But this means that the *experienced* eye is also blind, albeit in a different way from the innocent eye. We learn to see by masking off, editing, ignoring, and overlooking millions of bits of optical data. If we saw everything that presents itself to the retina or the optic nerve or the visual cortex, if we registered all the stimuli bombarding our senses, we would be overwhelmed with sensory overload. We would be plunged into the opposite of darkness and obscurity—into a plenitude of optical sensations, a vortex of light. When novelist José Saramago sets out to describe a society beset by a terrifying plague in his novel *Blindness*, he depicts the blindness not as a darkness, but as an even more horrifying *whiteness*, as if darkness would be the more comforting sensation, a kind of restfulness, in contrast to the painful, dazzling dissolution of visual field that occurs in snow blindness, for instance.[3] Blindness is relatively acceptable; it is the condition that Oedipus seeks as a refuge from his sin. It is the moment of blinding itself that terrifies. The tragic emotion of pity is for the blinded Oedipus; the terror is in the blinding.

The other major focus of invisibility and blindness in the visual field is the presence of other seers. The primal scene of vision is not the separation of light from darkness, but the encounter with the face of the other, usually of the mother. In his classic essay, "The Look," Sartre describes the encounter with the gaze of the other as a kind of hemorrhage in the seer's visual world.[4] Lacan's dialectic of the "eye and the gaze" is a recognition that the visual process is as much about being seen as it is about seeing.[5] We are caught, and "caught out" in the gaze of the other, and we know this with the kind of certainty that comes from our own experience of wanting to catch things that we see, to reach out and grasp them, touch them, make them our own. The scopic is rightly named as a "drive," not merely a cognitive or perceptual process, a weaving of the optical and tactile, just as surely as the vocative drive is a weave of hearing and speaking. The eye is a hungry organ, voracious and thirsty for the milky luminosity of the world. (*Invidia*, the envious, evil eye, notes Lacan, has the legendary effect of drying up a mother's milk.)[6] Only God has a benevolent eye, and only for the brief, passing moment of the creative act when he looks upon his creation and "saw that it was good." But then the trouble starts. He makes the mistake of introducing other minds and other eyes into his world. They see things differently. They want to do more than merely live; they want to know, to see. They are not content with the Tree of Life, but eat of the Tree of Knowledge, which "opens their eyes," and also makes them understand that they are *seen* by God and by each other. The taboo on nakedness, the secrecy of sexual difference, perfectly illustrates the blindness of the experienced eye. Adam and Eve are blind to their nakedness when they are innocent. When they attain experience, the knowledge of good and evil, it is at the price of enforcing a new blindness and invisibility on themselves, concealing their "parts of shame" from each other.

Of all the media and genres of imagery, landscape is the one that makes the constitutive blindness and invisibility of the visual process most evident. We notice this even in the most common injunction in the presence of a landscape prospect: "look at the view." What does that mean? How can one "look at a view"? One looks at objects, figures, faces, bodies, and signs. Our visual system learns to pick out *things* that have names: this tree, that house, those fence posts. So what are we looking at when we look at the view? Everything and nothing. The view is the totality of the objects in our visual field, the relations among them, the entire system or syntax that underlies the language of vision. Looking at the view is like looking at the grammar of a sentence, while forgetting what it is saying. Or it is like "looking at looking," a process that invariably reveals to us the paradoxical invisibility of vision itself. We will never quite see what vision is, no matter how precisely we may describe or depict it.

The paradoxical character of seeing landscape, "looking at the view," is materialized for us most vividly in the phenomena of walls and gates, the things we build around ourselves to obstruct the view, and the holes we punch in those obstructions to allow ourselves to pass through, visually and bodily, what we have erected precisely to prevent such a passage. The wall and the gate (or the window, of course) are what give the *fort-da* game of "now you see it, now you don't," of "peek-a-boo," a physical field of play. They are the architectural manifestations of the scopic drive as a dialectic between what geographer Jay Appleton calls "refuge" and "prospect," the impulse to see and show, on the one hand, and to conceal and hide on the other.[7]

Figure 2.1. Gilo Wall, Jerusalem, c. 2002. Photo: W. J. T. Mitchell.

Consider two recent works of landscape art that dramatize this paradoxical process, the Gilo Wall in Jerusalem, and Christo's *The Gates* in New York City's Central Park. The Gilo Wall (fig. 2.1) was built on a hillside to protect an Israeli settlement in East Jerusalem from snipers in Beit Jala, the neighboring Palestinian village on the hillside facing it.[8] But the settlers, though grateful for the physical security, were unhappy with the ugly visual obstruction of the wall, so they decorated it with a trompe l'oeil painting of the hidden Palestinian landscape (fig. 2.2). When viewed from above and the side, the wall reveals itself as a seam or scar in the landscape, a site that simultaneously divides a lived, social space, and overcomes that division by veiling it with an illusion. The wall is precisely an erection of a blind spot in the landscape, but a blind spot (unlike the larger security wall that is being built to protect Israel

Figure 2.2. Gilo Wall, Jerusalem, c. 2002. Photo: W. J. T. Mitchell.

from the Palestinians) that conceals itself with a veil of illusory transparency. One also sees immediately the contrast between the real and the depicted Palestinian village. The real village is populous, covering the adjacent hillside with housing. The painted village is a picturesque Arabian pastoral, a depopulated landscape dotted by ruins. It shows with remarkable candor the long-standing wish of many Israelis to simply "disappear" the Palestinians along with the signs of their habitation. But not, it should be noted, to disappear them completely. The ruins remain as reminders, a comforting acknowledgment of what and who will have vanished, a kind of melancholy recognition of disappearance that is the central aesthetic emotion of the Romantic picturesque.

This is in sharp contrast to the other kind of candor, the brutal destruction wrought by the Israeli security wall, which extends and extrudes the brutalist architecture of the settlements for some hundred miles, slashing into the West Bank, cutting off Palestinian farmers from their fields, splitting families and friends with the naked simplicity that reminds us of the Berlin Wall and (even more ominously) of the wall around the Warsaw Ghetto.[9] The euphemistically named "fence" (made of concrete slabs ten meters high) will, when completed, take up much more space in the tiny land of Israel/Palestine than the entire city of Jerusalem. This "separation barrier" comes, of course, with numerous gates, and the West Bank more generally has become a land of (usually blocked) gateways. In January 2004, according to the United Nations Office for the Coordination of Humanitarian Affairs (OCHA), there were 59 permanent Israeli checkpoints in the West Bank, 10 partial checkpoints, 479 earth mounds, 75 trenches, 100 roadblocks, and 40 road gates, all designed to disrupt or halt the circulation of Palestinian traffic.[10]

The wall is routinely declared to be a merely "temporary" measure, but it is also widely suspected of being the key tactic in a permanent annexation of Palestinian land that will make the emergence of a viable Palestinian state in a contiguous, sovereign territory an eco-sociological impossibility. Which is worse, the Gilo Wall that disappears itself at the same time as the Palestinians, securing an illusion of peaceful neighborliness in the landscape, or the brutal frankness of the security wall?

Christo's *Gates* invites an even more complex and elusive meditation on the dialectics of landscape and vision (fig. 2.3). *The Gates* drew tourists from around the world, some attracted, no doubt, by the fame of Christo's previous landscape installations, and the very ephemerality of the construction. *The Gates*, unlike the Israeli security walls, was erected with a strict time limit. It literalized by temporalizing the *fort-da* game of appearance and disappearance in the landscape. But the initial reaction to *The Gates* seems to have been one mainly of puzzlement and disappointment. I confess that my own reaction was one of being underwhelmed, feeling that I did not know what to look at or what to make of it. Of course *The Gates* was "pretty." The saffron fabric, when fluttering in the wind, produced a kind of ornamental fringe, adding a surplus enjoyment to what is arguably the single most famous artificial landscape garden in the world. But Central Park was already beautiful. What did *The Gates* add to it? What could it possibly be saying to us that the park itself had not already said?

Figure 2.3. Christo and Jeanne-Claude, *The Gates*, Central Park, New York, 1979–2005.

Photo: W. J. T. Mitchell.

Many of the reactions to *The Gates* were symptomatic of this kind of frustrating elusiveness, the refusal of *The Gates* to "say" anything, or even to *show* anything very surprising. It marked out the winding paths, to be sure, but we already knew that the paths of Central Park are sinuous, variable in width, snaking picturesquely over the hills and through the woods and across the fields. Did we need Christo to show or tell us this? This elusiveness may have been the reason there were so many comparisons of *The Gates* to other things, comparisons that often seemed to be disrespectful. The gates were "seen as" giant croquet wickets, or as a kind of walk-through equivalent of the curtained tunnels of a car wash (fig. 2.4). The color of the saffron fabric was objected to as unfortunately similar to the orange fabric that adorns the temporary fences of construction sites. And the larger purpose of *The Gates* was disturbingly vague, perhaps even vacuous. *The Gates* appeared to suffer in contrast to Christo's *Wrapped Reichstag*, which took a deeply troubled historical monument, the central symbol of Germany's traumatic role in the twentieth century, and seemed to transfigure it, releasing it from the spell of nationalism and resurgent fascism, delivering it as a kind of gift to be unwrapped for a new stage in German history.

The harmlessness and innocence, even prettiness, of *The Gates* seemed at first glance to render it trivial, a passing sensation whose primary virtue was its ephemerality. It was especially disturbing to me that Central Park, a purportedly public space, had only a few months earlier been declared "off limits" by the city of New York for a massive political demonstration against the Republican Party during its August 2004 convention. The reason given was the danger of damage to the Great Lawn, which would have been trampled by the large crowd, and perhaps torn up if the demonstration had been accompanied by rain. "So," I said to myself, "it is okay to take over the entirety of Central Park for a harmless art project, a bit of innocuous urban beautification. But it is not okay to use Central Park as a gathering place for political demonstrations." Like many others, I thought that the time for *The Gates* was past, that it would have made sense when Christo initially proposed it, back in 1979, when it would have helped to transfigure what had become a dangerous jungle, a hideout for muggers and murderers, into a liberated and pacified public space.

But the dialectics of landscape and vision are not always revealed to us at first glance. Sights and sites are memory places that may continue to work on us long

Figure 2.4. Christo and Jeanne-Claude, *The Gates*, detail, Central Park, New York, 1979–2005. Photo: W. J. T. Mitchell.

after our first—in this case, our only—glimpse of them. And, in fact, I think that Christo's *Gates* will continue to resonate for some time to come, if only because its very elusiveness and vagueness will elicit a continued "filling in" by the imagination, an interpolation of meaning, and a long incubation of images in memory and the photographic record. Part of this filling in will be prompted, I suspect, by the formal character of each individual gate, which mirrors the formal structure of the entire park in its combination of a rigid, geometrical, rectangular frame with a fluctuating, undulating interior. This formal mirroring of the whole in the part is what arrests and entices the beholder simultaneously, one moment urging the walker to stop at each gate, to use it as a frame for a new vista, to pause and reach up to the saffron veil just high enough for an adult to reach on tiptoe, and then to be propelled onward, to stride through. Like those minimalist corridors to nowhere designed by Robert Morris in the 1960s, *The Gates* lures us onward and stops us in our tracks at one and the same time. It creates open-air corridors that end, not in an inaccessible cul de sac (as with Morris) but in the open, in a state of indeterminacy, "looking at the view" — i.e., at everything and nothing at the same time. The uncertainty about which of these things we are supposed to do is, I think, one of the things that initially struck beholders as a kind of vagueness and pointlessness, as if we were being presented with a whole new set of playground equipment in the park that was designed for a game we have not yet learned how to play.

But the game is only beginning, as Christo's work (often dismissed and misunderstood before) has demonstrated time and time again. The retro-spect is, in Christo's work, just as important as the immediate pro-spect, and in fact the ephemeral, temporary prospect is only constructed as a kind of "photo op" for an open — in principle endless — series of retrospective "takes." We have to ask ourselves what *The Gates* made visible that was previously hidden from view, and what appeared that could not have been seen without it.

Such questions provoke exactly the sort of retrospective assessment that seems constitutive of landscape "prospects" as such. Here are a few of my answers, a list that should be seen as necessarily incomplete.

The formal dialectic of rectangularity and sinuosity (which may be dismissed as "all too obvious") is a provocative for a deeper reflection on this feature as a key to the specific character of Central Park (not only its ground plan, but its internal ground-level views with the interplay between foliage and architecture and irregular interior and regular, vertical framing). It also activates an awareness of Central Park's embeddedness in a deep tradition of landscape aesthetics that is defined by precisely this alternation between the stable structure and the moving, dynamic appearance, between artificiality and naturalness, between design and control and unbounded randomness. This is a tradition that transcends period and national styles of landscape architecture, uniting the neoclassicism of Alexander Pope, whose "Windsor Forest" is predicated on a *concordia discors* of light and shadow, form and flux —

Here hills and vales, the woodland and the plain,

Here earth and water seem to strive again;

Not chaos-like, together crushed and bruised,

But, as the world, harmoniously confused

—with Robert Smithson's analysis of picturesque Central Park as a "dialectical landscape."[11] Christo's gates make the form of the landscape stand up on two legs, pictorializing it like the empty frame of a Magritte painting in the midst of the view, and de-pictorializing it by inviting us to walk through the frame again and again.

One of the original features planned for Central Park (rejected ultimately by Olmsted) was a set of entrance gates that would have been monumental, heavily ornamented, and closed against the public at night (Olmsted recognized that the park would turn into a wilderness when the sun went down, and the gates were originally designed as a public safety measure). The notion of democratic openness prevailed, however, and *The Gates* is a reminder of this piece of the deep history of the park. It evokes the notion of the gate as a barrier to passage and an open invitation to it at the same time. The translucence of the saffron curtains is the coloristic analogue to this double message. Rather than an illusion of transparency (compare the trompe l'oeil on the Gilo Wall), translucence allows the passage of sunlight and shadow through a moving surface, an effect that almost every visitor registered as a source of delight, especially when a burst of sunlight would illuminate the fluttering fabric with the tracery of bare winter branches from the trees overhead. Christo reminds us that curtains are not just there for privacy; they are "part-objects" that simultaneously occlude and illuminate, foregrounding the mediation of visual experience as such. Their resemblance to the orange warning fabric around a temporary construction site is, in this light, not a blemish but a deeply suggestive feature.[12]

The long temporal process (1979–2005) of bringing this work to fruition rendered visible exactly what the park is as a civic, political, and economic institution. Central Park is a public space, but what exactly does that mean? The coincidence of Christo's aesthetic appropriation of the *entire* park with the forbidding of public appropriation of *any* part of it had the happy effect of deconstructing any simple illusion about the control of this space. While Central Park was originally designed as a free gift to the public, it was also an incredibly complex political institution, and was largely designed to provide a magnificent front yard for the newly minted millionaires of Knickerbocker-era New York, who rapidly bought up all the surrounding real estate. An Irish shantytown and a well-established African American village (complete with a church) had to be forcibly removed by the police. Like the Palestinian landscape, like all of North America, Central Park is the site of "disappeared villages" and the ghosts of vanished races. One thing *The Gates* makes hypervisible in the landscape of the park is the movement of the air, the necessarily invisible (or translucent) medium through which all spatial perception must travel. In the fluttering saffron draperies, one seems to feel the motions of these invisible presences, the specters of visitors and residents, past and present, who have moved along the pathways, passing through Olmsted's sacred public space in order to purify themselves with an escape into "nature" from the constraints of the city. These invisible presences, felt only in the breezes, are the *genius loci*, the "spirits of the place," that reveal themselves passing through the gates, which can then be "seen as" something like Native American dreamcatchers. Although the park is now technically "public land," it may be rented for private use, and areas may be temporarily fenced off for private functions. Christo rented the entire park, in effect privatizing the whole thing, in order to erect a construction that symbolically evoked the control and fencing of land, proliferating a vast number of the most salient feature of walls, borders, and controlled checkpoints, and then transfiguring them into their exact opposites—gates without walls, gates that open up corridors that lead us into infinite space. In a time when commodities and credit circulate more and more freely in a global economy, and human bodies are confronted increasingly with walls, borders, checkpoints, and closed gates, one is compelled to admit that *The Gates* has an uncanny perfection in its sense of timing.

Between them, then, the Gilo Wall in Jerusalem and *The Gates* of Central Park exemplify some of the range of possible meanings of vision and landscape, and especially of the dialectics of transparency and opacity, visibility and invisibility, passage and obstruction, that make up the enigmatic pleasures and meanings of landscape. Both involve sites and sights unseen, the one providing a veil to conceal the occupation and dispossession of a sacred landscape, the other offering the gift of a new perspective on a very familiar place.

NO STATE OF GRACE

Martin Jay

Violence in the Garden

IN 1975, MY WIFE AND I MADE WHAT IN RETROSPECT WAS OUR SECOND wisest decision—second only, that is, to our getting married a year earlier—which was to buy property in the San Francisco Bay Area. Along with the house came with what in Berkeley was a reasonably sized garden, which had several generations of previous plantings waiting to surprise us when the seasons changed. I can remember in particular my feeling of delight when in February a profusion of delicate yellow petals on tall stalks above a cluster of clover-like leaves broke through the ground seemingly everywhere. Each day brought new outbursts of these stunners, glinting with reflected sunlight in virtually every flower bed in the yard.

Figure 3.1. Buttercup oxalis (*Oxalis pes-caprae*). Photo: M. Jay.

My reverie, however, was short-lived, as my wife, a native of California and the daughter of a serious gardening family, informed me that what I was so innocently admiring was, in fact, the dreaded weed oxalis, which ruthlessly invaded beds meant for other flowers and was extremely difficult to eradicate. If we wanted a decent garden, she insisted, we had to do all in our power to stamp it out. With a certain regret, I made the paradigm shift and began to see the little yellow flowers as the enemy (fig. 3.1).[1] And what a formidable foe they were! For every attempt to pull them out by the roots left a tiny residue behind, a little nodule on the base of their root, which always rejuvenated the following year. Finally, after several seasons of Sisyphean labor, I resorted to chemical warfare and brought in toxic weapons to do the job, in particular the aptly named "Roundup," which succeeded in reducing the menace to a manageable level. Although eternal vigilance is the price of an oxalis-free garden, I find myself feeling enormously superior to the other Berkeley gardeners who have given up the battle, allowing what is a horticultural version of urban graffiti to overwhelm their defenses.

I begin with this trivial anecdote not only to make the obvious point that our distinction between flower and weed is an entirely cultural one, but also to introduce the vexed topic of violence in the garden. For there can be no doubt that my war against oxalis mobilized all of the sadistic and aggressive impulses I normally keep under control, and allowed me to vent them against a stubborn and resilient foe. For every intentional plant that I coaxed into healthy maturity or whose premature demise I mourned, there were hundreds of oxalis weeds that I gleefully uprooted or chemically annihilated. Whatever psychic benefit I was gaining from the activity flowed as much from the outlet for my anger as the opportunity to exercise my nurturant instincts.

What I discovered in my own modest attempts to garden has become a theme of considerable importance in the discourse about landscaping in general. Linking the human desire to mold the environment for aesthetic purposes with the domination of nature in its more brutal forms is, in fact, now a commonplace. As W. J. T. Mitchell puts it in his hard-hitting essay "Imperial Landscape": "We have known since Ruskin that the appreciation of landscape as an aesthetic object cannot be an occasion for complacency or untroubled contemplation; rather, it must be the focus of a historical, political and (yes) aesthetic alertness to violence and evil written on the land, projected there by the gazing eye. We have known at least since Turner— and perhaps since Milton—that the violence of this evil eye is inextricably connected with imperialism and nationalism. What we now know is that landscape itself is the medium by which this evil is veiled and naturalized."[2] Not only have we come to acknowledge what John Barrell called "the dark side of landscape" in his 1980 book of that name, the toilsome labor that the ideology of the picturesque banishes from view, but we have also come to question the costs of the gardening impulse itself.[3]

Perhaps the most extreme version of the argument comes in the work of the Polish-born sociologist, now resident in Britain, Zygmunt Bauman, the author of such books as *Legislators and Interpreters*, *Modernity and Ambivalence*, and *Modernity and the Holocaust*.[4] Inspired by Foucault's analysis of the corporeal normalization of modern disciplinary societies, as well as his claims about the imbrication of knowledge and power, Baumann extends their scope beyond panoptical architecture, dressage of the body, and techniques of social control to an essential cultural attitude underlying modernity *tout court*. Here the complaint is not only against the hypertrophy of the visual and the disincarnation of the contemplative eye, as it often is in critiques of landscape painting or design, but also against the exercise of the more proximate tactile sense in working directly on the soil. For in addition to the surveillance abetted by the clearing of the land are the activities of pruning and grafting, as well as weeding.

Following the distinction of Ernest Gellner between "wild and garden cultures,"[5] the former reproduced spontaneously, the latter dependent on organized control over the environment exercised above all by the nation-state, Bauman has described the modernizing elite as "gamekeepers turned gardeners." "The power presiding over modernity (the pastoral power of the state)," he argues, "is modeled on the role of the gardener. The pre-modern ruling class was, in a sense, a collective gamekeeper."[6] Its decline opened the way for the rise of a new managerial elite, intent on rationalizing time and space and imposing its superior knowledge on both a recalcitrant natural world and a human population in need of its benevolent care. "Gardening and medicine," Bauman writes, "are functionally distinct forms of the same activity of *separating and setting apart useful elements destined to live and thrive, from harmful and morbid ones, which ought to be exterminated.*"[7] Lest there be any doubt about the enemy of the gardening impulse, he adds: "The weeds—the uninvited, unplanned, self-controlled plants—are there to underline the fragility of the imposed order; they alert the gardener to the never-ending demand for supervision and surveillance."[8]

In the early modern era, these included all those residues of popular culture and indigenous communities that were in the way of the Faustian project of rational development. But as modernity progressed, the costs of weeding grew even higher. Bauman goes so far as to claim that the gardening impulse, foreshadowed in the social engineering of Enlightenment despots like Frederick the Great, found its apotheosis in the totalitarian utopias of the twentieth century. He cites a passage by R. W. Darré, written in 1930 (three years before he became the Nazi minister of agriculture), to make his point:

> He who leaves the plants in a garden to themselves will soon find to his surprise that the garden is overgrown by weeds and that even the basic character of plants has changed. If therefore the garden is to remain the breeding ground for plants, if, in other words, it is to lift itself above the harsh rule of natural forces, then the forming will of a gardener is necessary, a gardener who, by providing suitable conditions for growing, or by keeping harmful influences away, or by both together carefully tends what needs tending, and ruthlessly eliminates the weeds which would deprive the better plants of nutrition, air, light and sun.[9]

Among the "weeds" to be "ruthlessly eliminated" were not only Jews, but also "carriers of congenital diseases, the mentally inferior, the bodily deformed. And there were also plants which turned into weeds simply because a superior reason required that the land they occupied should be transformed into someone else's garden."[10] In short, ethnic cleansing was a child of modern social engineering, which was itself an expression of a sinister gardening impulse that had no difficulty analogizing between the oxalis in a suburban flower bed and inferior human races. Even the most well-meaning vegans, it would seem, show complicity with the violent domination of nature and the annihilation of human "weeds."

How plausible, we might wonder, is Bauman's rant against the gardening impulse as the ultimate cause of such twentieth-century horrors as the Holocaust? Is it just a loose metaphor or does it express a hidden affinity that is occluded in the normal celebration of gardens as blissful islands of serenity, play, contemplation and sensuous enjoyment? As a heuristic device, Bauman's work has, in fact, had a certain success. It has been sympathetically received, for example, by some students of totalitarianism, including those specializing in the Soviet variety, who stress a utopian goal of radical improvement of the species and reliance on impersonal bureaucratic means.[11] But many other critics have resisted Baumann's self-consciously postmodernist attempt to link the project of modernity, understood reductively as the domination of man and nature, with such terrible outcomes.[12] As in the comparable cases of Heidegger's blaming the technological worldview of the West, or Horkheimer and Adorno's "dialectic of enlightenment," these critics worry that Bauman's theory allows the specific responsibility of Germans for their actions to be subsumed under a more general explanation that is so broad it makes us all somehow equally culpable. Indeed, others have wondered about the plausibility of Bauman's wholesale characterization of modernity itself with its impoverished notion of rationality as little more than bureaucratic instrumentalism. As one of his most trenchant critics, Michael Crozier, has put it, "It would seem that Bauman himself has engaged in a bit of trimming and pruning on his garden metaphor in order to topiarize a complete picture of modernity."[13]

But in addition to essentializing modernity in a simplistic way, does Baumann do a serious disservice to the historical variations in gardens themselves, which cannot all be understood in terms of violent weeding or ruthless pruning as their essential *raison d'être*? It is, in fact, the case that many of those variations have been interpreted in ways that support Bauman's point. Thus, for example, it has become commonplace to note a sinister relationship between the great formal gardens of early modern European monarchs or landed nobility and their desire to project overwhelming power. It was not coincidental, students of the period have claimed, that the frontispiece of Hobbes's great treatise on sovereign power, *Leviathan* of 1651, shows a gigantic ruler composed of his individual subjects looming over a miniature landscape spread out before him (fig. 3.2).

The calculated expansion of interior architectural control to the adjoining natural exterior, arrogant defiance of the laws of gravity in the elaborate use of fountains, and extension of the Cartesian perspectivalist scopic regime from urban to rural sites were costly exercises in hubristic artifice that have been easy targets for critics. Even in his own day, Louis XIV could be chastised by Saint-Simon for choosing to "tyrannize over nature" as well as his human subjects.[14] A typical recent account reads: "The Baroque landscape of the seventeenth century turned gardening into a species of martial construction. Techniques developed by military engineers—mensuration, irrigation, fortification, to say nothing of optics and hydraulics—transformed the park into a symbol of power. Versailles, Herrenhausen and Schoenbrun each owe as much to Vauban as to Le Nôtre, to Charbonnier or to Fischer von Erlach."[15] Lest this impulse be seen as confined only to the megalomania of the West, it has been possible to find it no less present in Eastern gardens like that of the Ming Emperor's Summer Palace in Beijing, whose beauty was often bought at the price of considerable human misery.[16]

Not only have the explicitly artificial formal gardens of imperial aggrandizement been accused of expressing violence and domination; so too have their apparent opposite: those gardens that sought to imitate wild or unconstrained nature. The exquisitely wrought miniature gardens of Japan, with their carefully balanced landscapes of flowing and still water, artfully arranged rocks, and subtly coordinated flora, have been condemned as no less an expression, if perhaps more subtly exercised, of the human will to dominate than the self-consciously artificial formal gardens of Versailles. The practice of bonsai reduction has likewise been seen as a torture of nature comparable to the topiary concoctions of baroque gardeners.[17]

A similar critique has been made in the case of European landscape aesthetics after the heyday of Le Nôtre and his geometrical designs. As is well known, the formal

Figure 3.2. Thomas Hobbes, frontispiece, *Leviathan*, 1651. Courtesy: Rare Books and Special Collections Library, University of Illinois, Urbana-Champaign.

gardens of the French court, their clipped hedges still bearing traces of the clearly demarcated borders of their walled medieval and Renaissance predecessors, were challenged beginning in the 1730s by the more informal, seemingly open "parks" of Lancelot "Capability" Brown, Charles Bridgeman, William Kent, and Richard Woods. Vast manicured lawns and wide panoramas supplanted intricate knot patterns and symmetrical flower beds.[18] The ideal Virgilian Arcadias depicted in the paintings of Nicolas Poussin and Claude Lorrain moved from the realm of the imaginary to the real. Here the god's-eye perspective necessary to make sense of French neoclassical gardens, a perspective that could be achieved only from the terraced heights of a great house, was replaced by a succession of pleasing pictorial scenes that were quickly immortalized by painters like Richard Wilson.[19]

But these examples of the picturesque—hovering somewhere between the beautiful and the sublime—have also come to be understood as only a more subtle form of theatrical, scenographic artifice, based on the invisible boundary of the hidden trench or ha-ha (whose purpose is more explicit in the French equivalent term *claire-voie*). Their attempt to conceal the agricultural exploitation of the land in the service of a horticultural fantasy of pastoral serenity made criticism inevitable. A certain violence to the land for aesthetic effect could be discerned in the production of these scenic wonders. Hills, after all, had to be reshaped to undulate in a pleasing manner, branches removed to open up vistas, land cleared to produce great lawns, and water diverted to fill serpentine lakes. The pastoral idylls such acts facilitated could be exposed as a sentimental ornament of the ethic of the great country house. Writers like Raymond Williams have critiqued that ethic, which exemplified a complicity with the economic order it pretended to forget.[20]

Becoming boringly predictable in their studied sameness, the pictorial park was in turn replaced by a rougher, apparently more spontaneous English garden, heavily influenced by the fad of asymmetrical and irregular Chinese landscape design in the late eighteenth century.[21] It was perhaps not by chance that this more radical version of unconstrained naturalism, deliberately shorn of Arcadian idealization, gained momentum in the 1790s at a time when any residue of French rationalism could be stigmatized by its association not only with Bourbon neoclassicism, but also with Jacobin terror. The diversitarian ethic of nascent romanticism found its horticultural parallel in a naturalism that threw away the Lorrain glasses through which the theatricalized pictorial scenes of Capability Brown were framed. This transformation was registered in the paintings of Turner or Constable, who proclaimed in 1822 that "a gentlemen's park is my aversion. It is not beauty because it is not nature."[22] The untamed Hampstead Heath became what Simon Schama has called "one of Romanticism's holy places." Accompanying this attitude was a new respect for totally unimproved natural landscapes, like the previously detested mountain ranges, whose sublime appeal was given moral, even spiritual value in the late eighteenth century.[23]

But even this style, in retrospect, has been decried as complicit with a certain violence. As Ann Bermingham has shown, replacing the wide panoramas of Brown's manicured pictorial landscapes, dotted with neoclassical temples, with humbler, smaller-scale, and less ordered versions of the picturesque was sometimes seen as echoing or reinforcing the British resistance to abstract continental theory and its allegedly terrorist implications.[24] In one political narrative, such a resistance was interpreted as the landscape version of an egalitarian, Wordsworthian celebration of rustic simplicity and individual sensibility—a place for solitary walkers rather than the choreographed collective fetes of the French court or its Revolutionary successor. As such, it might come to symbolize a benign combination of equality and liberty without any violent overtones. But alternately, the wild English garden could also be understood to express the conservative defense of an allegedly organic social hierarchy most famously mounted by Edmund Burke in his critique of the French Revolution. In the conservative reading, the abstract leveling of a French geometrical garden, and perhaps even the reshaping of the unruly natural landscape that produced the sweeping vistas of a Brownian park, was emblematic of the leveling produced by both tyrannical despotism and vulgar democracy. In his *Reflections on the Revolution in France*, Burke explicitly excoriated "the French builders, clearing away as mere rubbish whatever they found and, like their ornamental gardeners, forming everything into an exact level."[25] In contrast, the unimproved preservation of what already existed was celebrated as the counterpart of cherishing the ancient liberties, time-honored customs, and unreformed idiosyncrasies of the British constitution rather than imposing an alleged universal system of human rights. It reinforced the sylvan utopia of what was called "greenwood freedom" before the Norman conquest.[26]

But for those less enamored of those allegedly immemorial liberties and customs with their valorization of traditional privileges and duties, the wild English garden could be understood as the perfect landscape expression of an unjust political status quo, with its covert violence towards those on the lower rungs of the ladder.[27] Still in some ways an artificial concoction, "sweetly disordered" rather than left to random chance, it could be seen as contributing to the ideological work of the aesthetic as a soft form of that hegemonic control decried by critics like Terry Eagleton.[28] Burke's loving metaphor of the aristocracy as "the great oaks that shade a country" seemed less than compelling to the smaller plants that wanted some sun of their own. The wild English garden also could be questioned for reinforcing nationalist impulses in a Britain anxious to set itself apart from its continental enemy. Perhaps, as W. J. T. Mitchell has speculated, there may even be a more than coincidental affinity between the imperial pretensions of the Chinese inspirers of the English garden and those they inspired.[29]

There was, to be sure, a reaction to the extreme version of naturalist aesthetics in the mid-nineteenth century, as various eclectic combinations of formality and informality came into and went out of fashion, but the "wild garden" began to enjoy a revival with its defense by William Robinson in Britain. Around the turn of the century, in Germany, the wild English garden really came into its own. Perhaps its most explicit manifestation came in the writings of the influential garden architect Willy Lange, who popularized the somewhat oxymoronic notion of a "nature garden" in such works as *Gartengestaltung der Neuzeit* of 1907.[30] Lange's aesthetic was based on a rejection of anything geometrical, boundaried, regular, or architectonic. Pruning was forbidden, as were the importation of non-native plant species and the creation of artificial lawns and flower beds. Instead of an extension of a house, a garden should best be understood as an extension of the surrounding countryside. Each region, moreover, had its own ecological integrity, which involved respecting local animals as well as plants. What Lange called "plant physiognomy," drawing on the lead of earlier writers like Alexander von Humboldt, meant that gardens should honor the harmonious appearance provided by their natural habitats. In so doing, the gardener would achieve an ethical balance with the natural world that had been violated by the tortured artificiality of previous gardening styles.

A great deal of recent attention has been paid to Lange's legacy and its political implications by the contemporary German scholars Joachim Wolschke-Bulmahn and Gert Groening.[31] And according to their reading, those implications are deeply troubling. Noting Lange's debts to the populist (*völkisch*) ideology of his day, with its exaltation of German national uniqueness and resistance to the rational abstractions of modernity, they argue that his mystical worship of nature bespoke a concomitant denigration of human civilization. His anti-anthropocentrism, they further contend, was laced with hostility to the Hebrew Bible and the "rootless" people who worshiped its God, which fit well with the anti-Semitic and racist tendencies in the *völkisch* movement. His cult of native plants, if sometimes transgressed in practice, echoed the suspicion of foreign cultures and alien races. The formal garden, Lange charged in 1933, was an expression of the inferior "South Alpine race." Even the seemingly benign ecological principles underlying Lange's aesthetic were suspect, if one recalls that the concept of ecology itself had been coined in 1866 by the Monist philosopher Ernst Haeckel, whose social Darwinist beliefs figure in any genealogical history of Nazism.[32]

Wolschke-Bulmahn and Groening go on to argue that both Lange's garden concept and his racist/nationalist worldview (*Weltanschauung*) found their fulfillment in actual Nazi "blood-and-soil" landscaping theories and practices (*Bodenständigkeit*). Such figures as Hans Pastor, Alwin Seifert, and Heinrich Friedrich Wiepking-Jürgensmann sought to restore alleged Teutonic landscapes, including the idea of the forest "clearing" (*Lichtung*), which was realized in Heinrich Himmler's SS "Grove of the Saxons" (and although Wolschke-Bulmahn and Groening don't mention it, became a central concept of Martin Heidegger's later philosophy).[33] Positing a specifically German feel for the landscape in which the people (*Volk*) were rooted and a biologically determined "Nordic feel for space," men like Pastor, Seifert, and Wiepking-Jürgensmann aimed to banish international influences on German gardening styles, despite the fact that much of what they advocated was already present in the wild English garden of Robinson and his predecessors. Likewise, they attempted to link the fight against non-native plants with the Nazi struggle against foreign elements, even using the rhetoric of a "war of extermination" against a certain variety of *impatiens parviflora*. Ironically, however, they had no difficulty in advocating the importation of the Nordic nature garden into those areas of conquered Poland that were destined for the expansion of German "living space" (*Lebensraum*). Thus in 1939, Wiepking-Jürgensmann, who was Himmler's special representative for landscape design, wrote a essay on "The German East: A Priority for Our Students" in which he enthused over the new opportunities presented by conquest to create a "golden age for the German landscape."[34]

Wolschke-Bulmahn and Groening's critique might be extended by acknowledging the ideological implications that have been attributed to German mountain-worship, which gave a specifically nationalist twist to the comparable appreciation of the sublime we have already noted in late eighteenth-century Britain. As Siegfried Kracauer pointed out many years ago in his analysis of the mountain films in Weimar Germany made by Arnold Fanck, Luis Trenker, and Leni Riefenstahl, who starred in one before directing her own, such films often combined a highly romanticized image of heroism amid the clouds with martial values.[35] One might say that mountains in these films serve as an ultimate version of the unregulated garden with humans reduced to ciphers in a landscape of awe-inspiring power. Pushing their argument to an extreme conclusion, Wolschke-Bulmahn and Groening contend that postwar German gardens often continue this ideology under the rubric of environmental or ecological correctness, while blithely forgetting its earlier tainted associations. Wiepking-Jürgensmann, they point out, became a professor in 1948 and trained a whole generation of new students at the University of Hannover.

Not surprisingly, their critique has been met with some skepticism by defenders of this movement, who point out that not everything the Nazis supported or accomplished was by virtue of their support inherently evil. Indeed, as Robert Proctor has recently shown in his unsettling book on *The Nazi War on Cancer*, their campaign against smoking and occupational carcinogens was in fact very much ahead of its time.[36] But even granting that much of what the Nazis promulgated in landscape design was ideologically motivated, it may be wrong to tar all natural gardening principles as equally odious. In a recent issue of the *New York Times Magazine*, a very laudatory article was devoted to rediscovering the Danish immigrant to America, Jens Jensen, who died in 1951 after a long and illustrious career as the inspiration for what became known as "the new American garden."[37] As in the case of Lange, Jensen was a fanatic believer in native rather than imported plants and abhorred artificial regularity. Against the static patterns of formal gardens or the vast panoramas of the English park, he preferred coaxing the visitor through unexpected, often shadowy passageways in a mysterious landscape. "No clipped hedges!" was his fervent motto, which earned him comparison with the great advocate of Prairie School architecture, Frank Lloyd Wright. Yet in political terms, Jensen's worst sin was to design the grounds for the Edsel and Eleanor Ford House in Grosse Pointe Shores, Michigan.

In a riposte to Wolschke-Bulmahn and Groening, the landscape architect Kim Sorvig has insisted on the distinction between, on one hand, sound ecological principles of land management, which follow the "location-fitness" of plants rather than their culturally determined "hominess," and neo-Nazi racist nature worship, on the other.[38] Without acknowledging Zygmunt Bauman, Sorvig in fact concludes: "if there is any valid horticultural equivalent of Nazism, it is the re-making of arid, tropical, or montane landscapes in the image of Versailles or Stourhead."[39]

Although Sorvig does not mention Bauman, his invocation of similar ideas turns us once again to the plausibility of his condemnation of the gardening impulse as a motor of modern totalitarian violence. Putting aside the question of how fair Groening and Wolschke-Bulmahn have been to the long tradition of nature gardening, their claim of a fit between the style exemplified by Lange and the Nazi *Weltanschauung* alerts us to the difficulty of accepting Bauman in all respects. Bauman posits some sort of inherent link between rationalist modernizing projects of development and improvement and the totalitarian desire to remake the world in a utopian way, yet Groening and Wolschke-Bulmahn show that a *surrender* of that rationalizing impulse informed much of the landscaping practices of the Third Reich. If landscape is the "dreamwork" of imperialism, as W. J. T. Mitchell has claimed,[40] it is clear that there is more than one kind of nightmare in the nocturnal imaginary of our species. Nazi landscape aesthetics promoted anti-modernist, anti-rationalist notions of regional specificity and resistance to internationalist mongrelization, in contrast to certain pseudoscientific elements of social Darwinism that might be seen as evidence of the mixed ideology that Jeffrey Herf has dubbed "reactionary modernism."[41]

But however imprecise the fit between Bauman's broad generalizations and the actual practices of Nazi landscape design, his argument helps to undermine the assumption that gardens are best understood as absolutely distinct refuges from the rest of the world, as Edenic places of a grace that is lost outside their boundaries. Michel Foucault, it may be recalled, included them along with cemeteries, places of crisis (e.g., menstruation huts or boarding schools), and places of punishment and treatment (e.g., prisons or hospitals) in the "heterotopias" he saw as radical counter-sites to normal spatial organization.[42] The word "paradise," it is often noted, comes from the Greek *paradeisos*, which means an enclosed garden or park. But the rhetoric of total otherness exaggerates the ability of the garden to keep at bay what it tries to resist. Gardens are connected to other spatial configurations with all of their ideological and cultural meaning not only when they are understood as extensions of architecture, but also when they are seen as its antithesis. Wherever we place them on the spectrum whose ends we designate with those impossibly vexed terms "culture" and "nature," gardens are hybrid entities with all of the complexities that status entails.

Moreover, Bauman's stress on the link between the weeding and pruning of plants and the sinister selection and breeding of humans, however exaggerated it may seem, alerts us to the importance of the nonvisual component in any analysis of the gardening impulse.[43] It is sometimes assumed that the hypertrophy of disincarnated vision is the main culprit in the domination of a nature that is then understood to be enframed for purposes of subjective control. Heidegger's influential critique of "the age of the world picture" is perhaps the *locus classicus* of this charge.[44] The strong interaction between pictorial representations of gardens and gardens constructed as if they were pictures, especially prevalent at the time of Capability Brown and Richard Wilson, would support this assumption. With the ha-ha as a symbol of eye-pleasing deception, such gardens can easily be chastised for their duplicitous hiding of the onerous labor and violation of the land that was necessary to create picturesque scenes to be admired from afar.

But by emphasizing the importance of the tactile dimension of gardening, the dirt under the fingernails that pull out the weeds or the blisters on the hands that prune the shrubbery, Bauman's argument points toward the proximate violence that is necessary to create such pleasing vistas. It makes us question the now conventional assumption that the replacement of qualitative notions of local "place"—defined by the lived experience of real human bodies, with ideas and practices of abstract, homogeneous and quantitative "space"—somehow ultimately causes the violence in the gardening impulse.[45] Such violence may just as well be caused by the desperate desire to reterritorialize ourselves in a familiar and comforting home as an antidote to our alienation into the abstract world of spatial grids and impersonal fields of force. If, as Marc Treib has speculated, "at the very bottom of the psychological urge to garden there also lies a sad and somewhat pathetic attempt to literally reroot oneself in a world of rapid change and rampant mobility,"[46] the desperation of that attempt may abet a certain violence all of its own. Or at least that would be one implication of the nature garden tradition in German *völkisch* culture.

Finally, Bauman provokes ruminations on the inevitability of violence in the garden. Some sort of ideological work of suppression and control is always being exercised, either directly on nature or indirectly on the humans who inhabit it. Contrary to the Edenic myth, it seems as if the apple is always already eaten and recovered innocence is an impossible dream. The necessarily intrusive agricultural cultivation of the land for purposes of human sustenance always lurks behind the horticultural fantasy of a purely aesthetic vision, despite the attempts of ha-has to mask the labor behind it. The ordered geometric patterns of the French garden, as Keith Thomas has pointed out, echoed the symmetry and regularity of ploughed furrows and planted orchards in rows or quincunxes, which also came into their own in the seventeenth century.[47] The unfinished epigraph inscribed on the tomb in Poussin's great allegorical painting of around 1755, *The Arcadian Shepherds*, may be an acknowledgement of the inevitable, perhaps even deadly, violence that lurks in every garden: "Et in Arcadia ego…" (I am also in Arcadia).[48]

But what does it really mean to say that violence is an inevitable moment in any garden? In fact, what exactly do we mean by violence itself? In her well-known attempt to distinguish violence from power, Hannah Arendt provided one answer. Power, she argued, requires numbers; it is based on people working in concert to achieve an end and gains its legitimacy from the initial act of people getting together. In contrast, violence can be the medium of one person or a minority to bring about an end through an instrumental extension of strength or force. It lacks legitimacy and can only undermine legitimate power, never support it. Its inherent tool is coercion, not persuasion. Arendt also sought to separate force, as "the energy released by physical or social movements," from violence.[49] The former, she argues, can justifiably be used to speak of the "forces of nature," but it is imprecise to speak of the violence of nature.

Building on her distinctions, I would argue that gardens are precisely the sites in which natural force and human violence are in a tense constellation with collective power. That is, the overwhelming power of natural force has necessitated the instrumental use of human violence in order to make possible the survival and growth of our odd species. The first gardens, we might justifiably speculate, were inventions to compensate for the relative scarcity or capricious fickleness of the natural environment in providing for human subsistence. Gellner's simple progression from gamekeeping to gardening, adopted by Bauman, fails to do justice to the fundamental role agriculture played in the earliest days of civilization as well as in modernity. Cultivation, even horticultural, has never lost its intimate connection with the instrumental violence humans had to employ to make up for the unpredictable and often cruel environment provided by nature. What changes, however, are the ways in which power in Arendt's sense of voluntarily acting in concert inflects and mobilizes that violence. Gardens, in short, are not places of prelapsarian grace, Arcadian heterotopias in tension with the rest of the fallen world, but rather are laboratories for the unending human struggle to get the balance right between natural force, instrumental violence, and the power we give ourselves to do both good and evil.

MOVING THE EYE

Marc Treib

PERSPECTIVE PLAYS SUCH A DOMINANT ROLE IN OUR VISUAL PERCEPTION THAT WE
often forget it is entirely a mathematical construct. As a graphic convention it is relatively new, denying both all sense of time as well as the symbolic, rather than optical,
construction of space. Prior to the codification of perspective in fifteenth-century
Italy, representational systems addressed the symbolic aspects of existence as more
central than its external appearance. Russian icons from the fourteenth century combined the elements of a religious scene in a field almost free of spatial continuity,
stressing through size and position the relative importance of the figure and its supports. Created on the cusp of "the rationalization of sight"—as William Ivins termed
the Renaissance development of perspective—Giotto's frescoes struggled to create an

architectonic continuity.[1] Yet on the other hand, they staged temporal and figural relations confidently, accepting in equal measure earthly matter and heavenly transfigurations. Ultimately these views concerned religious convictions, and of course artistic practice; they did not fetishize the search for the objective rendition of space.

Stories tell that the painter Paolo Uccello was overheard saying: *"Que miraviglia questa prospettiva!"* (What a wonder this perspective!). One can share his sense of adventure. Here was a method for transposing the metric regularity of the then-evolving ichnographic plan (credited to Leonardo) with the subjectivity of the view. Perspective was a way of translating factual dimensions into pictorial space.[2] At the same time, it portrayed psychological impressions as believable, or as Erwin Panofsky noted: "The result was a translation of psychophysiological space into mathematical space; in other words, an objectification of the subjective."[3] But there was a downside as well: perspective is not really how we perceive the world physiologically, and as a result, we lose much of our immediacy of sensation. To see in perspective, the world would need be flat; we would have but one eye set on an immobile body, and there would be no atmospheric or chromatic distortion. Perspective denies that the information received on the retina is inverted, causing the brain to process and make sense of a world read upside down, and that the essentially physiological construction of vision sets a narrow cone of foveal vision and a rapidly moving eye against a broad peripheral field.[4] Studies show that the eye moves differently when it is scanning a scene—the so-called saccadic movement—than when it is tracking a specific object.[5] But the eye is always in movement, even when seated, even when at rest.

Despite these serious shortcomings, drawn perspectival representation possesses considerable merits. For one, by codifying representation it established a basis for objective comparison. Ivins discussed the importance of these conventions for the development of science in his *Prints and Visual Communication.*[6] Until more objective systems of representation were developed and broadly accepted, he argued, a naturalist could not determine whether the differences witnessed in drawings of plants were due to differences in the actual vegetation or disparities in the manner by which they were drawn. For Ivins, perspectival drawings, representational typologies, and ultimately the camera helped to eliminate that problem of disparity, and to some degree he was right. But as John Berger, and a host of critics thereafter have noted, no photographic representation is truly objective. We make photographs, we don't take them.[7] Seeing—and *visuality* as described by Hal Foster—involves the mind as well as the brain, and vision is a sense with a cultural location.[8]

Perspective also sets near and far, and helps us get from here to there, despite our inability to distinguish stereometry at distances over about thirty feet. To compensate, we learn to rely on clues such as overlapping and occlusion to interpret spatial constructs. We learn through experience that two objects cannot occupy the same space at the same time. Therefore, if one object screens another we assume that it stands before the second object, which we mentally position to the rear. Visual perception, then, becomes a process whereby we try to resolve the conflicts between what falls on the retina, how the brain processes that information, and how prior experience informs our interpretation of that visual data.[9] Studies have shown that we must learn to see in perspective, or let us say, to coordinate our living experience with its representation in perspective. We also must learn to read the systems behind particular media, for example film and television. A classic perceptual psychology vignette tells of African tribespeople watching for the first time a film made of their group. As one man walked off screen in the film, everyone got up and looked in back of the screen to see where he had gone, presumably due to a lack of experience with the two-dimensional capture of three- and four-dimensional experience and its projection across space. Over time, we learn to see in perspective and to experience the world in its terms, and in terms of the representational system it propels.

Although the body supports the head, eye and body do not always remain or travel in complete accord. The body may remain at rest, with the eye freely active; or the eye may precede while the body follows after it; or the eye and body may move at the same time but not necessarily engaging the space together in the same way. This disparity between the eye and its supporting figure—its exaggeration or its elimination—has been a major factor for the designing of landscapes of extreme beauty and at times, great force.

Formal, geometric garden designs in Western Europe—the French gardens of the *grand siècle*, for example—have stressed the regularity of spatial definition and the linear path of the axis, tracing depth through rhythmic repetition and the judicious placement of spaces, statuary, and vegetation. Where practicable—for example, at

Versailles—the path inspired nonstop travel to the vanishing point—although visual stumbling blocks may have encumbered the way (fig. 4.1). In the gardens of Italy around the time of the Renaissance, the perspectival thrust was rarely of great consequence, except perhaps as a means to fool the eye. The trip could be hastened by forced perspective, but only visually. Given that so many of the fortified villas for which the gardens were created occupied hillside sites, there was little opportunity to develop gardens with the grand sweep that would come within two centuries to a kingdom in Italy's northwest.

In gardens such as the sixteenth-century Vicobello outside Siena, each of the terraced garden rooms were fitted to the hillside through judicious excavation (fig. 4.2). There is a planning ideal of sorts behind these gardens—similar to the one proposed by Carl Franck to explain the siting of the villas of Frascati. Franck asserted that in creating the site plans for these late Renaissance villas in the outer reaches of Rome, a consistent idea guided the positioning of the villa, its garden, and views, ideally maintaining a visual connection back to Rome. Due to contingencies of orientation and topography, however, this ideal was realized in its entirety only rarely.[10] On any given hillside, the lay of the land coerced the plan and thwarted any achievement of perfection. Even the celebrated garden at the Villa Lante—with its axis folded into terraces, its perfectly balanced casinos, and its symmetrical parterre—is ultimately just terraces carved from a hillside. Although the linear structure of the garden predominates in plan, features positioned on the axis preclude bodily movement along the center of the route. As a result, the eye stutters in jumps and starts, at first trying to grasp the grand idea but acquiescing and focusing instead upon individual areas. The Villa Lante ultimately comprises a sort of saccadic garden experience, and like the tracings of the eye, one must piece together the fragments of experience almost in the manner of a cubist collage. The schematic idea determines the design, but it is sensed more than conclusively perceived—that the plan of the garden abuts three squares comes as a surprise to most visitors. Thus, the jump in scale from the juxtaposed terraces of the Italian Renaissance garden to the formal French gardens of the seventeenth century was momentous.

The sweep of a garden by André le Nôtre, such as Versailles or Vaux-le-Vicomte, can be overwhelming. Although they share similar root ideas of order and control,

Figure 4.1. André Le Nôtre, Versailles, axis in garden, c. 1660s. Photo: M. Treib.

Figure 4.2. *Limonaia,* Vicobello, Siena, late sixteenth century. The lack of available flat land instigated terracing and directed the garden as a series of outdoor rooms. Photo: M. Treib.

these two grand gardens differ considerably in their development. Vaux, in many ways, embodies a gross expansion of the Villa Lante idea, wherein the widened axis embraces the most important features of the garden. Its principal axis encompasses the château and its parterres; it is a grand line that leads the eye ever onward to the next feature and its terminus at the statue of Hercules. Vaux, like the Villa Lante, employs a three-zone plan, in this case, enjoining the forecourt, the parterre garden, and the sloped green on the far side of the canal.[11]

Vaux's site in the Île de France is relatively flat, which allowed exploitation of the terrain and the extension of the views at grand scale. One focuses less on the immediate elements than those seen for the future; the thrust continually moves the visitor to the end of the axis and the sky beyond. This play pits near and far, intricacy and grand gesture. Most commonly the body moves through space as the eye traces its path. Only the surprising events such as the cross-axial canal arrest the body, although the eye continues its inexorable march to the horizon. This disjunction, of course, can either frustrate or heighten the sense of pleasure.

Plans, like perspectives, can be misleading. The oft-reproduced plan of Versailles, for example, stresses the central axis of the park, with writers commonly noting the path from Louis XIV's apartments, over the Latona and Apollo fountains, and on to the heavens—an appropriate visual procession for a Sun King. The axis dominates first perceptions of the garden, at least from an upper floor, or once the grand terrace has been traversed.[12] But the terrace breaks the link between château and axis, and in its place creates a zone set parallel to the château. Once upon the axis, however, eye and body are brought into accord. The immediate elements matter little, although statues modulate the rhythm of the path. These are minor incursions on the advance to the horizon, however, where the mature woods have been shaped and function like horse blinders that ensure the eye will not wander. Without doubt, the axis, which continues as the grand canal, is the backbone of the garden and optical directive—but the axis is not everything.

The scheme undergirding the gardens at Versailles develops as a woods and a series of clearings that complement and, to some extent, soften the thrust of the axis. These clearings provide prime settings for experience within the garden. Banquets, musical and theatrical performances, and even amorous trysts occurred in the bosks, and on the axis only for grand spectacles. The circulation network crisscrossing the park featured a series of bounded paths that restricted the eye and widened voids that permitted the eye to wander. In the gardens of Versailles, Le Nôtre and his colleagues created an analog to the modern subway system with its dark tunnels and its bright stations. Likewise, the eye and body traversing the garden suffer tantalizing foreplay and subsequent release contributing to the mildly erotic nature of its experience.

Yet more interesting, perhaps, is Le Nôtre's work at Chantilly, because here he so brilliantly mined the existing conditions to maximize the aesthetic effect. This was no blank canvas upon which the landscape artist could paint: the earliest existing image of the medieval castle dates to 1579.[13] The moat and surrounding landholdings had been developed long before Le Nôtre arrived on the scene in 1662; he continued working on the landscape of Chantilly until 1692.[14] Thus, fully integrating the building into a new landscape intended to perfect nature in accord with Enlightenment norms was clearly impossible considering the conditions, available technology, and economies. To please his client, the Grand Condé, Le Nôtre devised a brilliant strategy: the axis would bypass the château, using the castle as a counterpoint in a scheme not unlike the flight deck and service tower of an aircraft carrier.

In plan, the axis connects the forecourt with the extensive field of water parterres set before the canalized river. The statue of the Grand Condé forged the pivotal point in the composition, but its role was far more evident in section—that is, as perceived by the moving figure—than in plan. Unknown to the approaching visitor was the dramatic grading that relied upon a shallow ramp, set adjacent to the château, as its principal vehicle (fig. 4.3). The power of the statue, read against the sky, increased as one drew closer, with the Grand Condé gesturing across the axis toward his familial seat and holdings. There was little hint of what lay ahead. After passing the statue, a stone solid balustrade veiled the drama that would ultimately follow: a sweeping vista over a field of regularly set pools of water animated by fountain jets, a grand parterre of water, and a view over the surrounding countryside (fig. 4.4). The body will follow, momentarily losing direction as it descends the stairs into the garden.

At Chantilly the effect is more powerful than that at either Vaux or Versailles because the view arrives as a revelation, informed by the eroticism of the voyeur but the ultimate pleasure of which is withheld to increase its effect. Here we see parallels

Figure 4.3. André Le Nôtre, Chantilly, c. 1673. The ramped principal axis skirts the existing château with little suggestion of the garden revelation to come. The statue of the Grand Condé functions as a pivot that directs movement as well as view. Photo: M. Treib.

Figure 4.4. André Le Nôtre, Chantilly, water parterres, c. 1673. Photo: M. Treib.

to a design idea that became part and parcel of the English landscape garden in the succeeding century—and, not incidentally, the Japanese stroll garden nearly contemporary with Le Nôtre's own landscapes. This impact derives to some degree from a discord between what the eye attends and where and how the body is allowed to walk.

The coupling of eye and body reappears, strengthened, in the eighteenth-century England landscape garden, although a time lag purposefully separates what the eye registers and what the body can engage. While this friction is endemic to all seeing, and to some degree to all landscape experience, its effects are heightened in these gardens despite their emulation of nature. Literature on the subject establishes the theoretical underpinnings for the gardens as a reaction to the formality of, or exhaustion of aesthetic fascination with, the French and Dutch garden styles of prior centuries.[15] If in the *grand siècle* across the Channel, "Grove nods at Grove, each Alley has a Brother, / And half the platform just reflects the other," as Alexander Pope once phrased it, the new garden would banish efforts at any perfecting of nature and be more accepting of what nature offered without human help.[16]

The condemnation of geometry was poorly founded of course; it was then, and it remains so today with the calls for the so-called nature or ecological gardens. To make a landscape involves making choices of order, earthen contour, and species; none of these choices produces a natural landscape. The inclusion of any architectural elements compounds the inherent artificiality of the garden. Thus, no matter to what degree the English landscape garden sought the natural, it could never escape the fact that it was a human construct. At Stourhead, for example, a river was dammed to create a lake, inundating land that had once stood above water level, and an entire village was rearranged for compositional effect. The architectural elements within the garden were significant. They played a semantic role as the bearers of associations and literary allusions, as well as visual punctuations in the compass of the planted landscape. These built elements—termed "eye catchers" even in the literature of their period of origin—led the eye on a merry chase that could be likened to a visual game of billiards, only here they were expanded more fully into three-dimensional space.[17]

In many gardens a preferred, if not always prescribed, route guided the visitor's encounter with nature. From the upper level at Stourhead one glimpsed the re-sited St. Peter's Church through gaps in the shrubbery, and slightly later on, the classical

Figure 4.5. Henry Hoare, Pantheon (from the opposite shore), Stourhead, c. 1741. Photo: M. Treib.

Pantheon standing on the opposite shore (fig. 4.5). Then one saw only vegetation, at least in seasons when the deciduous plantings remained in leaf. Descending to the level of the lake, a visitor could catch another glance at the Pantheon; and then it was gone. The serpentine path wound through the masses of carefully positioned plantings, ultimately bypassing the Gothic Cottage, and setting up the dominating view of the Pantheon at the path's (seeming) end (fig. 4.6). From the portico of the Pantheon, the Temple of Flora and the village buildings appeared neatly framed, and slightly further on, the Temple of Apollo entered the retina and the visitor's consciousness — luring the visitor to follow this architectural temptation.

This lag between what was seen and what was perhaps ultimately touched instigated a desire for movement, to achieve with the human figure what the eye had first proposed. To effect the magic required a visual structure of architectural ele-

Figure 4.6. Henry Hoare, Pantheon (from the pondside path), Stourhead, c. 1741. Photo: M. Treib.

ments that functioned doubly as individual constructions with semantic or recreational purposes, and collective forms to goad the body into action. Aspects of this matrix had existed in the French and Italian gardens, of course, as it had in many garden traditions throughout history. But it had never been exploited in quite this way, except perhaps in Asia. It is interesting that Lancelot "Capability" Brown described his compositional tactics in terms of orthography. In a conversation with Hannah More shortly before his death, Brown asserted: "Now *there* . . . I make a comma, and there," pointing to another spot, "where a more decided turn is proper, I make a colon; at another spot, where an interruption is desirable to break the view, a parenthesis; now a full stop, and then I begin another subject."[18] Brown exchanged clumps of trees for architectural elements, in a more subtle way accomplishing the project of earlier garden designers such as Henry Hoare, Charles Bridgeman, and Alexander Pope. What they achieved in building stone, Brown attempted in vegetation. The semantic dimension melted into one of experiential syntax.

In terms of aesthetic strategies, the designers of the English landscape gardens translated elements from pictorial conventions into spatial constructs. The normal references cited are paintings by Nicolas Poussin, Claude Lorrain, and Salvadore Rosa, but to some extent this dismisses the inherent differences between painted representation and actual space. William Hogarth, for example, spoke of the serpentine line as the most beautiful, effectively destroying the urge for the straight line in painting or the straight path in the garden—especially when in the three or four dimensions of space, the eye could be more effectively manipulated.[19] Certain conventions that characterized the drawn view or painting did find application in a garden's composition. A *repoussoir* element, often a tree branch or dark trunk, anchored the foreground; the prime subject occupied the middle ground; and a more general massing of vegetation paved an unobtrusive background. But garden design can never simply apply pictorial ideals unadapted because the garden introduces the dimension of time, and quite commonly, bodily movement. A painter need only control the movement of the eye upon the surface of his work, while the garden designer must correlate the movement of eye and body, either in accord or in disjunction, as he or she deems fit.

In his 1777 *Composition des Paysages* (An Essay on Landscape), René de Girardin described the ideas and methods by which he realized his own garden at Ermenonville (fig. 4.7). Influenced by the philosopher Jean-Jacques Rousseau, Girardin took umbrage with the formality of the previous century. In particular, Girardin condemned the use of symmetry: "Symmetry certainly owed its origin to vanity and indolence," he wrote, "to vanity in attempting to force the situation to accord with building, instead of making the building suit the situation; in idleness, because it was more easy to work upon paper, which will allow of any form, than to examine and combine the real objects, which can only take the form that suits them: hence all the views are sacrificed to one point, the exact center of the house." The multiplicity of views, which are supposedly limited in the formal garden by its axis and vanishing point, become very important here. In Girardin's writing there is a special place in hell for Le Nôtre, who confined the view within masses of hedges, so that "the prospect from the house

Figure 4.7. René Girardin, Ermenonville, late 1770s. Photo: M. Treib.

[was] limited to a flat parterre, cut into squares like a chess-board, where the glittering sand and gravel of all colours, only dazzled the eyes." Unrelenting, he ended his commentary with the note that "the nearest way to get out of this dull scene became the most frequented path."[20]

As an antidote, Girardin proposes naturalism. He imagines a garden as "a deep sequestered valley that this stream, which we have heard the sound of at a distance, finds its way amongst rocks covered with moss. Advancing into it, the valley closes, leaving room only for a rough and crooked path. Then how beautiful the scene which suddenly opens to us."[21] Closure and openness, restriction and release: these are frequent themes in the planning of the naturalistic garden according to painted conventions.[22] Girardin mocks the formal tradition using an elevated tone: "if he [i.e., the visitor] begins by the admiration of picturesque landscapes which pleases the sight, he will soon seek to produce the moral landscapes which delight the mind." The eyes are the window to the soul, and the naturalistic garden provides the best balm for immoral eyes. Only when taste is present, however, may "nature smile with all the graces of elegant simplicity, its infinite variety will never cease to amuse, and it will produce that secret charm of which no feeling mind can tire."[23]

In all probability, Girardin acquired his ethical pronouncements and stance from Rousseau, who had stayed at Ermenonville for extended periods and who was enshrined there—at least for some short period. In *La Nouvelle Héloïse* (1761), Rousseau chides both patrons and architects who despoiled nature through formality under the rubric of garden making in the past. Instead Rousseau prefers a garden with an aspect so natural that one forgets that it has been made: "All is green, fresh, vigorous, and the gardener's hand is nowhere to be seen." In the garden of Julie, the novel's protagonist, the boundaries of the landscape, once so obvious, have all but disappeared. "These two sides," crows Julie's guest Monsieur de Wolmar, "were closed in by walls. The walls have been hidden, not by trellises, but by thick shrubby trees which make the boundaries of the place seem to be the beginning of a wood." Time and neglect have been key ingredients in Julie's garden. Julie has overcome the formality of orchard and path, as her visitor notes: "This place is charming, it is true, but uncultivated and wild. I see no marks of human work." Julie responds: "It is true . . . that nature has done everything, but under my direction."[24] In Julie's garden the visual aspect—and the eye always finds a new subject upon which to rest—leads to escape rather than to movement. It is a place of "prospect and refuge," where one experiences nature as removed from civilization.[25] This despite the obvious contradiction of a garden made and tended, even in the mildest way.

The German view of the English landscape garden tradition may be found in Johann Wolfgang von Goethe's *Elective Affinities* (1809), a part of which addresses the remaking of estate and graveyard in accord with contemporary, that is romantic, ideas. The quartet of the novel's leading characters shares many philosophical inquiries which do not exclude those concerning the garden. Although mention of the view almost always enters their conversations, one senses less an interest in the moral—or even the beautiful—than in the estate as aristocratic amusement.[26] Pavilions are constructed within the garden as destinations for pastimes such as conversation or dining, replacing to some degree the pleasures of the eye with corporal gratification that wine and cuisine provide.

To the English, at least as they appear in early nineteenth-century literature, there is pleasure in the garden as a *topos* for the walk, and it is a theme that recurs in the novels of Jane Austen. In *Mansfield Park,* for example, the subject of estate improvement reappears several times; Humphry Repton is even cited by name. The values, in the minds of several characters, are simple. "'Mr. Rushworth,' said Lady Bertram, 'if I were you, I would have a very pretty shrubbery. One likes to get out into a shrubbery in fine weather.'" There is little discussion of any particular view or any particular feature, unlike the gazebos of *Elective Affinity* or the follies of Stourhead, Stowe, or West Wycombe. Like Julie and her guest across the Channel, Miss Crawford, the Bertrams and the Rushworths take pleasure in shrubbery so dense in its planting that it may be termed a "wilderness." It was hot, "insufferably hot" as Miss Crawford points out, and then asks, "Shall any of us object to being comfortable? Here is a nice little wood, if one can but get into it." The passage then describes "the wilderness . . . was a planted wood of about two acres and though chiefly of larch and laurel, and beech cut down, and though laid out with too much regularity, was darkness and shade, and natural beauty, compared with the bowling-green and the terrace. They all felt the refreshment of it, and for some time could only walk and admire."[27] In Jane Austen's England, visual pleasure follows movement through the garden or park. In the work of British artists Richard Long and Hamish Fulton, where the significance of the walk supersedes any evidence remaining after travel, that tradition continues today.[28]

While at times propelled by different ideological and aesthetic intentions, like pictorialist garden makers in the West, Japanese gardeners used the judicious placement of landscape elements to manipulate the quality and apparent dimensions of garden space. Historically, the representation of space in the Japanese graphic arts was non-perspectival, with depth rendered through the layers set parallel to the picture plane, or painted in oblique dimetric projection. The famous woodblock prints of the nineteenth century followed several centuries of Western contact, despite the closure of Japan to foreigners in 1638.[29] In fact, as Henry Smith and others have demonstrated, a number of the most celebrated woodblock artists tried to integrate the indigenous representational systems with a rudimentary knowledge of linear perspective gained through books and prints.[30] This notion of layered space underlay the demarcation of here and there in the graphic arts and to some degree in garden making as well: a completely visual construct to be enjoyed primarily while sitting, and more complexly, in the larger gardens for which bodily movement was an essential ingredient.

Japanese garden culture was hardly homogeneous, either synchronically or diachronically. While it is convenient to talk about styles neatly following one another in simple succession, garden making was actually more of an enfolding and reinterpretation of previous ideas. The paradise landscape typology, rooted in direct experience rather than religious ideas alone, dated to at least the ninth century, when lavishly planted gardens enriched temples as well as palaces. In time, garden forms were brought into closer accord with religious ideas, however, and by the twelfth century, the paradise garden had become a consequential vehicle for the Jōdo (or Pure Land) sect of Japanese Buddhism. Here the garden was intended as an evocation of the celestial paradise of the Amida Buddha, who rested in his Western Paradise awaiting the enlightenment of all sentient beings. The paradise garden was thus a visual feast for the eyes, lushly planted, with a pond as its central feature: the transparency and mirrored surface of the pond suggested purity. Paths traversed the garden and joined the architectural forms of temple or palace; paths restricted the array of routes but movement was not truly choreographed as it would become in later centuries.

Like English garden makers, Japanese creators used a manner that David Slawson, in his excellent study *Secret Teachings in the Art of Japanese Gardens*, has translated as "the principle of three depths."[31] This is essentially the configuring of foreground, middle ground, and background to maximize the perceived dimensions of gardens constructed where flat space was limited. To some extent the eye was drawn *into* the view by elevating receding objects or layers in space; but for the most part depth developed from occlusion, from the convoluting of shore lines, and from the skillful positioning of trees. The late fourteenth-century garden at Kinkaku-ji—the celebrated Temple of the Golden Pavilion—is an excellent example of this twisting of shorelines,

Figure 4.8. Ashikaga Yoshimitsu, The Temple of the Golden Pavilion (Kinkaku-ji), Kyoto, c. 1395. Planted islands and convoluted peninsulas increase the sense of space and depth. Photo: M. Treib.

and it is believed to be one of the earliest mature applications of the practice (fig. 4.8).[32] From any of the verandas of the pavilion's three floors, the eye dances across the pond. With planted peninsulas and islands as deflecting mechanisms, the eye ricochets from one stand of clipped pines to the next until it finds rest within the folds of the distant mountains. Other than by boat, there is no way for the body to follow its optical trajectory, as a circumferential path around the pond is the only true promenade. Here, then, we see an almost complete disjunction between what the eye can engage and what the body may traverse, a trait common to much Japanese landscape design.

If the body cannot move toward the scenery, the landscape must be brought to the body. To effect this transference, Japanese garden makers perfected the practice of *shakkei*, or "borrowed scenery." According to landscape historian Teiji Itoh, this annexation may be passive or active, reaching a culmination of sorts in the "capturing alive" of the landscape as if it were a part of the garden.[33] Here again, the principle of three depths governs, but the primary relationship lies between foreground and background, with the middle ground serving as a crucial mediating agent. The middle ground must screen unwanted elements to effect a stronger bond between the near and the far, smoothing the transition so that the distant mountain seamlessly fits within the small garden without regard for the disparity in their respective scales.

The seventeenth-century garden at the Buddhist temple of Entsu-ji in northern Kyoto well illustrates the basic manner of borrowed scenery. A field of stones within the garden precinct is arranged in a roughly radial pattern, its spread countering in form the shape of Mt. Hiei in the misty distance. A hedge on the perimeter intercedes, separating and yet linking mountain and stone, moss and clouds. The clever planting of trees on both sides of the hedge undermines any verdict that the trees are either inside or beyond the garden's bounds. Garden and woodblock print share this sense of space, where the crucial middle layer becomes the conceptual pivot that propels the eye to the mountain and retrieves the mountain to the garden. Using mimesis more directly is the garden at Raikyu-ji in Bitchu-Takahashi, also dating from the seventeenth century. Here a large crane-shaped stone at the far edge of this temple garden corresponds to the mass of the mountain far beyond. A cluster of plants and stones screens unwanted elements beyond the limits of the garden, while the shape of the rock mimics the profile of the mountain, rendering more tangible the bond between the two.

In southeastern Kyoto, one may encounter the mastery of Kobori Enshu in his garden for the Joju-in (circa 1629).[34] The temple complex rides a ridge extending outward from the Higashiyama slopes, a shelf that falls abruptly into a ravine just beyond the northern edge of the garden marked by a low hedge. Enshu was known for his adroit mixing on formal, semiformal, and informal elements, embodied here in the clipping of the shrubs and the shape and setting of the rocks (fig. 4.9).[35] The central feature, reflected in a small pond, is the *eboshi ishi*, a stone named for its resemblance to the *eboshi*, the hat worn by Shinto priests. But Enshu appeared unsatisfied with the meager dimensions of the land available for development. Within the garden he placed a stone lantern, and then set a corresponding lantern on the hillside more than two hundred feet away. The far lantern is said to be almost twice as tall as its sibling, and the surrounding vegetation is usually clipped to allow sunlight to fall more readily upon it. In some light conditions, despite its bulk, the lantern is lost in shadow. At other times of day, however, the connection between near and far is lucid: like the two parts of the sight on a rifle the brace of lanterns forge a line almost palpable. This virtual line in space draws the eye from its seated position on the veranda into the bamboo and maples of the distant hillside, correspondingly linking the idea of the garden with the preserve of the larger landscape. The body rests; the eye travels extensively.

Extensive travel, however, can be disquieting, and to relax this nervous saccadic movement yet another Japanese principle came into play: what Slawson terms "single-depth perspective." Linguistically, the phrase is somewhat of an oxymoron, but it nevertheless conveys the intention to reduce eye motion from near to far and back again, which is optically tiring and detrimental to contemplation. To counter this, the garden elements are clustered in the middle ground, with a simple field of gravel, moss, or sand forming what is essentially a forecourt to the garden's subject. A wall encloses the background, reinforcing the grouping of the central constellation within the garden space. The minute rock garden at Daisen-in, a part of the Daitoku-ji monastery complex in Kyoto (circa 1509), illustrates this principle succinctly, although there is so little available space that the perspective could hardly be other than single-plane (fig. 4.10). The rocks are clustered to create a composition that works well from either side of the temple's corner, animated by a stream of gravel that suggests a river and spare planting. Slawson notes that rocks that taper at the top, or those with vertical

Figure 4.9. Kobori Enshu (?), Joju-in, Kyoto, Edo period. A second lantern on the far side of the ravine, barely discernable in this photo, corresponds to the large stone lantern within the garden, strengthening the power of the borrowed scenery. Photo: M. Treib.

Figure 4.10. Daisen-in (sub-temple of Daitoku-ji), Kyoto, 1509. Photo: M. Treib. The compressed dimensions of this tiny garden create what has been termed "single-plane perspective," drawing the eye and the contemplative mind into the composition.

striations, conjure a greater sense of the soaring, "making them appear to tower precipitously over the stone bridge and gravel stream below."[36]

At the seventeenth-century Leaping Tiger Garden at Nanzen-ji, few elements articulate the predominant field of raked gravel. Unlike Ryoan-ji, for example, where the composition dynamically pits rock against rock, and the rock groupings against the rectangular boundary wall, the arrangements in the Nanzen-ji garden tend to cluster. The eye will scan and pause laterally upon stones and shrubs, but there is little depth of movement from the eye on the veranda to the rocks across the gravel plane.

In some ways, single-depth perspective is the opposite of borrowed scenery. Where borrowed scenery joins near and far in a continuous traversing of distance, single-depth perspective stays at home, comfortably ensconced within its delimiting wall. It accepts stasis; it prefers to *consider* rather than to *see*, to focus internally rather than externally. Thus, in the seventeenth century, single-depth perspective became a useful vehicle for the practice of *zazen*, or seated meditation.

The development of the tea ceremony reinserted the human body into the designed landscape. As a link between mundane daily life outside the garden and the rarified realm of tea within it, the garden was cast as a transitional path. Available spaces tended to be small, and the short walk from street to tea house entry was convoluted both physically and psychologically to expand the sense of distance traversed. In the *roji*—the "dewy path," as the tea garden was termed—the stepping stone was used more consciously and effectively than in gardens past. The great sixteenth-century tea master Sen no Rikyu introduced a mood of longing and time into the experience of tea, and the preferred tone for the ceremony was muted and autumnal. The favored twilight hour meant encountering condensation from temperatures below the dew point, making the clay soils of the path muddy and slippery. The stepping stone was first used as a functional vehicle for keeping the foot from the potentially hazardous earthen surface. Furthermore, a body wrapped tightly in a kimono may take a step barely one foot in length, and being shod in sandals or *geta*, or wooden clogs, makes walking an exercise in purposeful movement. The stepping stone, then, functioned not only as a visual pattern, but also as an inscription of movement within the garden. By making stones long, straight, and smooth, the pace could be quickened. By using rough stones spaced more broadly, movement could become more deliberate, perhaps turning the body to break concentration or reveal a preferred view (fig. 4.11).

The lessons learned in the tea garden were applied broadly in the stroll gardens of seventeenth-century Japan, roughly parallel in era to the French landscapes of André le Nôtre. Although the size of these gardens was miniscule when compared to their French counterparts—or even to the aristocratic enclaves of Japan's twelfth-century Golden Age—stroll gardens such as the Sento Gosho maximized the effect of the space using every clue at hand. Here the body transported the eye, at times aligned, at times allowing the eye to precede the legs that followed at a far slower

Figure 4.11. Prince Toshihito, Katsura Villa, Kyoto, seventeenth century. To the kimono-clad guest, the shape, surfaces, and arrangements of stepping stones concerned more than visual patterning: they directed speed and direction of movement as well as view. Photo: M. Treib.

pace. The primary path maintained the pond to its right, exploiting to the maximum the principle known as *miegakure*, or hide-and-reveal.[37] Here we see the same methods stressed by Girardin in constructing *jardins à la anglaise*, judiciously mixing constriction and openness with sequential obstruction and revelation. These contrasts provided surprise and pleasure, and continually renewed ways of viewing and experiencing nature.[38]

The stroll garden in Japan addressed not only mass and void, but also species and seasonal color. Perhaps no other culture is so imbued with the passage of the seasons, a sensibility that informs everything from the foods consumed to the patterns on a kimono. In the garden, the flowering cherry might serve as a visual target that transforms a simple background into a short-lived foreground. But the colored specimen tree, even in the autumn, can greatly affect the movement of the eye and ultimately the psychological perception of the space and movement through it. In the Sento Gosho, for example, the tone is a consistent green in summer with a soft play of verdure against the cool gray of stone. The eye bounds from gravel to stone bridge and beyond, turning subtly at an angle to the primary path. In autumn, however, a middle-ground tree turned a vivid carmine arrests the eye although the body continues its march. Here heightened titillation derives from the apparent discord between optical and corporal progress.

The imperial stroll garden at the villa of Shugaku-in, set in the hills of northeast Kyoto, summarizes many of these ideas and practices. Built in the 1660s, the estate actually comprises three gardens, the uppermost of which centers on a pond garden created by constructing an enormous earthen dam. Hedges and terraces conceal the extent of the earth movement; the fields between the gardens host productive rice paddies. A curving *allée* of pine trees turns the view upward with a slight sense of apprehension and leads to a small waiting area before the gateway to the upper garden. Stepping in, the world constricts enormously, into a narrow path barely three feet wide with hedges so high that the eye can look only forward. Eye and body now act in complete accord, climbing the stone steps in tandem while curving gently away from what one intuits to be the true subject of the garden. As one arrives at the upper level, and the head rises about the hedges, one senses something behind, turns, and experiences a magnificent vista over all of northern Kyoto (fig. 4.12). This is a tremendous display of borrowed scenery, and one that gains in power from the discord between a figure stopped in its tracks and the boundless sweep of the view. In many ways, this is the antithesis of the contemplative garden, where the view projects *into* the garden rather than *over* it. On the other hand, both garden types pit visual access against corporeal confinement—that is, until at Shugaku-in one descends into the garden and follows its spatial choreography.

Awareness of these properties of vision and guided movement, whether the static body with a moving eye or the peripatetic body with a mobile eye, have contributed to the making of sensuously—and at times, contemplatively—rich gardens

Figure 4.12. Emperor Gomizuno-o, Shugaku-in Villa, Kyoto, c. 1660. Emerging from the constrictive enclosure of a narrow stone staircase this grand panorama of northern Kyoto appears by virtue of a judicious
massing of tree forms. Photo: M. Treib.

that acknowledged perception, its possibilities, and its limits. Neither manner is inherently better than the other; no culture can lay claim to aesthetic or perceptual superiority. Garden design develops within a cultural matrix produced by its people, its land, and its time. To some designers in the modern era, any constriction in movement or restriction in vision has become an anathema. The axis, any axis, is the enemy, and multiplicity of view and movement is the keyword. But that's another story, or at least a possible extension of this one.

LANDSCAPE AND GLOBAL VISION 5

Denis Cosgrove

MY SCHOLARLY INVOLVEMENT IN "LANDSCAPE" (WHICH DIFFERS FROM MY emotional, aesthetic, or sensuous attachments to specific landscapes) is rooted in two intellectual passions: my discipline of geography, and understanding the role that vision has played in the way that people come to know and understand the external world. Geography leads me both to regard landscapes as phenomena wherein physical processes and human agency are inextricably linked, and to stretch the scale of landscape from immediately local spaces to territorial, planetary, and indeed extraterrestrial worlds. My concern with vision supports and extends these geographical predilections. Vision usefully encompasses both sight and insight, allowing the inclusion of imagination as an element in the active human shaping of physical nature. In terms of spatial scale, vision is the most flexible of the human senses. Imaginatively always, and, over the past half-millennium, through ever more sophisticated prosthesis, human vision has extended far beyond the capacity of the unaided human eye, whose ambit has conventionally defined the scale of landscape, at least in its modern usage. Thus, some twenty years ago I argued that "landscape is a way of seeing" through which human relations with other humans and with the physical world are figured and represented. This way of seeing has its own techniques, which it shares with other areas of cultural practice.

One principal expression of this convergence of geography and vision is mapping and its graphic product, the map.[1] The connections between mapping and landscape are profound, both epistemologically and historically. Epistemologically, landscape always involves a territorial inscription and a bounding act, however informal, whether these proceed through law, property, or graphic design. Landscape thus always involves a mapping process if not always an actual map.[2] Historically, and not only in the West, landscape art—in painting, gardening, rural planning, and urban design—has depended quite materially upon mapping acts, and has frequently shared techniques with more formal survey- and map-making.[3] An obvious example is the control and management of water courses in sixteenth-century Italy or in seventeenth-century France, where surveyors and mapmakers provided the technical expertise without which Tuscan and Venetian villa gardens or Le Nôtre's grand parklands would have been impossible.[4] The intimate connection between sketching, drawing, and painting topography and land military survey (of land territories by army surveyors, or of coastlines by naval chart-makers) is another.[5] Landscape tastes, developed in the arts, have long informed choices over content, design, color, and symbolism in maps, especially the national topographic series that grew out of the chorographic tradition in modern European states.[6] This relationship between landscape vision and mapping was central to both the capitalization of land in Europe and the colonialist appropriation of extra-European spaces, as has been amply demonstrated by two decades of scholarship. If, in W. J. T. Mitchell's memorable phrase, "landscape is the dreamwork of imperialism," survey and mapping have been its wakeful fieldwork.[7]

My concern is not with the conventional topographic and chorographic scales at which landscape has generally been limned, but the geographic, and even the cosmographic, scales of landscape. As mapping terms, "topographic," "chorographic," "geographic," and "cosmographic" derive their meaning from Claudius Ptolemy's work *The Geography* (second century CE), whose outline of methods for projecting the globe as planisphere and whose list of coordinates for geographical locations have long been held responsible for reintroducing scientific mapping techniques into the modern West. The four terms define a scalar hierarchy from the most local and immediately visible "topography" to the universal scale of "cosmography" (with "geography" referring to the scale of the whole terraqueous globe and its principal parts). But the meanings of the terms are much richer and more labile than a simple hierarchy of scale suggests. Historically, they also denoted different ways of envisioning space—in fashionable parlance, different *spatialities*. Thus topographic mapping conjures the physical form of land: hills and plains, river lowlands and mountain plateaus. It would be related in the eighteenth century to the soldier's vision, looking at landscape as strategic space for realizing military objectives. Chorography incorporates a strong sense of territoriality, of human occupation and historical rootedness. As *choros* implies, it involves a sense of place. Chorography was the concern of local landowners in their relations with emerging state rulers and administrators, and of antiquarians seeking a pedigree for local identities.[8] Mapping at the geographical level was long associated with the mathematical questions of projection, scale, and accurate fixing of locations on the theoretical grid of longitude and latitude. Geographical mapping secured a true image of the globe and the distribution of its lands and seas, and this was equally the concern of strategists, diplomats, and scientists. In this respect, geographical mapping might be regarded as most distant from landscape, with its strong local and pictorial associations. This is only partially true, as I hope to demonstrate.

Finally, there is cosmography. Now obscure, cosmographic mapping represented for a long period the most complex form of vision and the most sophisticated and totalizing form of spatial representation. Conceptually it assumed the existence of formal and structural correspondences between elemental and celestial nature (earth and heavens); methodologically it involved both mathematically accurate mappings of those correspondences, and both written and pictorial descriptions.[9] In a pre-Copernican world its universal reach extended the cosmographic vision into metaphysical worlds. Its scope was not confined to a given spatial scale or order, so that cosmographic mapping could represent the microcosm as fully as the whole created universe. Cosmographic mapping had strong contemplative, religious, and moral associations. What characterized—and ultimately doomed—such mapping, especially in the context of secular science, was precisely its attempt to envision and represent the totality of its object in all its complexity and beauty, and its refusal to separate the physical from the metaphysical.

In early sixteenth-century Europe, cosmography seemed to offer a graphic way of comprehending a material and moral episteme undergoing radical change. Erasmus himself posed rhetorically the cosmographic question: "what spectacle can be more splendid than the sight of this world?" Those who sought to answer it included makers of great maps and globes of the earth and heavens, to be sure, but also artists working on tiny, but minutely detailed, canvases. Painters such as Joachim Patinir, Louis Cranach, and Albrecht Altdorfer in the early sixteenth century and members of the Brueghel family in its later years effectively invented a new form within the emerging genre of landscape painting.[10] Walter Gibson has aptly termed these images "world landscapes," for among their most striking features is the impossibly high viewpoint from which they are observed, allowing the viewer a window onto a vast world of varied physical and human incident, stretching across distances that can only be described as global.[11] The space depicted often terminates at a gently curving horizon. The image is full of detailed incident, structured by a narrative that itself often has a "global" significance, for example the Holy Family's Flight into Egypt, the battle of Issus in which Alexander of Macedonia defeated Darius's Persian empire, or Icarus's fall from the heavens to earth. But, if cosmic in conception and spatial scale, these were commonly tiny, jewel-like, panel paintings that consciously disrupted scalar expectations, seeking to capture "the world in a grain of sand." Such landscapes were regarded by early German humanist scholars as a more adequate format than language or text for describing the universe, and were often described as cosmographies. Albrecht Dürer wrote, for example, "the measurement of the earth, the waters and the stars has come to be understood through painting." World landscape emerged as a genre of painting in precisely the same cities that new techniques of map projection were being developed—Nuremberg and Augsburg, and later Antwerp, and both practices co-evolved. Landscape artists were close acquaintances of mathematical cosmographers and mapmakers: Altdorfer of Martin Behaim, Regiomontanus and Pirckheimer in the last years of the fifteenth century, Peter Brueghel or Abraham Ortelius a hundred years later.

Shared acquaintance in fifteenth-century south Germany or sixteenth-century Flanders seems to have accompanied a shared vision between artist and mapmaker. We might still call that vision cosmographic, had not cosmography disappeared as a respectable project with the rise of analytic science and the Enlightenment's rationalistic defeat of metaphysics. I shall therefore refer to it by the more contemporary term "global," and in what follows I shall address the matter of "global landscape" as a distinctive way of representing that vision. Global vision seeks to encompass and represent the earth as a whole, acknowledging its surface variation of lands and seas, mountains and plains, but subordinating this variety to an emphasis on surface and to a sense of unity and completeness. Global landscapes are no more innocent of the complexities of meaning and authority than more localized landscapes, although their totalizing rhetoric tends to obscure these complexities. That synoptic discourse of unity and harmony, traceable to cosmography and promoted by global landscapes, is a deeply ambiguous discourse, of continuing moral and political relevance. On one hand global landscapes speak to the unity of earth, together with the biological and physical processes that shape it and the human population that inhabits and transforms it. On the other hand, inevitably positioned, as they are, these landscapes become enmeshed with universalizing visions of power—with the geopolitics of empire.

The most obvious example in our own days is the Apollo 17 photograph of earth taken from space in 1972, a global landscape that became the very icon of holism in the late twentieth century.[12] As the satellite image of earth suggests, global vision is strongly, indeed entirely, dependent upon graphic images, which I call global landscapes, that frame and map the earth's surface or a goodly part of it. Global landscapes share with cosmography the pretense of capturing the wholeness and unity of the earth; they seek to make visible the whole earth or a significant section of it: hemispheres, continents, and oceans. They operate at a scale that could never be seen physically (certainly true for the spherical global figure). Therefore global landscapes employ such conceits as the ultra-high oblique angle, the imaginary flight, or the atlas: that collection of individual views bound together according to a textual logic of completeness.

Global landscapes are still produced: the atlas is a familiar but little remarked vehicle of knowledge; a way of viewing the whole earth that is today somewhat threatened by the more flexible medium of the computer. Yet the atlas might be regarded as an early example of precisely the hypertextual flexibility offered by computers. The atlas is a systematic and indexed collection of cartographic representations (images and texts) bound into one or more volumes. Its content is organized according to overlapping systems of spatial significance: scale, locational proximity, familiarity, power, etc. The atlas further extends the scope of nonlinearity that is characteristic of maps themselves. Its user can leaf through the atlas in any direction and across scale changes, connecting images to each other in innovative and imaginative ways. Nonuniformity of scale permits mobility: a virtual journey over and across earth space, which is vastly more flexible than physical movement because it permits simultaneous activation of scale, direction, and distance. The atlas may be regarded as a tool of mobility for picturing and witnessing global landscape.

Such value is explicitly acknowledged in Abraham Ortelius's *Theatrum Orbis Terrarum*, a work that has commonly been regarded as the earliest example of the genre insofar as it attempted a systematic and comprehensive coverage of the globe from the scale of the whole earth and its continents down to local areas illustrated through chorographic maps. It was first published in 1570, became an international commercial success, and was expanded, elaborated, and copied over the succeeding century (fig. 5.1).[13] The work's historical and cultural significance has generated a huge scholarly literature. Four less remarked aspects of the *Theatrum* are of particular interest here: its title, the opening world map, the prefatory texts to the volume, and its inclusion of images that are less strictly maps than landscape sketches. Each of these suggests the cosmographically inspired global vision as the proper way of seeing the contents of the atlas.

Ortelius's title, a "theater" of the whole earthly globe, differs significantly from the title "atlas" first used by his competitor Gerardus Mercator for his slightly later parallel project. In 1570, "theater" had a very specific meaning, denoting both a rhetorical space and a "conspectus" in which the totality and logic of a class of objects

Figure 5.1. Abraham Ortelius, *Typus Orbis Terrarum*, 1570. This is the first printing of the opening map of Ortelius's atlas. Courtesy: UCLA Library.

could be presented and understood.[14] "Theater" appears as a title for collections of other phenomena, both natural and artificial: devices and machines, the human body and its illustration in anatomy texts. This synoptic usage remains today in the "lecture theater"—a space for presenting the order and logic of things. In Ortelius's work, the theater of the whole earthly globe within the logical, harmonious, and beautiful "world" could be made visible and comprehensible. The world theater was, as Shakespeare said in the same years, the stage of human tragedy and comedy, so that the atlas, in revealing the vastness and variety of the globe, reflects our humanity back to ourselves. In this sense the atlas has a contemplative role—fully in keeping with its author's religious quietism. The atlas is a moral space.[15] Ortelius shared this aspect of the global vision with his close friend Peter Brueghel the Elder. Ortelius and his contributors emphasized this aspect of the atlas in its opening map and in prefatory prose and poetry.

The *Theatrum*'s world map, *Typus Orbis Terrarum*, was among the most influential spatial images in early modern Europe, so instantly popular and widely reproduced that the printing plate had to be replaced in 1587. It shows the known distribution of lands and seas across the globe, denoting the continents in distinct colors. Most significant to this discussion are the epigrams that Ortelius attached to it. In his initial version, the Latin subscript reads "For what can seem of moment in human affairs for him who keeps all eternity before his eyes and knows the scale of the universal world?" This Ciceronian quotation was augmented in the 1587 version with four other Stoic passages taken from both Cicero and Seneca (fig. 5.2).[16] Each reinforces the message that the vision of the earth's surface is a moral act that raises the viewer toward the divine and stimulates philosophical contemplation. This Stoic trope had long been associated with the moralities of vision over landscape—it was the basis for Petrarch's famous contemplation on ascending Mt. Ventoux, sometimes regarded as the precursor of a modern landscape sensibility in the Latin West. The same set of ideas is elaborated in the passages that preface the illustrated pages of Ortelius's atlas. Here its compiler is compared to the god Apollo, whose chariot passes through the heavens permitting a coolly rational and distanced perspective over the whole theater of human affairs. In his own discussion of the atlas, Ortelius celebrates its capacity to allow the scholar to travel the whole world, comparing states and nations, seeing the earth's variety and its unity without the dangers attendant upon bodily

Figure 5.2. Abraham Ortelius, *Typus Orbis Terrarum*, detail, 1587. Detail of the second version of the map, showing oculus in top left corner. The quotation from Cicero translates as follows: "For man was given life that he might inhabit that sphere called Earth, which you see in the center of this temple." Courtesy: UCLA Library.

travel. Each of these introductory elements—title, world map, and text—reinforces in the reader's mind at the outset the idea that the atlas is a mobile way of seeing the earth, where mobility is that of imaginative flight.

But the *Theatrum* has a more complex relationship to mobility and landscape vision. Appended to the pages that map the contemporary world is a collection of other images, mainly maps of historical and biblical significance (the extent of the Roman Empire, the voyages of St. Paul, etc.). Scattered among these are some quite specific landscapes, including two classical *loci amoeni*: the valley of Daphne and the groves of Tempe (fig. 5.3). Of the latter, Ortelius comments: "after this long and tedious peregrination over the whole world, I should bethink myself of some place of rest, where the painful students, faint and wearied in this long and wearisome journey, might recreate themselves; I presently, as soon as I awaked, went about it: and while I survey all the quarters of the huge globe of the Earth, behold the noble TEMPE, famous for their sacred groves."[17]

We know from the illustrations of his journey through Italy to Messina that were included in the *Theatrum*'s companion city atlas, *Civitates Orbis Terrarum*, that the northern humanist Ortelius witnessed for himself the classical landscapes of Italy (fig. 5.4). It is clear that his world atlas invites a way of seeing the globe as surface, as landscape, on the grandest scale and that it attaches to that vision a moral quest connecting local landscapes to the cosmographic picture.

The politics and moralities of this virtual journey to witness the globe through the medium of atlas maps and landscapes are complex: they incorporate both an implicitly imperial perspective that appropriates all the world's diversity to a European mastery (as Ortelius's title page makes strikingly clear), but also a cosmopolitan embrace of the world's variety and diversity through the Stoic recognition of global harmony and unity.

Similarly complex politics are apparent in a more recent and more immediately ideological mid-twentieth century atlas project. September 11, 2001, reminded us that "war is God's way of teaching Americans geography." That aphorism comes from the event to which the 9/11 outrages have often been compared, the Japanese attack on Pearl Harbor on December 7, 1941. Precipitated into global war that winter, Americans were ill-prepared to grasp the geographical scale and nature of the conflict they had entered.[18] This was only partly a function of poor geographical education. It was

Figure 5.3. Abraham Ortelius, Sacred Groves of Tempe, *Theatrum Orbis Terrarum*, 1570. Courtesy: UCLA Library.

the inevitable consequence of a wholly new scale of warfare, most especially in the Pacific Ocean, an area one-third the size of the globe, whence came the most direct threat to the territorial integrity of the United States, and of a wholly new strategic environment, constituted by sea and air rather than land. The Pacific war was fought across an entire hemisphere, a global space composed of tiny islands separated by vast stretches of ocean. The islands, together with U.S. Navy ships, acted as aircraft carriers for launching a struggle that was waged in large measure in the air—from the Pearl Harbor attack itself to the nuclear bombing of Japan. A crucial question for U.S. leaders and opinion formers in the early 1940s was how to communicate to the American public these novel aspects of war in an exotic landscape and thus to foster understanding of the war's goals, strategies, and meanings. If they were to win the

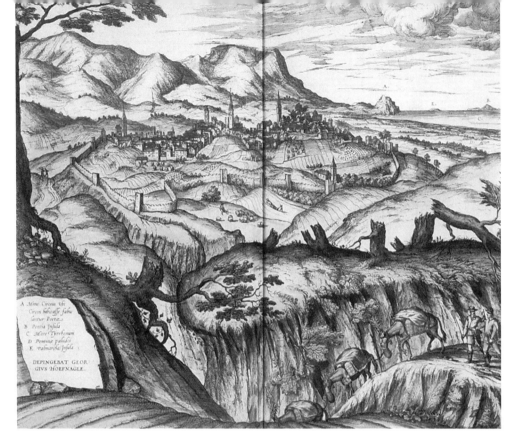

Figure 5.4. Georg Braun and Frans Hogenberg, *Civitates Orbis Terrarum*, c. 1580. The northern humanists Ortelius and his companion Jorge Hoefnagel follow the coast of Italy on the Grand Tour. Private Collection.

struggle and shape the peace, Americans had to think globally or, to use the catch-phrase of the early 1940s; they had to adopt "the airman's view." The poet Archibald MacLeish, writing in 1942, suggested that the conflict would be won or lost in the air and that this synoptic perspective would give the airman a vision that would deter-mine the nature of the world to emerge from global war. Never in all their history have men been able truly to conceive of the world as a single sphere in which there is no center because every point, or none, is center—an equal earth which all men occupy as equals. The airman's earth, if free men make it, will be truly round: a globe in practice, not in theory.[19]

To achieve this goal, ordinary Americans had to attain in imagination this air-man's global vision. Conventional maps and images were deemed insufficient for the task. When President Roosevelt asked that every American family consult a world map while listening to his fireside chat of February 23, 1942, many felt that the Mercator projection provided by map sellers and newspapers failed to do justice to the round earth and to the global vision necessary to grasp his words. Responding to this problem, it was artists rather than scientific cartographers who created new ways of representing the global surface as landscape, indeed as a theater of human action and moral purpose. A number of U.S. magazines and newspapers illustrated the conflict as it unfolded in a series of novel spatial images, and suggested that their readers collect these to build into atlases. *Fortune* magazine called upon the services of Richard Edes Harrison, architect and illustrator, whose maps were collected into the separately published volume *Look at the World.*[20] The *Los Angeles Times* staff artist, Charles Hamilton Owens, produced weekly over the course of the war dramatic colored images covering a full page of the newspaper. For both artists the goal was to make the conflict visible as a highly mobile action, viewed from the air as it played out across global space.

Harrison's are the best-known images.[21] He drew upon two types of mapping technique. One was to employ unorthodox projections: the azimuthal equidistant, centered at a pole or other arbitrary point in order to emphasize unexpected spatial relations, and the orthographic projection, in his words, "the most nearly pictorial of all formal projections," similar to the technique employed by an architect to draw a circular building. Both projections emphasize the globe's sphericity. Perhaps more pertinent are those images where Harrison abandons projection for high-angle, oblique perspectives, a purely pictorial device that dramatically suggests the airman's vision. In these we seem to sweep across onto the European peninsular from the east, as if coming in as an attacking fighter pilot high over the Caucasus, or across the Pacific toward Japan and the coast of Asia (fig. 5.5). Terrain is shadowed and colored to suggest relief and dramatically foreshortened to give the impression of strategic movement and direction. Futurist painters had used similar techniques during the 1920s and 1930s to suggest the new spatiality of powered flight. Harrison's maps serve a number of functions: as his atlas title suggests, his goal was to have Americans *look* at the world, and to change the way they *saw* it. His images challenged isolationism insofar as it was founded on the idea (promoted by conventional world maps) that the United States was a quasi-island, separated from the rest of the world by two oceans.

Figure 5.5. "Europe from the East," from Richard Edes Harrison: *Look at the World: The Fortune Atlas for World Strategy*, 1944. Orthographic picture map of the eastern Eurasian landmass. Private Collection.

Thus these images emphasized air and sea as spaces of movement, and the altered spatial relations of air power. They also revealed the arbitrariness of political boundaries, showing that at the global scale the world's physical landscapes paid no attention to human territoriality and that from the air such divisions, over which humans were struggling and killing each other, were invisible. Global synopsis was the airman's vision, and it promoted in contemporary terms Seneca's sentiment, reproduced by Ortelius on his own world map: "Is this that pinpoint which is divided by sword and fire among so many nations? How ridiculous are the boundaries of mortals!"

For its Los Angeles readers, directly involved in the Pacific War, Charles Owens offered a different but equally global suite of war landscapes. Owens had begun his newspaper career as a sketcher in the years before the widespread use of news photography, providing immediate and dramatic illustrations of news events: crime scenes, natural disasters, human triumphs and catastrophes. Outside his *Times* work Owens had also gained a reputation in the 1920s as an illustrator of California landscape for *Touring Topics*, the magazine of the Automobile Club of Southern California (which had 100,000 subscribers). Owens's landscape sketches and watercolors

Figure 5.6. Charles Hamilton Owens, "New Headquarters Building, Automobile Club of Southern California," from *Touring Topics*, March 1923. Courtesy: UCLA Library.

appeared in color on the cover of ten editions in 1923, and his pencil sketches appeared throughout 1926. Although his subjects were conventionally picturesque, the theme was mobility through technology. Whether Owens depicted an old Spanish mission, native *Washingtonia* palms, Joshua trees, Death Valley, or a lone pine on the California coast, an automobile was always placed strategically within the scene. For the March 1923 issue of *Touring Topics*, Owens painted the auto club's new headquarters building, a Spanish Revival block in downtown Los Angeles (fig. 5.6). Automobile use in those pre-Depression years was more closely associated with glamour and leisure than work, and car trips had turned California's coasts, mountains, and deserts into *scenery*, landscapes for visual consumption, a mode of vision encouraged by *Touring Topics*: "The term [scenery] is appropriate here, not only because it appears so frequently in the tourist literature of the day but also because of its associations with two other loci of urban visual consumption, theater and film. 'Scenic' implies seriality and movement from one visual setting to another, unlike the static connotations of the picturesque."[22]

Owens's engagement with mobility and seriality in landscape was reinforced by his direct involvement with the movie industry. In 1929 he produced a series of sketches to illustrate motion picture studios for the *Ladies Home Journal*, which he later exhibited at Stanford University. By the time he came to illustrate global war, Owens had developed a range of pictorial techniques to suggest synopsis, seriality, and motion. The unique character of the war landscapes he produced each week depended upon their combination within the limits set by the newspaper page. An immediately striking feature is their use of color, virtually unknown in newspapers at that time. While the palate is unsubtle and color is used principally to differentiate territories, color dramatically enhances the impact of the images in relation to familiar news maps of the period. Each work is a combination of text, map, and illustration (fig. 5.7). Text comprises the headline (oriented portrait, although the main image was often landscape), toponymy, and inserted narrative blocks, with occasional statistical information. These maps did not illustrate written articles; they were stand-alone news items.

The cartography is highly pictorial, created by adopting a similar high-angle oblique perspective to Harrison's, but here even more dramatically foreshortened. Each image emphasizes globality through a curving horizon at the top. This earth curvature is consistent regardless of the spatial scale shown: from the entire Pacific to tiny islands and atolls such as New Britain or Truk. On the horizon we see distant strategic goals—the next islands to be captured, the coast of Asia or Japan itself, viewed in low profile as if emerging into view from an advancing cockpit (fig. 5.8). Arrows and other directional devices reinforce this sense of forward movement across physical space.

The third element in the images is the "sky space" over the global horizon. This is occupied either by place icons for "exotic" locations being mapped (Sphinx for the Egyptian campaign, Colosseum for Rome, Eiffel Tower for Paris, London

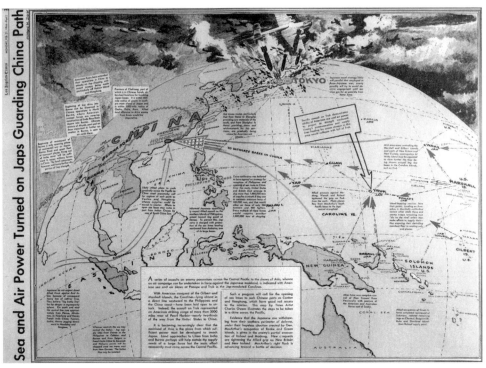

Figure 5.7. Charles Hamilton Owens, "American Advance Across the Pacific," from *Los Angeles Times*, February 21, 1944. Courtesy: UCLA Library.

Bridge for London) or by action images of battle—commonly air or naval warfare—using graphic techniques common in war comics of the period. Battle scenes radically increase the dramatic impact of the cartographic image, connecting global strategy to local tactics. They are not close-up renderings of the battlefield; rarely are individual figures seen engaged in combat. Owens pictures a landscape of mechanized war fought with ships and aircraft, naval guns and bombs across global space (fig. 5.9). The landscape view simultaneously distances and connects the viewer and the specific horrors of bloody, hand-to-hand fighting in the Pacific war. In Owens's most dramatic images these battle scenes invade the map: Flying Fortresses, Tokyo, and spouts of water explode from the ocean surfaces (fig. 5.10).

It is impossible not to read these global war landscapes in the cultural context of Los Angeles's movie-making (and Owens's specific association with it) and of the

Americans Ready to Settle Score With Japs on Wake

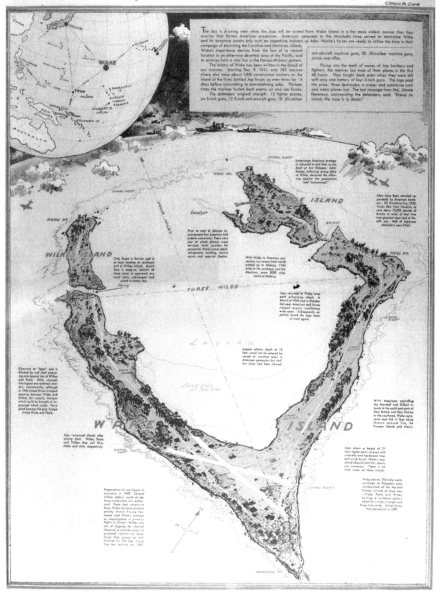

Figure 5.8. Charles Hamilton Owens, "Wake Island," from *Los Angeles Times*, March 4, 1944.

Courtesy: UCLA Library.

Figure 5.9. Charles Hamilton Owens, "Gibraltar Air Battle," detail, *Los Angeles Times*, December 28, 1942. Courtesy: UCLA Library.

city's close involvement with aircraft and ordnance manufacture and naval transport of troops to the Pacific front. They are highly mobile landscapes that capture with considerable imagination, precise technical skill, and some artistry the airman's vision of global landscape. Brought together as an atlas, they construct a spatial narrative of global war observed through the seriality of specific and local scenes.

Landscape has always been polysemic. Traditionally, its dominant meanings have had to do with locality, whether in the substantive and legal sense of close attachment of a group to defined area of land or in the more pictorial sense of landscape art, painting and design. But today, landscape is appreciated as a spatial concept principally for its capacity to connect specific place to geographic setting, spatial connections and the cultural context it both shapes and is shaped by. Landscape's claim to synoptic vision is, we know, always compromised; it deceives as much as it reveals. This is obviously true of the landscapes I have been considering here. Through the

Figure 5.10. Charles Hamilton Owens, "U.S. Warplanes Bombing Tokyo," from *Los Angeles Times*, December 11, 1944. Detail of war map of France and Iberia showing Gibraltar air battle sketch. Courtesy: UCLA Library.

macroscope of global landscape, both Ortelius and Owens seek to reveal scenes invisible to the unaided eye. But at the global scale, too, the landscape vision is duplicitous: at once cosmopolitan in its embrace of a harmonious unity of earth and humanity, and violent in its projection of a partial and singular perspective. These images remind us that spatial art and spatial science have always worked closely together in producing and mobilizing the landscape vision.

The atlas's participation in the discourse of landscape reminds us that landscape can never be restricted to a static picture of achieved spatial relations, but involves kinetic and serial experience as we move through space. The best landscapists have always recognized this and developed varied techniques to enhance it, above all through the manipulation of scale. The global scale of landscape is not a contemporary phenomenon; it has a long, complex pedigree.

PART

ENVISIONING PLACE

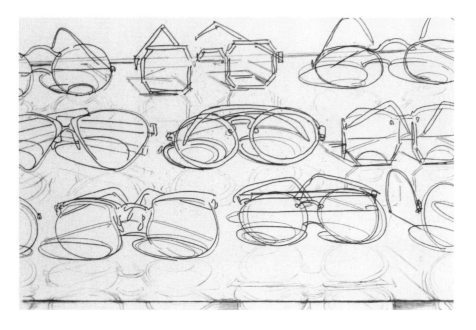

Wayne Thiebaud, *Eyeglasses,* 1994.

ANCIENT ROME THROUGH

THE VEIL OF SIGHT

Diane Favro

ANCIENT ROME IS IRRESISTIBLE. OVER THE CENTURIES, INNUMERABLE ARTISTS HAVE
attempted to capture the original appearance of the great capital city in paintings,
etchings, reliefs, models, and films (fig. 6.1).[1] Today, digital modelers exploit new media
to fashion images of the great capital city as it appeared in antiquity (fig. 6.2).[2] The
challenge is daunting. While extensive archaeological research has been done on
select monuments, buildings, or even certain urban areas, vast portions of the ancient
city have not been excavated. The lack of data hampers full-bodied reconstructions
of the cityscape. Scholars ponder how (or even whether) to represent undocumented
urban infill, unevaluated original topography, unpreserved skylines, and unrecorded
street patterns, among other aspects essential for the depiction of an expansive

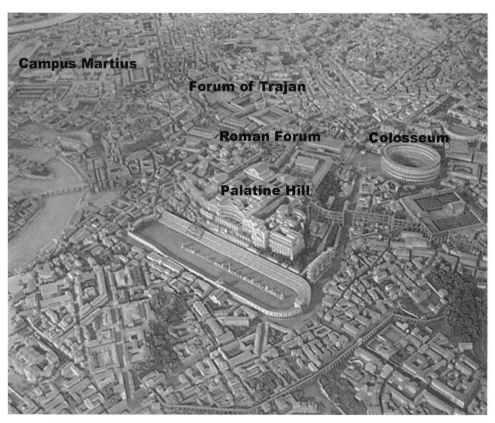

Figure 6.1. Rome in the early fourth century CE, plaster model created during the Fascist era, Museo della Civiltá Romana, Rome. Photo: D. Favro.

urban panorama. Such debates deflect attention from the consideration of how to view the ancient city. In the last twenty years research has been conducted on the gaze in antiquity, exploring how power, identity, and gender impact the reception of art.[3] Studies have considered how Roman residential architecture was shaped by view-planning, and how visual alignments impacted the siting of specific structures.[4] Far less attention has focused on how the ancients looked at Rome.[5] While numerous ancient images recorded the appearance of Roman urban environments, the cityscape of Rome is conspicuous by its absence in the pictorial record.

Figure 6.2. Roman Forum in late antiquity, virtual model. Reproduced with permission of the UCLA Cultural VR Lab.

The term "cityscape" appeared in the mid-nineteenth century as an urban counterpoint to landscape. The term implies a totalizing view of a city in a pictorial rather than sociological or experiential sense.[6] Thus the focus is on the potent exchange between the observer and the broad urban vista, not on urban planning, smaller urban visual vignettes, architecture, or city life. The cityscape in antiquity was impressionistic in both the literal and artistic sense. The ancients had few opportunities to observe urban environments from above. As a result, their ideas about the cityscape derived either from actual vistas seen from relatively low sites, or from imagined aerial perspectives. In contrast to a map, a cityscape attempts a more realistic three-dimensional presentation. The famous geographer Ptolemy, in the second century CE, carefully distinguished between mapping and pictorial representations. He defined geography as encompassing carefully measured depictions of the world. In contrast, he described chorography as localized, noting it concentrates "more on the quality of places than on their quantity or scale, aware that it should use all means to sketch the true form or likeness of places and not so much their correspondence, measure or disposition among themselves or with the heavens or with the whole of the world."[7] This more pictorial, more interpretive, more portrait-like chorographic approach approximates the modern definition of cityscape, whether seen directly or represented in images.

The differences in visual methods, interpretations, and capabilities between antiquity and today are staggering. Viewing is not just physiological, but culturally constituted. In the 1970s, art historian Norman Bryson coined the term "visuality" to describe seeing as mediated by culture.[8] Unfortunately, we can never see clearly through Roman eyes. Not only did the ancients lack optical enhancements such as glasses, but their modes of seeing drew upon shared experiences and ways of thinking that are difficult to reconstruct. The challenge is to consider the "period eye" for antiquity—how cultural mores influenced the interpretation of images, and upon what visual repertoire ancient viewers drew.[9] Invaluable attempts to reconstruct ancient visuality have been taken with studies of artworks, buildings, and viewsheds in broader rural contexts.[10] Yet what did Romans "see" when they looked at a city?

The Romans enjoyed expansive views. Architectural design, legal provisions, ancient texts, and pictorial representations all affirm a love of broad panoramas. The built fabric provides the most tangible evidence. The architectural vocabulary of Roman cities included public plazas and unobstructed augural platforms on high-points, as well as towering public structures with ample places for viewing such as the Colosseum with open arcades at every level.[11] Residential architecture boasted broad windows, jutting balconies, porticos, terraces, roof gardens, and other forms ideal for urban viewing (fig. 6.3).[12] In antiquity, as today, the upper classes preferred elevated hilltop sites; such locations were safer and more airy, and indicated wealth since the owner had to have sufficient slaves to carry water up the slopes. Once urban density increased in major cities such as Rome, urban construction frequently blocked residential views. In response, urban neighbors entered into legal private agreements or servitudes to protect prospects.[13] Ulpian, in the early third century, recorded, "in the case of the prospect, the dominant owner has this particular advantage, that nothing may be constructed so as to prevent his having a pleasing and unimpeded view."[14] Other decisions stipulated that shrubs on a roof be removed if they grew large enough to block the view, or that the sight of a specific public building should be maintained.[15] Shrewd city dwellers in Rome also exploited an expansive law guaranteeing city dwellers the right to sufficient light to conduct daily activities.[16] By protecting access to light, property owners often, though not always, preserved views as well. Remarkably, such architectural and legal evidence for the pleasure taken by Romans in urban views is not bolstered by literary sources. Overt admission of enjoyment in panorama centered almost exclusively outside the city.

Figure 6.3. Late Republican fresco, Villa of P. Fannius Synistor at Boscoreale. Courtesy: The Metropolitan Museum of Art, Rogers Fund, 1903, 03.14.13a-g.

The Romans considered viewing a pleasurable activity best indulged in the proper context, by the proper class of people. The most extensive evidence centers on villa life where wealthy Romans enjoyed a life of leisure (*otium*). Villa literature is filled with effusive descriptions of broad vistas encompassing hills, the sea, woods, other villas, and the coast. For example, Pliny the Younger recorded how his villas were laid out to frame optimal views of nature; he described the vistas from the dining couch in his rural residence at Laurentum, "at your feet you have the sea, behind are the villas, and from the head (of the couch) are (seen) the woods."[17] In a few instances, villa owners commissioned frescos that apparently mirrored the actual views of distant cities from the site.[18] City dwellers attempted to approximate villa environments in their residences. Throughout Pompeii, owners emulated villa decorative programs with faux painted vistas and landscape vignettes.[19] Significantly, such views rarely included cities as the primary subject, perhaps because urban environments were traditionally characterized as the place of work (*negotium*). The exceptions are notable; paintings of coastal cities such as those surrounding the Bay of Naples may have appeared because these vacation centers were known as much for *otium* as *negotium* (fig. 6.4).[20]

Most frequently, cityscapes occurred in pictorial narratives, tourist art, and state propaganda. Urban images above all identify place. In numerous ancient visual narratives, the inclusion of a cityscape succinctly located the action of a story. Since not many Roman observers had mental libraries filled with images of distant cities, realism was largely unnecessary. Not only could few viewers recognize actual cityscapes, but the environments shown were either mythic (Troy), or much transformed from the time of the narrative (Dido's Carthage). Identification depended on the overall context within the narrative storyline. Thus, a viewer familiar with the myth of Daedalus and his son Icarus would assume that the representation of a generic cityscape in conjunction with a youth wearing wings should be identified as Knossos, where the fatal flight took place. Simply, observers relied upon their familiarity with the stories to identify cityscapes, rather than on specific knowledge of how a city actually looked. Cityscapes were also frequently reduced to schematic representations of known urban types: the walled city, the port city, etc. In other instances, a prominent building or statue stood as an icon for the urban whole; for example, the lighthouse at Alexandria (just as the Eiffel Tower for Paris) was an effective urban sign.[21] Specific urban portraits

Figure 6.4. Wall painting of coastal cities, detail, Stabia, 55–79 CE, Museo Archeologico Nazionale, Naples. Photo: D. Favro.

were rare, usually employed to depict cities well known to contemporary viewers. They appear most often in official state art.[22]

Roman cityscapes also appeared in tourist art. Travel was a popular activity of the wealthy in antiquity.[23] Ancient travelers sought distinctly different images of cities from those required for pictorial narratives. Concerned with way-finding, they relied upon such travel aids as written itineraries and maps, including smaller pocket (or rather "toga-fold") versions. Pictorial travel maps (*itinerarium pictum*) were especially favored. A famous example is the medieval Peutinger table, believed to be a copy of a third- or fourth-century chorographic map.[24] This strip map measured 6.75 meters by 34 centimeters, a format selected to suit the material (parchment) and the Roman linear conceptualization of travel as a process of moving directly from one point to another. In such a context, accurate orientation, topography, and the actual appearance of each city were less important than the sequence, comparative scale, and type of notable physical features en route. On the Peutinger map, simplified typological icons efficiently and succinctly conveyed pertinent information about cities and their relative locations. Notably, the most important cities were represented not as architectural pictograms, but large personifications. Rome, Antioch, and Constantinople all appeared as enthroned goddesses (fig. 6.5).

Ancient travelers, like those in all periods, purchased souvenirs both as personal mementos and as documentation that they had indeed visited faraway sites. The type and class of objects varied widely. At Ephesus, tourists clamored for miniature replicas of the great Temple of Artemis; at Antioch, they bought small versions of a famous statue.[25] Images of cityscapes were also available. Tourists with limited means purchased inexpensive objects such as portable terra cotta oil lamps embossed with urban images, generally shown in bird's-eye views.[26] Such aerial panoramas allowed the purchasing tourists to show salient urban features and to claim the represented city as their own. More detailed urban illustrations appeared on mementos addressing the upscale market. The famous cut glass vials depicting Baiae and Puteoli specifically portrayed the recreational facilities frequented by wealthy tourists (fig. 6.6). Rather than a true urban panorama, the carvers showed baths, theaters, piers, and parks in elevation with identifying labels, as if these individual components, rather than the cityscape, characterized the seaside resorts.[27] Presumably, the targeted wealthy consumers of both the glass vials and the recreational facilities depicted preferred to do their panoramic viewing in the leisure of their villas.

The popularity of touristic urban representations implies an accepted social context for viewing. One can well imagine world travelers' proudly displayed mementos, mosaics, wall paintings, and maps of sites visited in their homes, where a guest's curiosity might spark a long discourse about past journeys.[28] Leisure travel implied a certain position or stature. Wealthy businessmen, senators, and the emperor all took extensive trips combining business and pleasure despite the challenges associated with journeys, from bandits to storms, plagues to uncomfortable vehicles. The

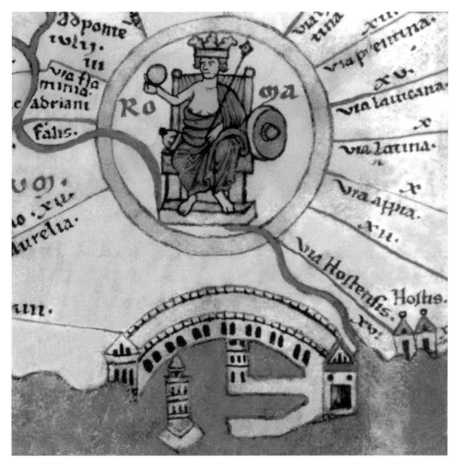

Figure 6.5. Dea Roma, Peutinger map, believed to be a copy of a fourth-century CE map of the Roman world. Photo: D. Favro.

emperor Hadrian spent the majority of his reign traveling. Just outside Rome he built an enormous villa incorporating the names and features of various buildings from across the Empire, as if encapsulating the built environments of the Roman world in his personal estate.[29] Through such a display Hadrian emphasized the extent of Roman power and his own partiality for the provinces. On a more generalized level he, like other tourists, claimed ownership of the places visited through the representation of cityscapes.

Figure 6.6. Drawing of recreational facilities and temple from Puteoli, Odemira glass flask, detail, third-century CE. Drawing: D. Favro after Ostrow.

The vicarious sense of ownership created by visiting (knowing) a place and possessing a secondary representation was a diluted reflection of the submission and control associated with images of conquered cities. In ancient literature and depictions, totalizing urban panoramas appeared frequently in relation to military and political submission. Before recounting the attack on New Carthage in 209 BCE, Polybius gave a comprehensive description of the city as if seen from on high by a military scout.[30] Seneca records that Gaius Marius, Gnaeus Pompey, and Caesar chose hilltop locations for their villas in the Campania, because, "This seemed more soldier-like, to look down from a lofty height upon lands spread far and wide below."[31] From the Republican period onward, the Romans proudly exhibited images of cities conquered in battle or possessed by other means. For example, generals often included models and paintings of captured cities in triumphal parades (fig. 6.7). Livy records that in 189 BCE, L. Scipio carried 134 simulacra of towns in his triumphal procession.[32] These cityscapes situated the military action and stood as visual trophies of territory acquired, above all justifying military expenditures. Though none of the exhibited cityscapes remain, they must have been similar to those preserved on numerous imperial monuments in Rome. In most, the viewer looks down upon the captured city, a potent visual shorthand for submission. The cityscapes on Trajan's Column display military towns and captured villages along the Danube seen from above, visually informing observers about the distant province and graphically contrasting the enemy's crudely constructed environments with the well organized layout of Roman cities and military camps (fig. 6.8).[33]

Bird's-eye views are obviously a logical way to depict large urban environments in their totality. However, the association with submission or possession should not be discounted. Aerial views of cityscapes also documented cities under imperial control. In 1998, excavators at the Baths of Trajan uncovered a remarkable fresco depicting a Roman city in an angled bird's-eye view, possibly one of several urban images on a portico constructed in the Flavian era. Despite a flurry of attributions of the city depicted (from Verona to London), its identity remains uncertain. Equally problematic is the identity of the structure on which it rests. The most convincing attribution is the porticoed headquarters of the urban prefect. Ancient sources locate the *praefectura Urbi* in this part of Rome; furthermore, Varro refers to speakers in the area looking at "painted Italy" (*Italiam pictam*).[34] La Rocca persuasively argues that representations of attractive, healthy cities would have been appropriate ornamentation for the municipal headquarters in Rome where urban information was archived. Furthermore, such prominently displayed images, even if no more readily identified by ancient than modern observers, would have effectively conveyed Roman beneficent control over other Italian cities.[35]

Rome was a magnet attracting thousands of visitors and new residents each year. Throughout the city they gazed at paintings, reliefs, and models of Athens, Syracuse, Carthage, and other cities on display in both public and private venues. Many must have wished to document their visit with a memento honoring the great capital. Remarkably, no ancient (pre-400) cityscapes of the most important city of all, Rome, have been documented.[36] Wellspring of Roman culture, locus of imperial collective events, and unchallenged center of power, Rome always occupied a unique position. In particular, the capital's size, status, and social context placed specific pressures on urban visuality, which may begin to explain the absence of visual representations.

On the most basic level, practical considerations provide a partial justification for the veil over depictions of Rome's cityscape. The capital was enormous, "stretching out indefinitely" according to Dionysius of Halicarnassus.[37] Unable to see Rome from an aerial perspective, most city dwellers saw the city either close up at street

Figure 6.7. Taddeo Zuccaro, *Triumphal Procession of Roman Soldiers Carrying a Model of a City*, drawing, c.1548. Courtesy: The J. Paul Getty Museum, Los Angeles.

Figure 6.8. Column of Trajan, relief sculpture, detail, c.112 CE, Rome. Detail showing urban constructions. Photo: D. Favro.

level or obliquely from slightly elevated locations. Vistas over the city from the hilltops, the old fortifications, or tall buildings provided only partial glimpses of the entire cityscape. By the first century CE, the city boasted a population of over one-million residents.[38] Legendary for the high price of real estate, Rome had a density of construction unrivaled elsewhere in the Roman Empire.[39] The capital's crowded conditions and dense construction further compromised viewing. In addition, pollution from thousands of wood fires obscured the city in a brown shroud. Industries such as metallurgy spewed more soot into the sky where it merged with river mists along with the smoke and steam from hundreds of bath buildings. On many days of the year pollution, described as *gravioris caeli* (heavy heaven) or *infamis aer* (infamous air) made seeing the overall cityscape a difficult proposition.[40]

Even if weather and viewing position allowed the great cityscape to be seen, was it appropriate to look? When presented with expansive urban vistas, the ancient Romans did not overtly exploit the opportunity, instead focusing on specific tasks. Thus soldiers assigned to peripheral lookout stations at high points, such as that on the Janiculum Hill, turned their backs on the city to scan westward for external threats.[41] Augurs on platforms atop Rome's major hills looked upward to read the signs sent by the gods, ignoring the cityscape at their feet. In fact, Cicero records that augurs ordered the demolition of a city house blocking their sightline to the distant Alban hills.[42]

Conceptually, the extent of Rome had potent meaning. While urban sprawl is today considered negatively, Romans perceived the untamed scope of the city as a positive attribute, equated with the physical area of the territory they controlled. In the first century BCE, Ovid succinctly wrote, "The extent of the Roman city and the world are the same."[43] Indeed, in contrast to other cities after the early pre-Republican fortifications, Rome was not constrained by city walls until the late third century CE. Jurisdictions extended to the always-changing edge of urban construction.[44] The city, like the Empire, grew ever outward; neither could be restrained or grasped by the human eye. Rome was also the beginning point of time, a fact reaffirmed by the Roman dating of events *a.u.c.* (*ab urbe condita*), "from the founding of the city."[45] To walk through the capital was to learn Roman history as embedded in urban buildings, spaces, and art. The strong link between places and collective memory was conveyed by Cicero in the late first century BCE, "Whether it is natural instinct or a mere illusion, I can't say; but one's emotions are more strongly aroused by seeing the places that tradition records to have been the favorite resort of men of note in former days, than by hearing about their deeds or reading their writings."[46] As Edwards has perceptively noted, such thinking resolutely linked viewing of the city with the flow of history.[47] Plutarch, in the first century CE, wrote, "A city, like a living thing . . . is a united and continuous whole. To create a multiplicity, or rather an infinity, of cities by chronological distinctions is like creating many men out of one."[48] Rome, with its long and complex history, could not be fixed in a single moment, like a fly in amber. Other cities might be possessed in representations on the walls of houses and tourist art, or on state displays of conquered cities, but Rome could not be.[49]

Only one category of observer had the status and vantage point to look at the ancient capital without shame: the gods who occupied the heavens.[50] Vitruvius explained in the first century BCE that temples should be sited, "so . . . that the greatest possible part within the walls of the city may be visible," implying that the gods were partial to urban views.[51] Beyond all other cities in size and stature, Rome could be seen (and thus possessed) only by those with divine powers or their representatives. Comprehensive viewing of Rome was not an appropriate human activity. In the second century, Aelius Aristides wrote of the capital: "About her not only is it impossible to speak properly, but it is impossible even to see her properly. In truth it requires some all-seeing Argos—rather, the all-seeing god who dwells in the city. For beholding so many hills occupied by buildings, or on plains so many meadows completely urbanized, or so much land brought under the name of one city, who could survey her accurately? And from what point of observation?"[52] The distinction was clear; the gods from their elevated stance could appreciate Rome's urban panoramas; humans who sought aerial perspectives, like Icarus, courted disaster.

Humans could, however, safely view Dea Roma (see fig. 6.5). Throughout the Mediterranean, the ancients represented the fortune of a city with a personification of the goddess Fortuna (Tyche) wearing a mural crown and carrying an appropriate urban attribute.[53] The goddess Roma at first glance seems to fit this typology, but as with all things connected with the capital, she is unique. Dea Roma represented not just the city or its fortune, but a more expansive conflation of the Roman capital, state, and people. The cult first appeared in the east during the Republican era, established by Greeks anxious to curry favor with the growing power in central Italy.

They associated Dea Roma not so much with the physical city as with the abstract conception of Roman political might, addressing her as the goddess of "the People of Rome," or "Rome and the Roman Benefactors."[54] The alternative spelling of "Rhome," based on the Greek word for strength, along with the deity's early depiction as a warrior, underscore this conceptualization. Thus when Romans looked at representations of Roma as an armed female or later as an enthroned matron, their minds filled with thoughts of the state's collective status and power, not of the capital city's appearance.[55]

In antiquity, the cityscape of Rome was a metonym for the powerful state and its people, as well as a stage for action and self-promotion. The acknowledged wellspring of Roman culture and ongoing center of power, Rome was the locus for significant political, religious, artistic, and major commercial undertakings. Senators had to reside in the capital at least part of the year and participate there in diverse political and religious proceedings. Certain momentous rituals could only occur in Rome, including the highest military ceremony, the revered triumph.[56] Ambitious individuals had to be known in Rome. During the Republic, building patrons competed avidly, constructing numerous memorials that advertised personal achievements; the emperors continued the tradition. Temples, commemorative arches and columns, and other buildings were effective urban advertisements inside the capital; outside Rome they were equally well known from images on coins and artworks. Every locale in the city also clamored for attention; each was associated with a *genius loci*, or spirit of the place, shaped and enriched by all events and structures linked with the particular spot.[57] A Roman looking at a site saw not only the extant buildings, but in his mind's eye also a full range of associations, as noted previously in Cicero's statement that places aroused emotions about traditions more strongly than deeds recorded through speech or writing.[58] Such readings reinforced the notion of Rome as composed of innumerable atomized interventions, a conceptualization that deflected any desire to visually represent the cityscape as a whole.

Romans looking at the city emphasized specific actions, events, or buildings, rather than the simple pleasure of an urban prospect. When Maenius sold his house in the first century BCE, he reserved ownership of one pillar for himself and his heirs so they could climb up to view the gladiatorial contests, but he did not acknowledge that such an elevated platform would also be ideal for looking at the city.[59] Similarly, Martial described looking out the window of his garret apartment to enjoy the sight of nearby laurel trees, not the larger cityscape.[60] Gazing at the sparkling marble buildings of the Augustan Campus Martius (a field to the northwest of the city center), Strabo took care to describe the impressive view as "present[ing] to the eye the appearance of a stage-painting," thus mediating his appreciation for a broad urban view through the filter of art.[61] Pictorial imagery likewise emphasized individualized events rather than urban appearance. On a pair of Hadrianic reliefs, the buildings of the Forum Romanum are barely visible behind figures taking part in various state acts under the emperor Trajan (fig. 6.9).[62] Urban appearance was secondary even when the architecture was the primary subject. For example, carvings on the tomb of a family of builders, the Haterii, show elevations of major buildings. Yet the image is not an urban vignette, but a visual list of the major works on which the deceased had worked (fig. 6.10).[63]

Other complex social factors further shaped Roman urban visuality. Property owners today associate status and value with expansive urban views and privacy. In contrast, the Romans privileged views toward and into structures, especially their homes. Drawing upon revered Republican sentiments, politicians demonstrated their integrity and *dignitas* literally through an open door and open window policy. During the first century BCE, an architect offered to design a house so that no one could look in; outraged, the client M. Livius Drusus ordered, "If you possess the skill you must build my house in such a way that whatever I do shall be seen by all."[64] The most prominent citizens left the doors of their houses open to indicate availability, lack of enemies, and overall honesty.[65] The principle of "nothing to hide" stimulated a preference for prominent, highly visible residential sites. Cicero boasted about his house on the Palatine, "My house, gentlemen, stands full in view of well-nigh the whole city."[66] Since sightlines are always reflexive, buildings visible to all Rome likewise proffered reverse views out over the cityscape. However, as objects of emulation and veneration, powerful citizens deigned to admit they enjoyed reciprocal views toward those of lesser standing. In this regard, another factor may also have shaped Roman urban visuality. Only the most wealthy, and lucky, of property owners were able to purchase highly visible houses in Rome. The majority of the populace lived in multi-

Figure 6.9. Hadrianic relief, detail, 117–118 CE, Curia, Rome. Depicts events in the Forum Romanum under Trajan. Photo: D. Favro.

unit apartment buildings, with the more affluent occupying larger dark apartments on the ground and lower floors. The less well-off lived in garret apartments with steep steps and no running water, but spectacular views.[67] Ironically, any boast about an expansive vista from one's residence could possibly be interpreted as an admission of comparatively limited resources, if not outright impoverishment. A person of stature spoke of rural vistas from his villa, not urban panoramas. Martial poetically described an expansive scene of the great capital city, but he took care to note that the vista originated from an appropriate viewing point: his cousin's villa outside the city.[68]

A high-born Roman who expressed delight at viewing Rome from within the city was open to criticism for being pleasure-oriented or irresponsible. In the late Republic, Cicero maligned his enemy Clodius by recounting his attempt to acquire a desirable hilltop house first by threatening to obstruct light to the structure and then

Figure 6.10. Tomb of the Haterii, relief sculpture, detail, early second century CE, Museo Laterano, Vatican. This detail may show buildings on which the deceased had worked. Photo: D. Favro.

by poisoning the unwilling seller. He followed with a more subtle, but equally powerful denigration, stating, "He [Clodius] had set his heart upon a portico with private chambers, paved to the distance of three hundred feet, with a fine court surrounded by a colonnade, on the Palatine Hill, commanding a superb view, and everything else in character, so as far to surpass all other houses in luxury and splendor."[69] By underscoring Clodius's preoccupation with views outward, rather than toward his house, Cicero implied his rival was inappropriately creating a villa-like structure in the city for personal leisure, with no concern for visual access by city residents. In the first century CE, Seneca the Elder asked students of rhetoric to determine damages in the following situation: a rich man offered to buy a tree blocking his view, but his poor neighbor refused to sell. The rich man then set fire to the tree, burning the neighbor's house as well. Each individual presented his case. The rich man contended that removal of the tree was essential since it made his house unhealthy by shutting off the sky and passage of air; he made no mention of a vista. In opposition, the poor neighbor flatly rejected the "reasons of health" justification arguing, "Here is fire being used to give the eye pleasure, to clear a view." He reinforced this powerful slur by contrasting his own modest desire to preserve the vista of a single tree in his small courtyard, with the rich man's attempt to have a broad, villa-like panorama of the city.[70]

Even the emperor responded to cultural mores about urban viewing. After the disastrous fire of 64 CE, Nero constructed a villa-like residence in the center of Rome. Like other elaborate country estates, the Domus Aurea maximized opportunities for expansive rural panoramas. Nero fabricated not only a lengthy viewing colonnade, but also numerous rural amenities to entice the eye, including, as Suentoinus records, "a pond too, like a sea, surrounded with buildings to represent cities, besides tracts of country, varied by tilled fields, vineyards, pastures and woods, with great numbers of wild and domestic animals."[71] Notably, the representations of cities (perhaps in the form of physical models) served as artificial, picturesque alternatives to the all too real views of Rome beyond the borders of Nero's urban "villa."

In the rural context of the villa, seeing dominated over being seen; in Rome the converse was true. Everyone watched prominent citizens as they moved through the capital with their vast retinues or unabashedly gazed into the homes of the mighty. Similarly, from throughout the vast Empire all eyes, like all roads, turned toward Rome.[72] Though everyone saw the great capital, their viewing was shaped by complex societal filters. Familiar to all, center of the ever-expanding Empire, the city could not be constrained in a fixed image. Furthermore, human observers had neither the appropriate vantage point nor the status to look upon the great capital. Distinctly different from all other cities in size and stature, Rome was too large, too powerful, too complex to be possessed by human vision.

Modern researchers have no such compunction about viewing ancient Rome. The visual power of historical recreations logically focuses attention on the activity of the eye. Impressive representations of the Roman capital, such as the plaster model of Constantinian Rome (see fig. 6.1), frequently gain visual authority, threatening to become more real to contemporary observers than the irretrievable appearance of the original cityscape. Today, new visualization tools are focusing even greater attention on sight. Virtual reality models allow modern observers to complement static images with dynamic interaction (see fig. 6.2). Observers move through recreated digital environments in real time, approximating the kinetic viewing experience of city dwellers. Real-time models allow viewers to move from the macro to micro scale, comparing the vistas of land-bound urban residents and the imagined panoramas of the gods from on high.

When evaluating ancient and modern re-creations of Roman cities, scholars tend to analyze the accuracy and comprehensiveness of the presentation, but rarely do they consider the visuality of the period depicted or of the reconstruction itself. Both are crucial. What researchers create, what they show, and what they see is mediated by their own cultural backgrounds, training, and disciplinary emphases regarding viewing. Understanding these factors can clarify and enrich findings and also promote exchange across disciplinary and national borders. Knowledge of ancient visuality can, and should, inform reconstruction work, providing insights about the placement, form, and orientation of historical buildings. Awareness of ancient viewing preferences and constraints promotes more accurate evaluations of extant historical recreations. Care should be taken to modulate the viewing experience. Too often presenters move through digital models at rapid modern speeds, rather than approximating the tempo of antiquity shaped by the type of conveyance, urban crowding, and the sequencing of experiences along a path. Most modern reconstructions present Rome in bird's-eye images. Such totalizing vistas allow the majority of the cityscape to be seen, yet they privilege a modern, not ancient, preference for panoramic viewing. Certainly, the Romans utilized aerial views of cities, but usually to convey a sense of possession. Modes of depiction, like modes of seeing, had meaning and varied according to the status of the viewer and the object of the gaze. By acknowledging how views of the cityscape were shaped by Roman visuality we can begin to understand, if not fully lift, the veil that obscured viewing of Rome in antiquity.

MAKING VISION MANIFEST

D. Fairchild Ruggles

Frame, Screen, and View in Islamic Culture

AN INTEREST IN VISTAS, IN WHICH THE VIEWER LOOKS FROM ARCHITECTURE TO landscape, is deeply embedded in Islamic history and culture. The landscape itself was a meaningful form that was given a shape, especially in elite gardens that expressed the human ability to cultivate and control the land, and the architecture of palaces and mosques often included windows, balconies, and pavilions whose purpose was to provide a place from which to regard the landscape from a fixed position. While in religious environments, gardens and representations of nature could be visual signs for the fecundity of the earth and the paradise promised to the faithful, in palaces and residential architecture the act of looking at landscape could express political hierarchy, territorial possession, and the material prosperity achieved under good stewardship.[1] Elsewhere I have examined the phenomenon of the *mirador* (a fixed site for viewing) as a mechanism for seeing not only space but the spatial field of landscape, and other scholars have studied the *jharoaka* (a projecting balcony for viewing and being viewed) as a ritual instrument of sovereign presence and identity.[2] The focus here is the difference between Islamic and Western visuality in order to understand how and why Western art historical analysis has been insufficient for explaining Islamic ways of seeing.

Although there exists an extensive literature on perspective, representation, and the psychoanalytic theories of vision, these works invariably address themselves to the Western eye viewing Western objects in space as conceived in Western terms. For historians of Islamic visual culture, this is deeply problematic. While Islamic ways of seeing can be addressed by these theoretical systems, some form of cultural translation is required to adjust for the fact that the keen interest in naturalistic spatial perspective found in European painting is subordinated to rich surface patterns in Islamic painting. Moreover, "looking" has historically had a very different social meaning in Islam than it does in Europe and the West. In the Islamic context, where book illustration and painting did not emerge as a significant artistic form until the thirteenth century, representation was less pictorial than spatial. Indeed, it often focused on landscape. To look through a frame before the thirteenth century meant seeing a "real" landscape through a window aperture, and although the scene was comprised of a great many natural elements—sky, rocks, and mountains—in conjunction with clearly constructed objects such as houses, farms, and city walls, it was perceived by eyes that had learned to read and interpret the view according to cultural modalities. In the Islamic context, therefore, the intimate connection of vision and landscape requires an examination of each individually as well as in conjunction with the other.

Landscape is an objective form that, like architecture, has volume and material presence. Also like architecture, its scale can be immense, surpassing what an individual viewer can perceive from one standpoint even when the glance is sweeping. Even more than architecture, landscape is often the object of representation in print, paint, and photography. Indeed, some art historians do not distinguish between the image of landscape and the landscape itself, so that "a landscape" has come to mean a landscape representation. Unfortunately, this conflation of image and thing suggests that the image emerges from the thing itself, instead of as a product of a human view-ing apparatus in which eyes, brain, and memory are engaged. Although the physiology of sight is universal (at least at birth), the ways that the mind learns to interpret the visual information conveyed by the eyes develops within a cultural context. Even the muscular action of eye movement is partially learned, so that eyes accustomed to reading from left to right will move slightly differently than those in a culture that reads in vertical columns or, as in the Islamic world, from right to left. Vision, particularly as a means of perceiving the spaces and forms of landscape, is a cultural construction.

The literature on vision and contemporary visual theory scarcely addresses either cultural formation or the built environment. Instead it reveals a preoccupation with the picture plane that intrudes between the viewer and the thing represented. The art historian Ernst Gombrich sometimes described this plane as a mirror in which we see our own reflection diminished or a sheet of glass on which the artist can, in theory, make a realistic transcription of the world. But he pointed out that consciousness intervenes to cloud the transparency of the glass and hinders the exact reproduction of the world, because it is not the world that is recorded by the artists but rather the world as seen or perceived according to a schema or visual mode.[3] For Gombrich, the world was simply material for producing representations of it; he was not particularly interested in the real complexity of its topography, weather, and built forms. Even when scholars such as Martin Jay shifted the emphasis from representation to vision itself, as in the idea of the simultaneous existence of "scopic regimes,"[4] there was an underlying assumption that the relationship between the viewer and the world is expressed in the representations that are made of the world (or representations of that viewer's ideas about the world). In this sense, even modern abstraction is a kind of representation because it is a trace of the artistic process, a metonymy in which a dribble of paint records the movement of an artist such as Jackson Pollock on the canvas. In the work of the op art painters of the 1960s, the picture plane seems to have an ephemeral fictive space caused by the eye's willingness to read abstract convergent lines and color juxtapositions as depicting three-dimensional space. In visual theory from the 1960s onward, the vision question has focused on representation, particularly representations made on two-dimensional planes—the canvas, photograph, or mirror. There has been considerably less analysis of three-dimensional space—architecture and landscape—and hardly anything on non-Western visuality.

Historically, the ubiquitous picture plane was absent in Islamic culture where neither representation nor mimesis was the primary visual activity. Islamic artists and viewers preferred to see the thing itself rather than a realistic or abstracted representation of it. Thus in glazed ceramic plates from Iran of the ninth through eleventh centuries (fig. 7.1) or calligraphic Qur'an pages (fig. 7.2), the only space was the two-dimensional surface of the ceramic or paper itself on which words are written. Here the script does not function as a representation. Although in linguistic terms, written words are signs for speech, in visual terms, once that transfer from speaking to writing occurs, the script loses the ability to represent itself. Hence, the elegantly written script on the page of a Qur'an manuscript does not depict another set of words in a mimetic sense—they aren't pictures of words, they are the very language of the Qur'an. While there may some artistic license in the style of calligraphy, the Qur'an itself is a fixed text written in Arabic, and there is no interpretive freedom whatsoever in choosing the words to communicate God's message. (Even *muezzins* who make the call to prayer and professional readers of the Qur'an are strictly trained so that the short vowels, which are not written in classical Arabic, are learned and spoken absolutely correctly.) This is not just a heightened form of realism, a matter of the "copy" being completely true to the original, because realism is predicated on the idea that there is a relationship between a thing and a representation of it. However, in reproducing script, that distance is collapsed. A manuscript or printed book does not represent the Qur'an; it *is* the Qur'an.

The distinction between words as images and words as language is important because script is one of the principal art forms in Islamic culture, and yet it is one in which mimesis has little or no place. It is an example of an Islamic art that, lacking representation, is inadequately addressed by the tools of traditional art history as well as contemporary visual theory. With the exceptions of the handsomely illuminated frontispieces, Qur'ans seldom figure in art history courses; they are more often studied as texts belonging to the realm of paleography.

To return to the picture plane: the Western picture plane represents things external to it (as an artist's canvas refers to a scene beyond itself). But this measurement

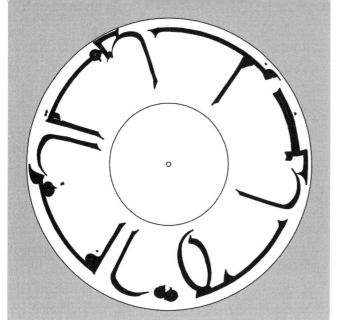

Figure 7.1. Glazed ceramic plate, tenth century CE, Iran. Drawing by Binaifer Variava.

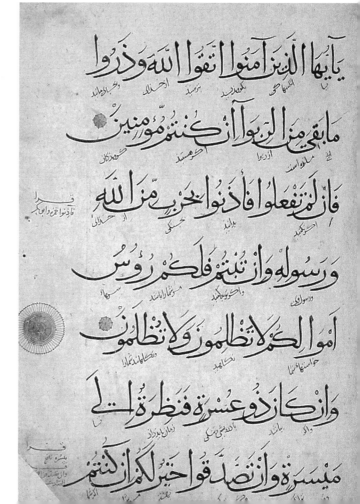

Figure 7.2. Qur'an page, thirteenth century CE, Egypt, Spurlock Museum, University of Illinois, Urbana-Champaign. Courtesy: Spurlock Museum.

of the distance between the external world and the artist's rendering is *not* the problem in Islam, because Islam avoids mimetic representation. And so, while the interrogation of "the real" by Derrida, Baudrillard, and others brought about a profound change in Western thought, such models are usually predicated on Western viewers and ways of seeing that have limited use elsewhere.[5] This European legacy, in which methodology is developed from a set of problems provoked by figural imagery, has shaped—or distorted—scholarly studies on Islamic art, architecture, and visual culture. First, the emphasis on representation has led to a devaluing of ornament as "minor" and even meaningless.[6] Because ornament is one of the primary visual vehicles in Islam, this relegates Islamic art to a secondary status vis-à-vis Western art. There is no Velázquez, no Picasso; there are just glassmakers, potters, and plate painters.

Second, the European theoretical legacy has caused scholars in both the East and West to seek to explain Islamic visual culture in Western terms, and this has led to the search for an Islamic iconography. The Islamic version of iconography does not seek to identify saints and their symbols because of course there is relatively little figural imagery and an active prohibition against representations of the Prophet or God. Instead, scholars find iconography in the selection of Qur'an verses displayed in architectural inscriptions and in the spatial location of architecture and its "appropriation of site." Oleg Grabar proposed an "iconography of appropriation" with his study of the Dome of the Rock (Jerusalem, completed 691), showing that the newly arrived Muslim conquerors claimed the highest point of the city of Jerusalem for their monument, which capped a rock of profound significance to the Jewish and Christian populations of that city (fig. 7.3).[7] The centrally planned, domed building with its ambulatory and golden mosaics appropriated not only the site but also a Byzantine architectural model, the martyrium. The inscriptions that encircled the inner rim of the dome stated the fundamental creed of Islam, "there is no God but God, he was not born, nor did he give birth . . ." These Qur'anic verses emphasized the fundamental difference with Christianity: the non-embodiment of God and rejection of the implied polytheism of the Trinity. What is astounding about this study is how Grabar was able to translate the absence of figural imagery at the Dome of the Rock—no Christ Pantocrator, no apostles, no sheep—into a brilliantly conceived iconographic model based on place, architectural typology, and epigraphy. While

Figure 7.3. Dome of the Rock, Jerusalem, completed 691 CE. Photo: R. Ousterhout.

the concept of an iconography of place has important ramifications for the analysis of landscape that extends well beyond the framework of Islamic culture, the emphasis on iconography, with its Western roots, has led a great many of the historians following after Grabar to adapt Western theory to fit Islamic art and architecture instead of developing an appropriate theory from within.

Islamic art in its formative period eschewed figural imagery in the public sphere, but the oft-repeated dictum that Islamic art lacks figural imagery is incorrect. Mural images of the human figure—even nude—were placed on bathhouse walls (such as Qusayr Amra in early eighth-century Jordan) and palaces (such as the Qasr al-Khalifa, Samarra, 836–839). Human and animal figures also appeared in textiles, metalwork, ivory, ceramics, book illustrations, and even large-scale sculpture. Only in specifically religious environments such as mosques and tombs and in religious

Figure 7.4. *Maqamat* page, 1237 CE, Paris Bibl. Nat, Ms. arabe 5847 (Schefer Hariri), folio 138, recto.

Courtesy: Biblioteque Nationale.

Figure 7.5. Perspective construction of Masaccio's *Trinity*, Santa Maria Novella, Florence, 1426–1428. Redrawn by Binaifer Variava.

texts such as Qur'an manuscripts, collections of *hadith* (sayings of the Prophet), and prayer books were such representations consistently forbidden so as to avoid the error of idolatry.

But the book arts, which began with a few illustrated exemplars in the late tenth or eleventh century and bloomed into an active painting industry in the thirteenth century (in part due to the availability of the new medium of paper), were often illustrated with figural scenes. Scientific manuscripts in the field of astronomy and medicine were sometimes illustrated. Early illustrated narrative manuscripts such as the *Kalila wa Dimna* and the *Maqamat* (fig. 7.4) contained scenes in which animals and people were depicted in three-dimensional space, yet the attempted realism took a form that did not emphasize an illusionistic depth of field. Trees and buildings were like flat stage sets with the figures placed next to or in front of them. In contrast, Western paintings such as Masaccio's *Trinity* in Santa Maria Novella in Florence, 1426–1428, used the single vanishing point of linear perspective to create the illusion of spatial recession (fig. 7.5). Just as the space receded into the picture plane, it also seemed to project outward from it, placing the viewer in the same fictive visual field as the canvas. But Islamic painting of that period and others offered no such spatial artifice. Not until the modern period did Islamic painters concern themselves with the realistic depiction of volumetric spaces.

In one of the scenes of the *Haft Awrang*, a mid-sixteenth century Persian manuscript copy illustrated with sixteen images, the planes that form the floor and inner and outer textile of the tent are ornamented with bright patterns that claim the surface of the paper as their own, visually negating what one intellectually knows is a spatial environment (fig. 7.6).[8] Even the leaves of the trees are flattened as if pressed against a glass surface, and where a shrub pushes out of the picture frame into the margin on the left side, it adopts the same sinuous forms as the marginalia so that there is a visual merger of the paper border and the scene within. Thus, even the frame shares the same two-dimensional surface as the picture. This is not Gombrich's glass; it refuses such transparency and insists on its own planar flatness. Because the space doesn't recede along neatly indicated lines toward the background of the painting, it also cannot extend forward into the space of the viewer. Instead, the viewer is positioned on the outside of the picture plane and is meant to stay there.

The lack of interest in figural and mimetic representation in Islamic art had ramifications for the way that space was treated in painting and the built environment. More importantly, it reveals a visual field that is very different from that of the West. In the Islamic visual field, the viewer is positioned not by lines receding into space, but by an insistent flatness that puts me-the-viewer *here* and the object-landscape *there*. But what mediates between the two? How is one connected with the thing seen? In Islamic art, not much intervenes between the world and the viewer's consciousness of it. Until the sixteenth century, Islamic architecture did not reproduce the viewer's experience of looking through painted landscapes and scenes, but instead framed vision so that the object—a real landscape of houses and trees—was presented as a view.[9] In other words, Islamic visuality is about *presentation*, not *representation*, with the frame as the mechanism that sets the exterior world off as an observable spectacle. The frame creates the positions of here versus there, or of viewer and view, and in so doing, it establishes subject and object in opposition to each other. In this area of subjectivity expressed (or realized) through the encounter with the world, Islamic culture and contemporary visual theory can speak to each other.

In the Islamic context, not only are the objects (the landscape and its architecture) "Islamic," but the entire apparatus of vision is culturally produced. While the anatomy of the retina, nerves, and brain cells may partially explain how an image moves from the eye to human consciousness, and Gestalt theory may demonstrate the existence of an underlying structure that causes all human beings to read some forms in the same way, precisely how forms are interpreted and understood (for example their size or distance) and how meaning is ascribed to things that are seen is a cultural

Figure 7.6. *Haft Awrang,* Iran, 1556–1565. Freer, Smithsonian. Courtesy: Smithsonian.

process that requires other forms of inquiry. There is no universal pair of eyes or physiology that explains every aspect of sight; some modes of seeing must be learned through experience. To give an example, the single vanishing point and converging lines of linear perspective work correctly as a mathematical construct and explain *one* experience of seeing—and it was a particularly convincing explanation for Renaissance philosophers and artists—but it does not explain *all* visual experience. As early as 1927, Erwin Panofsky, in *Perspective as Symbolic Form*, critiqued the supposed accuracy of linear perspective by pointing out that human beings do not stand in a fixed position with a single unmoving eye.[10] And certainly the oblique and reflected glances in Velázquez's *Las Meninas*, the nineteenth-century experiments with binocular photography and the stereoscope, Mary Cassatt's dialogic visual axes, and the Cubist interest in refracted volumes are evidence enough that single-point perspective reigned for a relatively short period of time.

In Islam, the linear perspective that was a product of the West's Cartesian way of seeing and thinking was absent, but the shunning of linear perspective was not due to an ignorance of mathematical theory, astronomy, and logic among Muslim scholars. To the contrary, many of the mathematical texts and works of classical philosophy that fueled the West's Renaissance were conveyed to Europe by Muslim, Jewish, and Christian scholars who flourished in the atmosphere of competition and patronage offered in Islamic intellectual centers such as Cordoba and Baghdad. Indeed, important works on optics and the physiology of the eye, such as Ibn al-Haytham's *Optics*, were produced by Muslim scholars.[11] Islam did not lack mathematics, but it did espouse a theology that led to a preference for abstraction over figural representation.

With respect to the visual field, instead of choosing to explore the relationship between viewer and world by means of pictorial representations, Islamic artists and architects found ways of commenting on how space and subjectivity are constructed by positioning the actual subject in the actual world. Instead of representation in the form of the occasional wall fresco, images and decoration were encountered in handheld objects such as ceramic, metalwork, and glass vessels, and in complex architectural environments. One of the principal ways that the constructedness of the two positions of the visual field—viewer and object of the view—was expressed was in the conceptual dichotomy between body/architecture and landscape.

Historically, in the Islamic cultural context, the acts of looking, seeing, and being seen were carefully controlled. For example, in all but the poorest class, the human body (of both sexes) was modestly covered so that it could not be seen. In urban space, the streets were narrow and angled to forbid long vistas. Gateways were constructed with bent entrances to allow movement but not vision. Windows were often veiled by screens that prevented sunlight from heating the building's interior but that also allowed the inhabitants to look outward without being observed. These architectural screens—called *jali* in South Asia and *mashribiyya* in the Arab world— draw attention to the windows that frame views of streets, gardens, landscape, and the world of human inhabitation. Even more importantly, they are vehicles that make evident the window frame's split between subject and object, body and world, architecture and landscape. In a sense, they are equivalent to the Western pictorial frame because both the Western picture and the Islamic *jali* screen require the viewer to look at the planar surface *qua* surface as well as through it to a real or fictive space. The pleasure for the viewer lies in the quick shift from plane to volume, from material thing to the world beyond it.

The architectural screens that allow and deny vision are among the very same decorative objects that Western art history dismisses as "minor" because they lack representation (and iconography). There is, however, one outstanding exception: the stone screen that fills the window of the sixteenth-century Sidi Sa'id Mosque in Ahmadabad, India. This screen has attracted a fair amount of notice and appears in many surveys of art and architecture that focus on Islamic culture.[12] In the *qibla* wall (the wall of the mosque's prayer hall nearest to Mecca, to which prayer is directed) there are five windows, two of which are filled by screens forming the image of a tree in their stone tracery (fig. 7.7). The tree seems figural (to a Western eye, perhaps even Christ-like) in its strong centralizing posture, with a trunk or body and arms outstretched. The windows in the Ahmadabad mosque are placed so high on the wall that one cannot look through them to anything; they merely serve as light filters that form a figural image, like a stained glass window (fig. 7.8). This screen does not behave much like a screen because it looks as solid as a framed painting or tympanum with a figural scene, and that is precisely how it is treated by scholars. There are equally ornate but much smaller *jali* screens with swirling vines in the Jami Mosque of Champaner (in

Figure 7.7. Window screen, exterior view, Sidi Sa'id Mosque, Ahmadabad, 1572. Photo: D. F. Ruggles.

Gujarat), which served as a dynastic capital in the fifteenth century until it was replaced by Ahmadabad. The two cities belong to the same orbit of patronage, but Champaner has received scant attention from historians.[13] Elsewhere, the pattern in *jali* or *mashribiyya* screens occasionally took the form of an interlacing vine, as in the screens from the tenth-century palace city Madinat al-Zahra' (Cordoba). But even among screens with vegetal designs, the powerfully presented central figure from the Sidi Sa'id Mosque windows is unusual. It has been singled out by historians not because it is typical of Islamic architecture, but because it is a mimetic representation that fulfills the criteria of an art object. Other less figurally suggestive screens

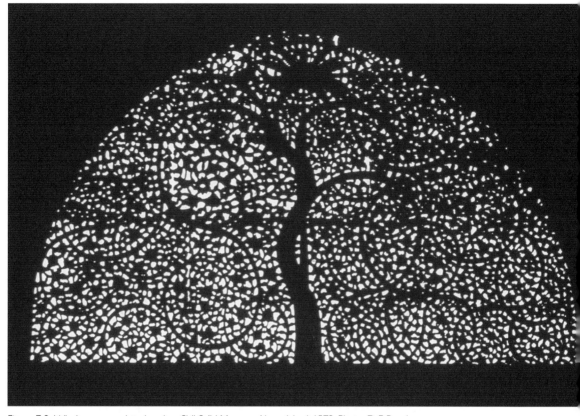

Figure 7.8. Window screen, interior view, Sidi Sa'id Mosque, Ahmadabad, 1572. Photo: D. F. Ruggles.

are ignored because they merely fill windows, and of course windows are the places in a building where the architecture is *absent*. However, they are the very locations where the landscape becomes part of the architecture, even to the extent of merging into it as an image perceived in the viewer's eye.

In Islamic architecture, beginning at least as early as the mid-ninth century, palaces were provided with windows that positioned the viewer to look toward the gardens within the palace walls and outward to the surrounding landscape. In Islamic Spain, this central positioning, and especially the elevation given to the viewer in raised pavilions or hilltop palaces such as the Alhambra, gave the viewer an enhanced social or political importance. The privileged view was a critical instrument of sovereignty and a metaphor in which the primary viewer was the king, the viewed landscape was understood to be his territory, and the act of looking mirrored his supervisory role as steward of kingdom and landscape. The frame of the window set the landscape up as a view; something that was both a *presentation* of a real working landscape as well as a *representation* of the Spanish-Islamic landscape in its entirety. The representation did not rely on mimesis—after all, there is nothing fictive about it—it was a real landscape of trees and earth that was observed from the palace windows, not painted substitutions; instead, the representation was achieved by metonymy, in which one tree stood for a forest, one mountain range stood for the kingdom's entire political boundaries.[14]

Because the frame separated the viewer's architectural space from the viewed space of the landscape, it delineated the positions of subject and object in the visual field. This articulation of the visual field appears over and over in Islamic architecture from the middle of the eighth century to the present and geographically from Morocco to South Asia. In Western architecture, too, there are famous examples of windows and framed views—Louis XIV's view from his centrally positioned bedchamber at Versailles is prominent among them—but windows have a particular primacy in the Islamic world. For example, the Mughal forts at Agra, Delhi, and Lahore were planned with the residential pavilions poised along the river's edge, overlooking the landscape from elevations that allowed for panoramic views.[15] At the Agra Fort, the seventeenth-century cluster of pavilions called the Khass Mahal, where the emperor Shah Jahan slept, stood above a four-part garden within the palace walls with pools, water channels, and ornately shaped garden beds, while outwardly it enjoyed a dramatic view of the Yamuna River and the opposite bank, green with orchards and garden estates. Similar views were possible from the golden *bangla* (curved roofed) pavilions that flanked the emperor's chamber and from every pavilion along the palace's riverfront façade (fig. 7.9).

The Mughal love of the framed view was quickly adopted by Hindu patrons with a vested stake in Mughal politics in the late sixteenth century. These were members of the Rajput warrior caste who became enmeshed in the Mughal administration by serving as their regional governors and by marrying their daughters into the Mughal royal house.[16] One such was the Rajput ruler who built the Amber Fort above the city

Figure 7.9. Bangla-roofed pavilion, Agra Fort, Agra, c. 1660. Photo: D. F. Ruggles.

of Jaipur at the beginning of the seventeenth century. The fort is an example of a non-Muslim palace that nonetheless reflects Mughal artistic taste. Rectangular in plan, it was built in successive phases, beginning at the south end. Of the two new courtyards that were added to the north by Mirza Raja Jai Singh I in the mid-seventeenth century, one was the raja's own sumptuous quarters and the other was a courtyard for semipublic reception. A monumental gate bearing an image of Ganesh, the elephant-headed god associated with auspicious beginnings, marked the threshold between them. This Ganesh figure was by no means the only explicit sign of the patron's religious identity. Other formal elements such as elevated rooftop terraces and a small Hindu temple inserted into a corner of this semipublic court likewise proclaimed the patron's affiliation. However, while Hindu motifs may have been explicit in the outer reception court, in the raja's private courtyard, Mughal architectural models were closely followed as a sign of political and cultural affiliation.[17] The raja's court adopted an elab-

Figure 7.10. Raja's court, Amber Fort, Jaipur, c. 1600. Photo: D. F. Ruggles.

orated four-part garden plan with a central water feature that was standard among Mughal palace gardens. Moreover, it stood on a hilltop above a stream that was dammed to create an artificial lake, following the typology of the classic Mughal waterfront garden at Agra.

The display of water was a prominent feature of the raja's courtyard garden. From the halls on the east and west sides of the courtyard, water poured down a chute (*chadar*) and over a panel of tiered niches (*chini khana*) to flow through narrow channels of white marble, collecting in the central star-shaped pool (fig. 7.10). At the Amber Fort, the gardens were walled and neither they nor their inhabitants were seen by the public eye of the outer world. However, the palace residents themselves saw magnificent views of the world around them by looking through the windows, or mounting stairs to the airy belvedere (*chhatri*) on the second story of the palace. Looking directly outward from this eastern face, they could see the dramatic profile

Figure 7.11. View from Raja's courtyard, Amber Fort, Jaipur, c.1600. Photo: D. F. Ruggles.

of rugged mountains (fig. 7.11); in the valley below, they saw the Maunbari garden, an artificial platform built in the lake that was divided into an ornate geometry of parterres by means of slightly raised stone partitions (fig. 7.12). The Maunbari garden is so strikingly two-dimensional in its symmetrical layout that it must have been intended to be read as a flat composition from the perspective of the palace above. It was viewed from a specific vantage point so that the garden below and the belvedere above, although distinct structures, were united in a single visual field. The concept of a visual field that unites architecture and landscape is important not only because it explains why architecture's reach extended far beyond itself, but also because in this duality the division between *self* and *space* becomes apparent.

By the late seventeenth century, residents on the western side of the Amber Fort could gaze upward toward the Jaigarh Fort where there was similarly a keen interest in the control and manipulation of vision within as well as beyond the garden.

Figure 7.12. Maunbari garden, Amber Fort, Jaipur, c. 1600. Photo: D. F. Ruggles.

Built about a half a century after Amber Fort by the same family of patrons, the Jaigarh Fort stands on a high peak and has stupendous views of mountains, deep valleys, lakes, and streams. The fort, which is in poor condition now, was closed to outsiders until 1983 and even today it is such a steep climb along a ruinous road that it receives few visitors.[18] There is no attempt to maintain the garden plantings or fill the ornamental pools. However, at the north end of the fortress enclosure, a large courtyard has the layout of a classic Mughal four-part garden (*chahar bagh*) with sunken quadrants. Its north-south and east-west axes are articulated by pavements that meet at a central pool (fig. 7.13). The courtyard is surrounded by high walls with parapets where guards once patrolled, but where the north-south axis of the four-part plan ter-

Figure 7.13. Courtyard, Jaigarh Fort, Jaipur, c. 1600. Photo: D. F. Ruggles.

minates at the wall, there is a huge triple-arched opening that invites the eye to survey the vertiginous mountain landscape. The present aperture was made at a later date, but it enlarged an already extant window.[19] It offers a stunning view of the water source that supplied the Amber Fort and settlements below. Another window on the west side looks down onto the Amber Fort itself.

The Islamic preoccupation with vistas was embraced here by a Hindu patron (mirroring the enthusiastic adoption of Hindu forms such as brackets and corbels by Muslim builders and patrons). However, the question of vision entails more than the adoption of a material element; it requires the adoption of a mode of perception and a social practice of positioning the body in the visual field. Not only was the landscape

151

view a sensory delight, but it was also read, by both Muslims and Hindus, as a sign of power and authority. At Jaigarh Fort, vision was directed on one side toward the valley's water source and on the other to the ruling family's palatine residence. The view of the valley was open and unimpeded, but the view of the Amber Fort below was blocked by a *jali* screen (fig. 7.14). Although during the colonial period many buildings lost their exquisitely carved stone screens, there are fortunately still many originals intact, as at the Jaigarh Fort. Hence, we can observe another aspect of Islamic visual culture: the denial or postponement of vision in architectural and landscape spaces by means of an intervening screen.

The most common practical explanation for these screens is that they offer protection from the hot sun while admitting cooling breezes into architectural interiors. Certainly in hot climates such as India and much of the Islamic world where exterior daylight may be five hundred times brighter than is desirable indoors, screens are used to filter the light, reduce glare, and subdue the heat in residential architecture.[20] However, the screens at the Jaigarh Fort do not significantly block the sun because their windows are protected by projecting eaves and they are in chambers that open through doorways on their opposite sides to a very sunny open courtyard. By the same token, in the dimly lit central chamber of the Taj Mahal mausoleum, the purpose of the ornate marble screen that encloses the cenotaphs is not to prevent the entry of sunlight. Instead, the screen marks the symbolic separation between the living and the dead—the most significant threshold imaginable. These screens also ensure privacy, especially for women. The screens can act as veils that deny vision to some (male non-kin and the public) and allow it to others (male and female members of the immediate family), but screens are also used in places like mosques and tombs (as in the example of the Taj), where women either were not present or where such screens did not serve to divide space according to categories of gender.

While *jali* screens play a functional role in reducing heat and a social role in providing visual protection, they also play an additional and more sophisticated role: to draw attention to the act of vision, much as a garden's fountain draws attention to the presence of water. Screens throw light in complex patterns onto walls and floors so that they appear textured, their surfaces dematerialized in such a way that challenges their solidity while insisting on their planar flatness (fig. 7.15). Placed across

Figure 7.14. View through screen, Jaigarh Fort, Jaipur, c. 1600. Photo: D. F. Ruggles.

windows and thresholds, screens intercept the view, or at least delay it. One *can* see through the screen to the view beyond, but only by first negotiating the intervening screen, an effort that makes the viewer more conscious of the act of seeing. Where formerly the window framed the view, setting it up as a thing out there to be looked at from in here, now the plane of the *jali* stands between the viewer and the view. One looks *at* the screen, which appears first as a material object, and then *beyond* it as it disappears from sight (fig. 7.16). The critical separation between the eyes that see and the object that is seen is made tangible in the screen. It teases the eye, making the viewer pause and, in that moment of hesitation, become aware of the very act of

Figure 7.15. Salim Chisti Tomb, Fatehpur-Sikri, 1571–1580. Photo: D. F. Ruggles.

Figure 7.16. *Jali* screen, tomb of Gaus Muhammad, Gwalior, c. 1600. Photo: D. F. Ruggles.

looking. The screen, then, is the embodiment of vision: it gives the visual field a membrane of material presence. Whereas the Western model of vision mimetically knits the viewer into the view and blurs the distinction between the two, the Islamic model proposed here constructs the visual field as disjunctured, clarifying and even emphasizing the distinction between the subject and object positions.

As a material form, the screen occurs in Islamic Spain, Syria, Egypt, and other areas of the Islamic world rendered in stone, stucco, and wood. In those areas it has practical and aesthetic functions as a window curtain for privacy, seen in the *mashribiyya* window screens of residential architecture in Cairo, and as an ornamental grille that filters and gives form to light, seen in the screens with colored glass that shower light from the dome onto the *mihrab* of the Cordoba Mosque. But in both north and south Indian temples dating from the sixth century onward, simple stone screens are also found, as for example in the early seventh-century temple at Aihole where they likewise illuminated the interior and created interesting visual patterns of light and dark reflected on walls and floors. It is probably pointless to attempt a typological genealogy of anything so ubiquitous as a carved screen that appears not only in Islamic and Hindu contexts but also in Byzantine and Western Christian churches, as well as eastern Asia. Although one cannot recreate the historical viewer and thus cannot know the precise experience of looking and its meaning within a given society, the material environment provides a guide that suggests the visual possibilities that did or did not exist. In South Asia, *jali* screens provided landscape views that were intended to be seen, yet at the same time temporarily denied to the viewer. This aspect of the *jali* screen seems to have appeared relatively late in Islamic culture, perhaps developing as a result of the conscious awareness of how architecture and landscape — the two halves of the visual field — were united. That momentary juncture between self and the world outside, or between body and nature, architecture and landscape, was embodied in the *jali*. In South Asia, it was a device that transcended religious difference, and its shared use, which demanded not only the adoption of an ornately carved object but also a particular way of seeing, was emblematic of the hybrid and complex nature of the Mughal Empire, in which both Hindus and Muslims were profoundly invested.

LANDSCAPES WITHIN BUILDINGS IN

LATE EIGHTEENTH-CENTURY FRANCE

David L. Hays

IRREGULAR GARDEN DESIGN EMERGED IN LATE EIGHTEENTH-CENTURY FRANCE IN
part through new interests in the view as a format of design, but the ways in which
vision shaped that development have yet to be fully described. Historians have focused almost exclusively on so-called "picturesque" design, which Dora Wiebenson
defined in her important study, *The Picturesque Garden in France*, as "the elements
of nature [. . .] composed into a series of highly controlled and sophisticated 'pictures.'"[1] In keeping with that formulation, Wiebenson concentrated on suburban
and rural gardens, the size and situation of which allowed designed spaces to be apprehended at a distance as if pictures. However, irregular design also flourished in
urban- to suburban-scale properties in France, where opportunities for such views
were limited.[2] Within such settings, the space-as-picture approach was physically

157

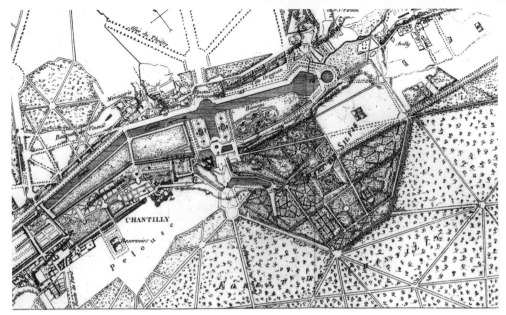

Figure 8.1. J. Mérigot, plan, Chantilly, from *Promenades ou Itinéraires des jardins de Chantilly*, 1791. Courtesy: Department of Rare Books and Special Collections, Princeton University Library.

impossible, yet vision could still be exploited in design. Many small gardens laid out or conceived in the 1770s and 1780s employed devices for masking walls while producing illusions of extension beyond them.[3] Those illusions at the margins were typically foregrounded, and thereby reinforced, by elements in real space.[4] In other words, the conventional approach to picturesque composition was inverted, or folded back, producing not space-as-picture but picture-as-space.

The picture-as-space approach, in which volumes appeared to exceed their physical limits, was well suited to small-scale settings enclosed by walls. Accordingly, it was readily applied in the lot gardens of Paris and its vicinity.[5] But the picture-as-space approach could also be applied in places of greater confinement, such as within buildings, as well as in contexts in which the container was designed and situated specifically in order to be exceeded. One such context was Chantilly, the vast estate and seat of the Bourbon-Condé family, situated about twenty-five miles north-northeast of Paris.

In the fall of 1772, or so the story goes, Louis-Joseph de Bourbon, prince de Condé (1736–1818), was walking at Chantilly in a swampy meadow close to the château.[6] During the walk, it occurred to him that the space—a visually open wedge

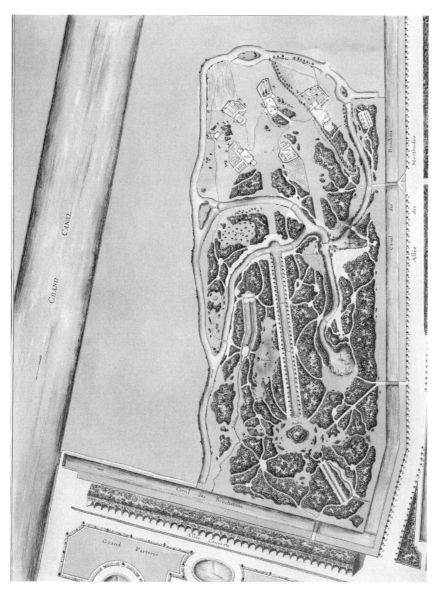

Figure 8.2. Plan, *jardin anglais,* Chantilly, from Chambé, *Album du comte du Nord,* 1784, fol. 15. In this image, north is to the left. Courtesy: Réunion des Musées Nationaux/Art Resource, N.Y.

between the Grand Canal to the north and the Petit Parc to the south—might be transformed into a so-called *jardin anglais* or irregular garden. He discussed the idea with his in-house architect, Jean-François Leroy (1729–1791), and the work apparently began immediately, as the garden was laid out in spring of the following year (fig. 8.1, center).[7] The new garden featured dense plantings of trees and undergrowth interspersed with a rich network of clearings, paths, water channels, and pools (fig. 8.2). The intervention occupied much, though not all, of the meadow and was separated from an untouched portion to the north and east by a broad stream, an arrangement that allowed pasturage to continue and be viewed in the vicinity. Within the *jardin anglais*, rockwork and architectural elements garnished several clearings. Among those features were a substantial rockery (*rocher*) rising up from a pool of water; a grotto and cave (*grotte et antre*); an open air drinking pavilion (*guingette*); and, at the east end of the garden, an artificial hamlet, begun in the fall of 1774 and completed by the following Easter.[8]

Designed by Leroy, the hamlet was a cluster of seven mock-rustic buildings that included three thatched cottages, a barn, an inn (*cabaret*), a water mill, and a dairy with a stable. Those structures were arranged in a rough circle in an area planted with grass, and each building included a separate produce garden (see fig. 8.2, right). On the outside, the hamlet hardly betrayed its artificiality. The baronne d'Oberkirch, who first visited the setting in 1782, noted that the barn was "surrounded by all things necessary to a good plowman."[9] On the inside, however, four of the buildings were fitted out not for rustic occupations but to accommodate elite social activity. One of the three cottages housed a lavishly appointed *salon*. The two others contained a billiards room and a library, whereas the barn framed a large dining hall. The watermill and the dairy, on the other side of a small stream, functioned as they appeared and provided bread and cream products for consumption by visitors to the hamlet. Other foods were prepared in a well-appointed kitchen housed inside the so-called inn. In short, the hamlet was like an elite domestic suite exploded into freestanding pavilions and rendered incognito, from the exterior, by mock-rustic façades and props.[10]

Among the four structures intended for elite occupation, the salon, the billiards room, and the library were fitted out in luxurious contemporary style (fig. 8.3, left side). In contrast, the interior of the dining hall was decorated not as a domestic space but as a woodland clearing (see fig. 8.3, right side). In other words, upon entering the

Figure 8.3. Plans, sections, and elevations of the salon (left) and dining hall (right) in the hamlet at Chantilly, from Chambé, *Album du comte du Nord,* 1784, fol. 16. Courtesy: Réunion des Musées Nationaux/Art Resource, N.Y.

building, one appeared to be once again outdoors. From the inside, the fabric of the building was completely obscured. The walls were painted to represent surrounding woodland growth, the windowpanes were partially painted over with leaves, and the vault above the room appeared as open sky beyond a ring of arcing limbs.[11] To reinforce that illusion, the scenery on the walls and vaults was foregrounded by elements in real space. The floor was covered with real grass, and the paths that led to the dining hall from the outside continued through its doors unobstructed (see fig. 8.3, bottom right). The path that entered the building from the northwest forked into two branches, one of which led east to a grassy mound—a green sofa—whereas the other led west across the room and back through another opening to the real outdoors.[12] A second grassy mound provided seating at the west end of the hall, and the remaining furnishings were composed of logs and branches.[13]

As an interior space garnished with imagery of the outdoors, the dining hall scheme had countless precedents. The most immediate of those was the theater at Chantilly itself, designed by the architect Claude Billard de Bélisard (d. after 1790) and built in 1767–1768 under Leroy's own supervision (fig. 8.4).[14] The walls inside the auditorium of the theater were painted with landscape views framed by an arcade of palm trees. Furthermore, a door at the back of the stage opened to offer a view of a real, outdoor fountain mounted into a wall, a device that produced an astonishing effect of reality by framing reality itself (see fig. 8.4, center). But as an interior conceived as if outdoors, in which the pairing of pictorial illusions and real-space elements obscured the reality of architectural enclosure, the dining hall had far fewer precedents. Symptoms of such a conception began to appear in the 1740s in decorations and festival scenarios in which vegetation appeared to penetrate architectural interiors.[15] In Jean-François de Bastide's erotic tale, *La Petite Maison*, the walls of a boudoir are lined with mirrors and decorative elements designed to make the space appear as if a quincunx. According to Bastide's text, "one believes oneself to be in a natural bosquet lit with the help of art."[16] The illusion is incomplete, however, as the room includes a niche with an ottoman set on a rosewood parquet. The walls and ceiling of a nearby water closet are decorated to evoke a garden room lined with a tall, clipped hedge, but Bastide's description does not mention the floor, which presumably remained conventional. A fully developed—if unusual and unrealized—precedent that

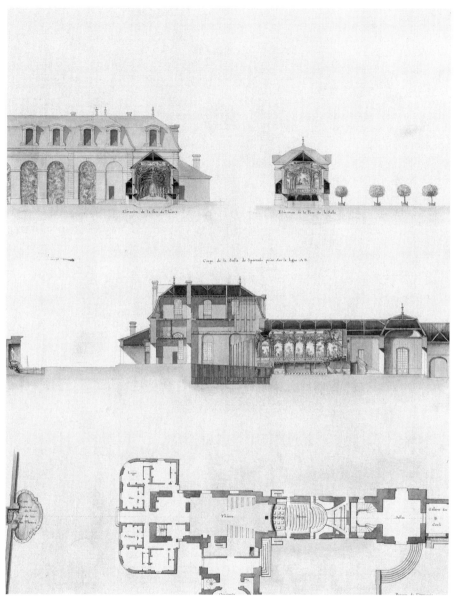

Figure 8.4. Plan and sections of the theater at Chantilly, from Chambé, *Album du comte du Nord*, 1784, fol. 11. Courtesy: Réunion des Musées Nationaux/Art Resource, N.Y.

Pl. VI.

Echelle de 5 10 15 *Toises*

Profil de l'Edifice sur la longueur.

Figure 8.5. Charles-François Ribart, section of the Éléphant Triomphal, from *Architecture Singulière*, 1758, pl. VI. Courtesy: Avery Library, Columbia University.

might have been known to Leroy was part of a peculiar theoretical project, a so-called "Elephant-Fountain-Private House," conceived by the engineer Charles-François Ribart and engraved by Pierre Patte in 1758 (fig. 8.5). Designed as a city residence for Louis XV, the building was intended for the middle of the Place de l'Étoile in Paris. On the second floor, in the hindquarters of the elephant, was a dining room decorated to appear as if a space deep within a forest.[17] Light entered the room indirectly, through leaves and branches, and a stream flowing across the floor appeared to trail off into the distance.[18] The furnishings in the room were made to appear as if objects in nature. For example, the buffet was shaped as if a boulder, and the water spigots were given the forms of aquatic birds.[19]

As a woodland hollow embedded in the rump of a colossal elephant, which in turn stood in the middle of an urban square, Ribart's dining room was doubly out of place.[20] In contrast, the dining hall at Chantilly was perfectly suited to its use as an amenity on the Condé estate. In combining the pleasure of dining outdoors with the sureties and conveniences of being indoors, every meal in the dining hall could be a picnic, regardless of the weather. Even so, the decision to situate the interior landscape specifically within a barn—an emblem *par excellence* of rustic enterprise—suggests that the space had deeper meaning than picnic pleasures.

In his guidebook to the vicinity of Paris, first published in 1786, Jacques-Antoine Dulaure stated that the disparities between interiors and exteriors surprised visitors to the hamlet.[21] Echoing that remark, historians have consistently interpreted the dining hall and its companion buildings as devices for provoking surprise.[22] Yet contemporaries did not necessarily respond to them in that way. For example, the baronne d'Oberkirch expressed no surprise about the dining hall in describing her first visit there for a festive supper in June 1782. Instead, she called the interior "comfortable, cheerful, unaffected, and perfectly well-imagined."[23] That response was undoubtedly shaped by some amount of foreknowledge. Garden buildings combining rustic exteriors and lavish or exotic interiors were well known by the early 1780s. At the west edge of Paris, for example, the design for the Jardin de Monceau by Louis Carrogis, known as Carmontelle (1717–1806), included a dairy that appeared rustic on the outside but was fitted with marble on the inside.[24] The baronne d'Oberkirch could easily have learned of such settings through visits, descriptions, or images, not to mention a reference (casual or now lost) to the hamlet at Chantilly itself. Furthermore, the baronne already knew such a setting—a thatched cottage with a finely appointed interior—from personal experience back in her native Alsace; she had even stayed overnight in that place a decade before visiting Chantilly.[25] Even without such knowledge or experience, however, it seems unlikely that a well-heeled guest would have approached the prince de Condé's hamlet as if an authentic settlement. Given the opulence of Chantilly and the theatrical way in which the grounds were presented to visitors, artificiality was to be expected. On that point, the prince de Ligne, an important contemporary commentator on garden design, complained that the exterior of the hamlet appeared too authentic, that "[b]y dint of being natural, it makes one regret at first that it had not been torn down."[26] At once a backhanded compliment to the architect Leroy and a reminder that the development of princely estates sometimes involved the destruction of peasant settlements, the prince's remark suggests that such veracity was considered inappropriate in the spaces of elite play.[27]

Whether or not the buildings of the hamlet were genuinely surprising, their association with that effect has been perpetuated by a convention of describing the setting from the outside in: region; estate; component garden; cluster of buildings; individual buildings; exteriors; and—finally—interiors, with unanticipated luxuries, amenities, and, in the case of the dining hall, illusions. The conceit of surprise, reinforced by this method of description, has distracted historians from questioning how the exteriors, interiors, and functions of individual buildings were related. That oversight is particularly ironic in the case of the dining hall, a staging of outside in that turned the view inside out. To account for that reversal—that is, to understand how vision was manipulated within the dining hall scheme—one must ask why a simulated woodland clearing, designed to occupy and visually exceed a sham rustic framework, was installed within the grounds of an estate renowned for its real woodlands. Said differently, one must consider how the dining hall was used, and how the theme of the woodland clearing related to the nested hierarchy of contexts within which it was embedded: a mock-rustic barn, within an artificial hamlet, at the edge of an irregular garden, within the grounds of a princely estate, within the larger landscape (see fig. 8.1). In the dining hall scheme, the picture-as-space approach, the setting within which it was realized, and the uses to which it was put were related through a strategy of occupying and exceeding rustic frameworks, a strategy pursued by the

Condé family in the 1770s and 1780s when a crucial symbolic territory of their privilege as nobles—the woodland—appeared to be in jeopardy.

According to Dora Wiebenson, "French interest [in the picturesque] reflected the retreat of the individual to nature and to the rural life in a period of political and economic decline."[28] Echoing that idea, historians have often described the hamlet at Chantilly as a place of retreat from urbanity. For example, one historian has recently suggested that the hamlet was "part of the 'peasant life' sought by those of Condé's class, for the peaceful countryside offered a refuge from responsibilities, and in games of make-believe even a Condé could momentarily lose his identity."[29] Whether the prince de Condé—a French Prince of the Blood, chief of protocol to the French court, and one of the wealthiest men in France—would or even could have effected such a loss of identity is doubtful. In any event, the arrangement and use of the hamlet as a setting for social dining suggests that doing so was not his intention. The paths of the hamlet were configured to accommodate the conventions of elite dining, with the dining hall as the starting point and the salon, a place for conversation, as the primary after-meal destination, from which guests could proceed to other places of diversion such as the billiards room and library (see fig. 8.2, right). In practice, the hamlet was a place not in which society was evaded but to which society was brought. Chantilly was heavily frequented by elite travelers from France and abroad, and the hamlet was one of a repertoire of settings—including the theater, the menagerie and its dairy, the stables, and the Maison de Sylvie, among others—displayed to guests during tours of the estate. Visitors to the hamlet within a decade of its completion included Marie-Antoinette's brother, Emperor Josef II of Austria (May 1777); the Grand Duke and Grand Duchess of Russia, traveling incognito as the so-called comte and comtesse du Nord (June 1782); and King Gustavus III of Sweden, who spent exactly six hours at the estate on July 20, 1784, during which time he visited the château, the theater, the hamlet, and the Island of Love.[30]

As a place of dining, the hamlet appears to have been used primarily for suppers (*soupers*), and occasionally for breakfasts (*petits déjeuners*) and light lunches (*déjeuners*), but not for the most formal type of meal: the dinner (*dîner*). To the modern sensibility, that restriction might suggest that dining in the hamlet was considered less intensive than dining in the château or other places where dinners were held, but that was by no means the case. The dining hall could seat 120 guests comfortably, and the amount of planning and resources required to cater meals there on that scale was anything but relaxed. Furthermore, in a culture in which skills of conversation and wit were highly prized, greater intimacy — in this case, supper in a garden pavilion — did not necessarily mean lesser intensity. The baronne d'Oberkirch remarked on that subject,

> [t]here are two types of guests: dinner guests and supper guests. Dinner guests are often, almost always [. . .] serious people, elderly, obligations, even bores; one dines easily in the city, so long as one's social circle is a bit wide. But supper is different. It requires qualities that are very difficult to bring together, the most indispensable of which is wit. Without wit, without elegance, without worldliness, anecdotes, the thousand bits of trivia that make up the news, one must not dream of being admitted to those charm-filled gatherings. There [. . .] one chats about the lightest topics, which are therefore the most difficult to sustain. It is a veritable *mousse* that evaporates and leaves nothing behind, but the flavor of which is very enjoyable. Once one has tasted it, the rest seems insipid and bland.[31]

Although the interior of the dining hall appeared to be outdoors, its arrangement followed the conventions of contemporary interior design. The green sofas at both ends overlooked four clumps (*touffes*) that loosely divided the room into a rectangular hall with semicircular end spaces, just as piers or column screens might have done in a conventional interior (see fig. 8.3, bottom right). The conformity of organic materials to social patterns "naturalized" elite space by implying that making nobles comfortable was part of nature's plan. In other words, the interior was structured not as a refuge from society in nature, but as an affirmation of society by nature. In the case of the dining hall, "nature" meant a simulated woodland clearing, with a continuous landscape of trees painted on the surrounding walls and vaults (see fig. 8.3, right side, upper half). The historian Louis Badré has suggested that, to the social elites of eighteenth-century France, real trees were perceived as rustic ornaments. Badré pointed out that Duhamel de Monceau, a member of the Académie Royale des Sciences and an important advocate of forest management, referred to trees as "the most beautiful decoration of the countrysides."[32] But trees were also signposts of social and economic power in France. Wood was a crucial material in construction and energy production, and it was always in high demand. Wood also happened to be scarce in France. Unchecked exploitation had left vast tracts of countryside deforested by as early as the fifteenth century, and chronic shortages persisted throughout the whole of the eighteenth century, particularly near cities and places of industry.[33]

Not surprisingly, the majority of the woodlands in France were owned by the crown, the nobles, and the church.[34] In the middle ages, control of woodlands had been restricted to those groups, but rights of ownership were subsequently liberated, and a small but growing percentage of French woodlands, mostly comprising small parcels, were owned by commoners and lay corporations.[35] In other words, ownership of woodland was not in and of itself a sign of noble or ecclesiastical status. In the context of possession by nobles, however, woodlands gained symbolic currency as attributes of nobility through their use as sites of hunting. The privilege of hunting was a cornerstone in the legislated construction of nobility in France. From 1396 until the Revolution, commoners in France were legally forbidden to hunt game animals, even on their own land.[36] Those who did so, or who harmed game for any reason, including defense of crops, were subject to punishments ranging from fines, to banishment, to conscripted service on galley ships.[37]

The association of woodlands with privilege was enforced by the laws that distinguished nobles from commoners in France. The priority of that distinction within the legal code is not to be underestimated. For example, article one, clause one, of the customs and ordinances of Senlis, the cathedral town situated two and a half miles east of Chantilly, stated that the law "knows only two classes of men: nobles and commoners. It distinguishes the former by the number of privileges which it refuses to the latter."[38] Hunting was key among those privileges, and its protection through legislation had significant impact on how woodlands were perceived by nobles and commoners alike. The nobility of woodlands was particularly explicit at Chantilly, where the exercise of hunting was pursued with a lavishness and intensity rivaled only by that of the crown.[39] The kennel at Chantilly had space for 250 dogs, and the palatial stables had stalls for 240 horses. Jacques Toudouze, first lieutenant in the prince de Condé's hunting administration, recorded in his journal the killing of 924,717 game animals during the course of his thirty-seven years of service, an amount that averages to just over sixty-eight animals per day for a run of 13,500 days. Needless to say, the prince de Condé enjoyed hunting, but he especially appreciated its social dimension.

Figure 8.6. Workshop of Michel-Barthélemy Ollivier, *Feast Given by the Prince de Conti for Prince Charles-Guillaume-Ferdinand of Brunswick-Lüneborg in the Woods at Cassan in 1766*, 1766. Châteaux de Versailles et de Trianon, Versailles. Courtesy: Réunion des Musées Nationaux/Art Resource, N.Y.

According to one description, he "preferred pack hunting, and he liked above all to include women in that pleasure. They followed the hunt in carriages; in the Chantilly forest were several *rendez-vous de chasses* (gathering points for hunting parties) where lunches were sometimes enjoyed on stone tables."[40]

To commemorate specific hunts, the prince de Condé commissioned works from painters such as Jean-François Perdrix and Jean-Baptiste Le Paon. Those images typically portrayed the height of action in the hunt: the "hallali" or moment preceding the death of the prey, with dogs in frenzy and courtiers all around in witness.[41] But the prince de Condé also commissioned scenes of the gatherings that took place in

Figure 8.7. J. Mérigot, view of La Table, from *Promenades ou Itinéraires des jardins de Chantilly*, 1791.
Courtesy: Department of Rare Books and Special Collections, Princeton University Library.

conjunction with hunts. One such picture, painted by Philippe-Jacques de Loutherbourg in 1765, represented a feast at La Table, a *rond-point* used as a *rendez-vous de chasse* in the heart of the forest of Chantilly.[42] Although now lost, that image might be imagined through two others. The first, a painting created in 1766 in the workshop of Michel-Barthélemy Ollivier, depicts a feast in the forest of Cassan, near l'Isle-Adam, an estate belonging to the prince de Conti, a cousin of the prince de Condé (fig. 8.6).[43] The costumes of the men, the setting of the meal beneath a tent in a *rond-point*, and the presence of numerous attendants with horses, hunting horns, guns, and dogs signal that a hunt is imminent. The second image, an illustration in J. Mérigot's *Promenades ou Itinéraires des jardins de Chantilly* (1791), offers a view of La Table within the forest of Chantilly (fig. 8.7). A circular tent garnished with pennants and stag heads occupies the center of the clearing while people, horses, and dogs garnish the surrounding space.

In his *Description des eaux de Chantilly et du Hameau* (1783), Nicolas Le Camus de Mézières referred to the interior of the dining hall at Chantilly as an *halte* (a stopping point) "that one would believe to be that of Diana, when, at the *rendez-vous de chasse* she rallied the different invited Nymphs to share her pleasures."[44] In his guidebook of 1786, Dulaure also referred to the interior as an "*halte* or *rendez-vous de chasse*." Mérigot concurred in his own guidebook of 1791 that the interior "recalls a *rendez-vous de chasse*."[45] Those remarks suggest that, within the context of a princely estate, the association of woodland and dining referred to hunting, even when the specific attributes of that activity were absent. As a *rendez-vous de chasse*, the interior of the dining hall was an explicitly elite space. In that sense, the simulated woodland of the dining hall and the sumptuous decoration found in other buildings of the hamlet resembled each other closely, even though they were formally very different. Both types represented effects of privilege inaccessible to commoners. That inaccessibility became pointedly ironic and provocative relative to the sham barn within which the woodland was embedded. In the dining hall—as in the salon, billiards room, and library—elite space occupied and exceeded a rustic framework. Nobles occupied the hearths from which commoners were excluded. With their mock-rustic exteriors exceeded by sophisticated interiors, the buildings of the hamlet resembled not virtuous common folk but nobles in costume.

The strategies realized in the dining hall also structured many of the activities programmed for the hamlet. The hamlet was a token of rustic production that functioned as a place of aristocratic consumption. During their visit to Chantilly in 1782, the Grand Duke and Grand Duchess of Russia were served a so-called "peasant's meal" in the dining hall that included "six soups, twelve entrées, twelve kinds of fish, three roasts, six poultry dishes, entremêts, and a table laden with oriental delicacies."[46] Consumption of cream also became an important activity at the hamlet. In June 1784, the baronne d'Oberkirch and the duchesse de Bourbon were served a lunch in the dining hall that featured cream products. The baronne wrote that the cream was the best she had ever tasted.[47] A month later, the king of Sweden's six-hour visit to Chantilly featured eating of cream at the hamlet.[48]

Meals at the hamlet were sometimes accompanied by rustic-themed entertainments in which distinctions between nobles and commoners were staged and rehearsed. Among those were diversions scripted specifically for the site by the in-house playwright, Pierre Laujon. In June 1777, Laujon staged a "Fête Villageoise" at Chantilly in honor of princesse Louise, the prince de Condé's daughter, who had recently completed her education at a convent in Paris.[49] The fete was a roving theatrical event with nine scenes set at different places within the *jardin anglais* and hamlet. The humor of the occasion was derived in part from the fact that local common folk were played by members of the prince de Condé's household and social circle.[50] In this case, occupying and exceeding rustic frameworks meant sporting costumes and assuming postures, manners, and patterns of speech in caricature of the local poor.[51] It also meant portraying the latter in acts of deference and self-humiliation. In Laujon's script, simple acts of seeing, saluting, and serving princesse Louise were shown to cause pleasure to common folk—sometimes even extreme pleasure, as in the case of the character Nicodème Louvet, who opened the gate to the *jardin anglais* and greeted princesse Louise by proclaiming, in thick jargon, "I have never felt so good as at the moment in which I have the honor of seeing Mademoiselle [. . .] and that it's me who has the honor of opening the door for you." Nicodème explained to princesse Louise that he was known by his first name alone because his two names together were "not easy to remember."[52] He then reported that, not being literate enough to read and memorize the compliment he wanted to present, a poet was on hand to express his sentiments properly.

After a brief recitation by the poet, who referred to Nicodème neatly as "the obliging villager," the guests moved to a nearby area of water where dugout canoes were waiting to convey them to the next scene. A boatman called to the princess that if she would honor him by getting into his boat, he "would never have had so much pleasure in the work and would row in a proud manner."[53] In the following scene, which took place at the grotto and cave, the portrayal of service as pleasure verged into absurdity when the local witch, played by Laujon himself, sought to please princesse Louise by bringing Nostradamus, the sixteenth-century mystic, back from the dead.[54] Once summoned, Nostradamus extended the compliment by explaining that his return to earth to the presence of princesse Louise was less of a challenge than a typical return from the dead because "leaving the stars to spend a moment with you was hardly like changing places."[55]

At the billiards room, redesignated as a school house in the "Fête Villageoise," the pleasure of seeing the princess became religious ecstasy for children who sang:

> *Ex hoc nunc et usque in sæcula a*
> (From this moment now and in perpetuity)
> *Gloria Patri et Filio*
> (Glory to the Father and to the Son)
> The two of whom have jealously showed you the Hamlet.
> The pleasure of seeing you is not of a day, nor of a week;
> But in *sæcula sæculorum* (forever and ever), *amen.*[56]

While the children presented flowers to princesse Louise, a nun played by Laujon offered a prayer:

> May her highness receive these flowers as homages that prove the satisfaction that the sight of her gives to all hearts. What happiness if we could read in her eyes, which are so sweet, so sparkling, and so gracious, that the god of pleasure [i.e., Laujon] who one sees here, as elsewhere, on his feet would sparkle no less through this gibberish.[57]

To that, the crowd answered in unison, "*Deo gratias* (Thanks be to God.)"

In the next scene, the group entered the Salon. Nicodème referred to the interior as "the metamorphosis of a thatched cottage into a salon," and he claimed that he had caused the change himself so that he could offer one specific pleasure to princesse Louise: that of not having to stand all the time.[58] In an earlier scene, the group assembled outside the dining hall and Nicodème addressed princesse Louise by asking, "Does Mademoiselle see the thatched building there? Well, by virtue of the witch's magic, I will change it into a forest."[59] As guests entered the Dining Hall, a fanfare was sounded and Nicodème anxiously asked the players to stop, pretending that the surrounding woods were swelling with hunters responding to the call, supposing mistakenly that a chase was about to begin.[60] Eventually, a hunter slipped into the room and Nicodème employed him for entertainment by making him sing an aria of Céphale from the opera *Céphale et Procris*.[61]

Laujon's script dramatized hunting as a constant potential of the woods, inherent and seemingly naturalized, invisible yet invocable at any moment. The success of that portrayal depended in part on the illusion of extension produced by the immersive arrangement inside the dining hall, where a space of specific depth was made to appear as a space of unspecific depth. As a gathering place set within an idealized space of hunting, the scenario inside the dining hall conformed to the hunter's dream of woodland as expansive and unkempt, conditions that would allow game to thrive and hunts to be pursued always within woods and according to the motive force of hunting, the flight of the prey.

In reality, of course, game moved according to instincts of survival and without regard for such abstractions as property limits. To ensure the chase for large-scale hunters, whose investment in the activity was both symbolic and financial, the crown granted the right of pursuit across property lines whenever a deer or boar had been chased for more than three leagues (about seven and a half miles).[62] Under Louis XIV, one hunt guaranteed by that clause ended up in the forecourt of Versailles, whereas another under Louis XVI finished on the boulevards of Paris.[63] For the crown itself, the ideal of the open chase was ensured against the realities of real estate through the legislation of hunting domains or *capitaineries de chasses*. Although the king could in principle hunt anywhere, according to his pleasure, he did so for the most part only within designated areas. Eleven hunting domains were maintained by the crown during the final decades of the ancien régime, all of them situated within the Ile-de-France.[64] Each domain was associated with a royal residence, but the boundaries extended well beyond the limits of crown property to include all space, even urban areas and the properties of other nobles.

As it happens, the prince de Condé's estate at Chantilly was fully immersed within one such domain: the *capitainerie* of La Halatte, which encompassed just over sixty square miles and included, among other places, the Cathedral town of Senlis and the forest of Ermenonville (fig. 8.8).[65] When land fell within a royal *capitainerie*, most proprietors—even though nobles—lost the right to hunt there.[66] Princes retained the right on condition of free access to their land by the king. But the prince de Condé enjoyed a supplemental benefit of great significance. Specifically, the captainship of the domain of La Halatte was made hereditary within the Condé household.[67] Through

Figure 8.8. The Royal Hunting Domain of La Halatte. "Carte de la capitainerie royale d'Halatte, ses evirons, et da la seigneurie de Chantilly avec ses dependences" (c. 18C). Archives Nationales de France: Cartes et plans, N III Seine 56. Drawing by David Hays.

that position, the prince de Condé enjoyed the privilege of hunting throughout the domain, even without the king's presence. Through the circumstance of privileged office, then, the area within which the prince de Condé could hunt far exceeded the limits of his own estate.

As a substitute for all-out possession, the assertion of hunting privileges was a meaningful expression of territorial power, especially when the self-interest of the prince de Condé ostensibly coincided with that of the king. The practice of hunting within the larger landscape pitted noble privilege against local economic interests and concerns.[68] Hunting also shaped the landscape through regulations and interventions meant to ensure the continuity of pursuit. With the exception of gardens attached to village houses, any new construction, excavation, or enclosure projected within the bounds of a royal hunting domain needed to be approved by the local captain, to ensure that the intervention would not hinder the progress of hunts through the area.[69] The prince de Condé was thus in a position to shape the landscape beyond his estate, if only through veto. Furthermore, hunting domains were garnished with set-asides, typically covering around one acre each, to provide shelter for game in places between larger areas of woodland. Set-asides were usually planted within fields, a situation that fostered damage to crops, and cultivation and grazing were forbidden within ten feet of such spaces.[70]

In May 1787, the English writer Arthur Young visited Chantilly and reported in his journal, "The forest around Chantilly, belonging to the Prince of Condé, is immense, spreading far and wide; the Paris road crosses it for ten miles, which is its least extent. They say the capitainerie, or paramountship, is above 100 miles in circumference. That is to say, all the inhabitants for that extent are pestered with game, without permission to destroy it, in order to give one man diversion. Ought not these capitaineries to be extirpated?"[71]

Young's comment about hunting showed his sensitivity to the impact of that activity on communities in the vicinity of Chantilly, but his account was otherwise highly exaggerated. His estimate of the size of the *capitainerie* exceeded reality by thirteen times. The Paris road (i.e., the ancient route that linked Paris to the *massif* upon which the château de Chantilly was constructed) crossed the forest of Chantilly for about 1,500 *toises* (1.85 miles), still a large distance but hardly the ten miles suggested by Young.[72] Furthermore, control of the forest—let alone the surrounding territory—was not as monolithic as Young suggested. The prince de Condé owned most of the forest of Chantilly, but not all of it.[73] Until the Revolution, a 340-acre tract in the northeast sector, north of La Table, remained in the possession of the Priory of Saint-Nicolas d'Acy, and a 13-acre tract along the south edge belonged to the Chapel of Saint-Martin.[74]

Although exaggerated, Young's observations shared a sense of expansiveness with the spectacle of boundless forest on display within the dining hall. The historian Robert Harrison has suggested, "the various ways in which forests are conceived, represented, or symbolized will give us access to the shadow of Enlightenment ideology—its fantasies, paradoxes, anxieties, nostalgias, self-deceptions, and even its pathos."[75] One such point of access was the dining hall in the hamlet at Chantilly. The fantasy of extensive woodland staged within the dining hall alluded to the extension of hunting privileges enjoyed by the Condé over the landscape surrounding their estate. But the dining hall also preserved the symbolic richness of woodland against factors that were jeopardizing those spaces in reality. Paradoxically, the practice of hunting had a compromising, even devastating, effect on woodland. Beginning in the mid-1760s, disputes within the prince de Condé's administration chronically pitted the *capitaine des chasses*, charged with ensuring the quality of hunts, against the *gruyer*, the man responsible for managing and regulating the forest as a financial resource.[76] The prince de Condé's passion for hunting made the work of the *gruyer* a perpetual ordeal. Relative to that situation, the simulated woodland, set within an area of the garden defended by water channels and locked gates, was an indulgent expiation.

The projected woodland was also far removed from circumstances within the larger landscape. In the wake of both the Seven Years War (1756–1763) and two difficult winters that led to widespread famine in 1762 and 1766, the crown introduced a new tax policy intended to bolster food production, particularly in the vicinity of Paris. The policy declared that any area of woodland cleared and turned to cultivation would be exempt from taxation for fifteen years. In a country where only the king and princes were exempt from taxes, that policy offered significant incentives to landowners, and the effect on woodlands was decimating. By 1770, only four years after the policy was announced, close to half a million acres (about 3.25 percent of the surface area of France) had been cleared of trees and converted to cultivation.[77] By 1780, tax breaks had been granted for almost 1.2 million acres, about 8.5 percent of the surface area of the nation). Although initiated to expedite recovery from crisis, the new tax policy smacked of a shifting attitude within the government in which, as Robert Harrison has put it, forests were "stripped of the symbolic density they may once have possessed" and reduced to "utility." Harrison pointed out that the entry for "forêt" in the *Encyclopédie*, written by Monsieur Le Roy, warden of the Park of Versailles, referred solely to trees and made no mention of wildlife of any sort.[78] By eliminating game animals from his account, Le Roy was able to ignore the symbolic aspect of woodlands in favor of economic concerns.

Historians have consistently couched the significance of the hamlet at Chantilly in terms of the other sham villages it ostensibly inspired, most especially the one built at the Petit Trianon at Versailles.[79] However, if one considers the hamlet in terms of the strategy of occupying and exceeding frameworks that determined its thematic contrasts, siting, and use, a more complex picture emerges relating the setting to a rich history of gardens as both expressions and instruments of territorial power. Furthermore, the manipulation of vision and forest imagery within the dining hall blurred to an unprecedented degree the traditional boundaries between architecture and landscape. At the time of its construction in 1774–1775, the dining hall departed radically from the conventions of French architecture, even as those pertained to such marginal structures as garden pavilions on private estates.[80] In doing so, however, the scheme anticipated the conception of interior space as landscape that became a powerful aspect of so-called "visionary" architecture in the following two decades. The interior of the dining hall was a landscape within a building—not a garden within a building (e.g., orangeries, glasshouses, hothouses, greenhouses, "winter gardens"), or a landscape seen from or through a building, or a landscape incorporating a building, or a landscape becoming a building, but a landscape occupying a building in such a way as to make the building disappear. Landscape occupied architecture while exceeding it from within, challenging its visual and spatial authority. The dining hall was not Laugier's "Primitive Hut" set within another primitive hut (i.e., a barn).[81] This woodland was not where architecture began but where it began to be dismantled. Seen in plan, the dining hall appears to be a roofless ruin, the interior of

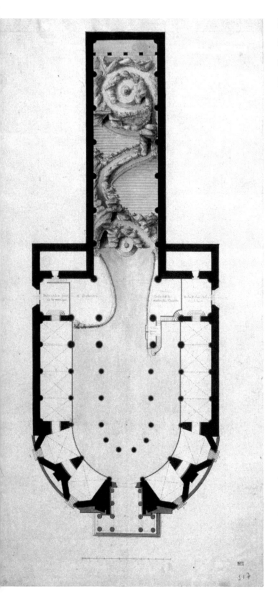

Figure 8.9. Alexandre-Théodore Brongniart, Project for the Mountain in the Cathedral at Bordeaux, Fête de la Raison, 20 Frimaire an II (December 10, 1793). Courtesy: Réunion des Musée Nationaux/Art Resource, N.Y.

which has been taken over by nature. The continuity of ground "ruins" architecture by demonstrating its insufficiency as a barrier between inside and outside. Seen from within, architecture disappears entirely. But seen in section, the mechanism of the illusion is apparent. The dining hall is a clearing within the woods within a building within a clearing within the woods. The sections of the dining hall reveal the power of architecture, at once practical and magical, to collaborate in its own undoing. The substance of architecture helps landscape make it disappear.[82]

As a landscape within a building, the dining hall scheme was a precursor, if not a model, for some of the most remarkable schemes in French architecture of the 1780s and 1790s, including Étienne-Louis Boullé's *Cenotaph to Newton* (1784), Claude-Nicolas Ledoux's "Elevation of the Cemetery of the Town of Chaux" (n.d.), and Alexandre-Théodore Brongniart's "Mountain" for the Festival of Liberty and Reason, constructed within the Cathedral of Saint-André, Bordeaux (1793) (fig. 8.9).[83] In echoing—if not emulating—a strategy pursued earlier in the dining hall at Chantilly, these examples demonstrate that the potential of landscape to inform and give direction to developments in architecture, an idea glossed over by modernism but recently renewed, has an important historical precedent in late eighteenth-century France.[84]

SITES OF POWER AND

THE POWER OF SIGHT

Elizabeth Kryder-Reid

Vision in the California Mission Landscapes

> From the first day I laid eyes on these beautiful arches and tiled roofs, it has been my consuming desire to restore what was lacking in the buildings. I visioned [*sic*] a venerable structure, grown mellow indeed with years, but still reasonably intact; and the sight of the vanishing walls and the weed grown sanctuary pained me exceedingly.
>
> Father St. John O'Sullivan, Pastor, Mission San Juan Capistrano, 1929

FATHER O'SULLIVAN'S DESCRIPTION OF HIS FIRST VIEW OF THE MISSION HE WAS TO serve is redolent with visual imagery.[1] Through "laying eyes" on the ruins, O'Sullivan's imagination was sparked to envision what might be. The priest had come in 1910 to the sleepy town of San Juan Capistrano south of Los Angeles in ill health and, the records imply, likely intended to spend whatever little time remained of his active

Figure 9.1. Father O'Sullivan's garden, Mission San Juan Capistrano, c. 1923. Photo courtesy: The Huntington Library. Father O'Sullivan's newly planted garden bears all the classic elements of a mission garden: edged paths, planted beds, draping vines, and blooming flowers.

ministry there. Whether it was the dry air, the sunny climate, or the passion to restore the mission, O'Sullivan revived and went on to lead a twenty-three-year campaign that not only restored the historic mission, but developed an entire complex with a new school, parish house, and a guide program to host the increasing number of tourists to the site. He also was instrumental in the installation of a garden in the formerly dusty courtyard (fig. 9.1). O'Sullivan's descriptive passage is also telling because, like any subjective text, it bespeaks his own perspective. The view of the mission as a ruin and a relic of a bygone era provided the starting point for O'Sullivan's restoration. The voices of those who might have borne witness to a different heritage or told of a different memory were not heard during the good pastor's campaign. In the void left by their silence, the past was rendered as a fountain-filled, rose-planted, and vine-draped Eden. This vision of the past, in turn, framed the views of the site for those who would follow.

Jasper Johns's *The Critic Sees* (fig. 9.2) offers a compelling image for the methodological challenges of understanding how vision has been constructed by diverse cultures throughout history. Johns's sculpmetal brick, with its protruding spectacles set with mouths in lieu of eyes, not only challenges us to question the perspective of critics (and perhaps architecture historians), but it is also an image that bespeaks the intertwining of language and vision through which we make meaning of our world. We understand what we see as we name it. This linguistic foundation of human thought is particularly cogent when attempting to understand the cultural perception of past landscapes.

For historical times we know the human experience of vision in the landscape through written words—a diary entry capturing private thoughts about a moment in a garden; travel literature written to evoke the experience of exotic landscapes to those who may never make the journey; a legal document recording the boundaries of disputed property; a letter describing the routine improvements to the farmyard so an absent son can picture the family homestead. It is accepted that each of these documents not only records a landscape, but also reflects the tropes, conventions, and discourses of their day and the cultural construction of vision that informs them. Similarly, visual records of landscapes in forms such as murals, sketches, textiles, carvings, prints, and paintings offer another line of evidence for understanding how landscapes

Figure 9.2. Jasper Johns, *The Critic Sees*, 1979, sculpmetal over plastic with glass. Courtesy: The Philadelphia Museum of Art © Jasper Johns/ Licensed by VAGA, New York, N.Y.

are represented, codified, and read in a particular cultural context. These textual and visual records are not only the historian's primary evidence for the three-dimensional physical landscapes themselves, but are also our sources for understanding the cultural construction and *reception* of landscapes.

For the archaeologist or landscape historian investigating "prehistory"—a time before written words—the challenge of understanding the cultural construction of vision becomes particularly acute. With vast timescales for which there are few images and no written records, how does one begin to decipher the visual vocabulary of perception? Assuming the vagaries of preservation allow one to recover at least some remnants of past physical landscapes, how does one learn to see them as they

ELIZABETH KRYDER-REID

were perceived in the past? Even accepting the mutability of landscape experience—the notion that "neither place nor context nor self stays put, things are always in movement, always becoming"[2]—what sort of theory allows us the interpretive traction to map even plausible ways of knowing the landscape in the absence of textual and visual evidence?

One response to this theoretical and methodological challenge is the assumption of some universal operations of landscape.[3] While the visual dialect is framed by the situatedness of the viewer's culture, gender, life history, even the context of the moment, we may still draw broader connections among humans and our visual experience of space that seem to operate across time and place. It is a premise of anthropological studies of landscape that humans both learn and express their place in the world through the landscape. Humans also negotiate their relationships with each other through landscape—in short, the ways we live in and on the land are inherently linked to our social lives. Furthermore, like language, when practiced in social settings, vision is a means by which we not only negotiate our place in the world, but our relationships with others. In this respect vision is an active and essential part of the exercise of power.

Not only does this understanding of the recursive relationship of humans and landscape build on the linguistic model referenced by Johns's sculpture, but it also equips us to interpret the vast diversity of modes of landscape reception and meaning. The same model that lays the foundation for understanding fundamental operations of landscape and human society across time also accounts for the uniqueness of culturally specific articulations of that relationship. Namely, the particular language we learn to speak molds our consciousness. It frames both the grammar of our thinking and the conceptualization of our thoughts. Our understanding of time, motion, the structure of the universe, our relationships to others are all fundamentally shaped by the words and linguistic structures of the language we speak.[4] The prominent peak that is a sacred locale, the chief's residence perched on an earthen temple mound, the cave entrance that is a passage between worlds—all these landscape meanings frame and are framed by the human experience of the world. Vision, like language, is constructed—a unique cultural vocabulary as fundamental to our experience of the world as the language we speak. It is a means of making meaning in and of the world.

The notion of vision and landscape as both culturally specific meaning making and as a timeless exercise of power is useful for a study of landscapes that span multiple times and cultures, and it is therefore a particularly apt approach to the deeply layered landscapes we know today as California. The California landscape not only has a history that spans pre-recorded and recorded history, but also includes indigenous peoples, Spanish colonizers, Mexicans, "Anglos," and the diverse citizenry of California with its emerging local, state, and national cultures. Within the broader landscape, the missions were a primary site of Spanish colonization and, as such, their landscapes were an instrument through which the Spanish and the indigenous peoples attempted to control and resist the imposition of power. The landscape was also the locus of colliding ideologies of landscape—radically different understandings of what it meant to be in and of the world.

The relationships of sight and power in mission history reside in the sites' eighteenth-century origins as a locus of colonial encounters between Spanish Franciscans and the indigenous peoples of California, the missions' development beginning in the second half of the nineteenth century as public sites including the invention of "California mission gardens," and their present incarnation as tourist destinations. While seemingly disparate settings, the imposition of Western power on native peoples and the creation of romanticized oases in tourist destinations are parallel in a number of respects, particularly in the control of vision. In the intersection of reconstructed sites and gazes lies some glimpse of their meaning and significance to those who inhabit these landscapes in the past and today.

There are twenty-one California missions located in a chain originally about a day's ride apart, or what is now an hour's drive, along the California coast and inland valley. The first site, Mission San Diego, was established in 1769. The last, Mission Solano, was founded in 1823, just ten years before secularization was decreed by Mexico's newly independent government. The missions were founded during the waning years of the Spanish empire in the New World by Franciscan missionaries under the leadership of Fr. Junípero Serra. Their purpose was simultaneously to claim what was then known as Alta California for Spain and to convert the indigenous peoples. These native peoples included many of the tribes of California, the most linguistically and culturally diverse area in North America. The area contained at least sixty-four and perhaps as many as eighty mutually unintelligible languages at the time of European contact.[5] The groups' social organization and subsistence practices ranged from the nomadic, loosely organized tribes of the Mojave Desert to the complex chiefdoms of the Chumash Indians, indigenous peoples of the central coast who thrived on the rich variety of marine and forest resources, particularly harvests of acorns that were a staple of their nonagricultural diet. The archaeological record of these native peoples of California extends back at least twelve thousand years and perhaps far earlier.[6]

Today all of the missions are open to the public in varying degrees of restoration or reconstruction. The majority are owned by the Catholic Church in one form or another—parishes, a seminary, and a university. Out of the twenty-one missions, only two, which are state parks, regularly receive governmental funds; most are supported primarily by charitable contributions and earned income from admissions and shop sales. The missions today are in a variety of settings. Some are in the midst of dense urban areas such as Mission San Gabriel near Los Angeles and Mission Delores in San Francisco. Others are more remote, such as Mission Soledad in the Salinas River Valley. Some have been catalysts for local tourism. San Juan Bautista's historic plaza is a favorite locale for picturesque picnics and filming movies, despite being directly over the San Andreas Fault. Santa Inés is part of the visitor's package tour of the small and unlikely "Danish" town of Solvang, and Mission San Juan Capistrano has become a vital engine of the tourist economy in its town an hour south of Los Angeles. The missions have a prominent place in California history as expressed in and inculcated by secular structures such as mandated fourth-grade state education standards and Catholic-sponsored publication series and symposia. The passage of the 2003 California Missions Preservation Act, along with a steady stream of visitors and growth of groups such as the California Mission Studies Association attest to the strong public interest in the sites and their histories. In addition, the missions' governing entities, whether parish churches or California State Parks, are dependent on entrance fees for the sites' continued financial support. Both the public interest and the opportunity for earned income continue to inform the presentation and the management of the sites with an emphasis on privileging visitor access and amenities.

One of the most popular features of these contemporary mission sites is the mission garden (fig. 9.3). Printed on postcards, featured in garden magazines and

Figure 9.3. Courtyard, Mission Santa Inés, 1993. In the courtyard, the garden is centered on a two-tiered fountain from which walkways extend among the four edged beds. Photo: E. Kryder-Reid.

coffee-table books, and marketed in tourism brochures, these vibrant garden images are emblems of the romanticized histories presented at these sites.[7] The archetypal mission garden lies in the heart of a quadrangle formed by the mission buildings—a pan-Mediterranean amalgam of tiled fountains and pools, cascading vines of bougain-villea, intricate edged flower beds and lawns intersected by paths and punctuated with columnar elements of palm or cypress. In addition to the small museums associated with most of the missions, many of the gardens display artifacts—either surviving remnants or more recent donations to the mission collections, in the landscape. Mission San Luis Rey's courtyard has examples of the traditional *maños* and *metates*, or grinding tools (fig. 9.4). At many missions bells are hung from arches or wooden supports or even molded into landscape lighting. Most of the gardens are articulated to the mission cemeteries, either physically or through interpretive signage, and many also incorporate surviving architectural elements or ruins in the gardens (tannery vats, a furnace, a granary, or portions of ruined walls and foundations). Mission gardens also include unique local features such as scale models of the missions (as at San Gabriel and San Juan Capistrano), folk art, and elements related to contemporary parish activities. These include picnic tables for a parish festival filling San Juan Bautista's forecourt, religious statuary at San Antonio de Pala,[8] and a memorial at San Rafael devoted both to the five thousand Native Americans who died at the mission "in memory of the 4000 humans executed daily without trial waiting birthdays . . . ."

In contrast to the relative uniformity of today's mission gardens, however, the history of these landscapes has borne witness to a wide variety of change over time—from millennia-old Native American architecture and subsistence practices, to Spanish colonial adobe construction, to crumbling ruins captured by nineteenth-century impressionist painters, to mission revival architecture, to tourist destinations. For each generation, the shaping of the land has been a way not only to inscribe their position in the world, but also to give it reference to a broader context, whether that be a mythical cosmology, an imperial mandate, or a constructed past. In each of these instances, it is the nexus of landscape and vision that naturalizes and reifies that position.

The essential challenge of understanding landscapes as a site of meaning making and the negotiation of power lies in interpreting the cultural context of the landscape—how it was perceived by those who lived in and acted upon it. Two brief accounts of the landscape along the central coast offer an entry point into two seemingly disparate ideologies of landscape. A little less than a hundred years ago, a Chumash woman named María Solares told a story to an anthropologist, John Harrington, who was collecting oral traditions from the last of the Chumash speakers. María Solares had been born at Mission Santa Inés and she told this story as an old woman: "There is this world in which we live, but there is also one above us and one below us. . . . Here where we live is the center of our world—it is the biggest island. And there are two giant serpents . . . that hold our world up from below. When they are tired they move, and that causes earthquakes. The world above is sustained by the great Slo'w,

Figure 9.4. Interior courtyard, Mission San Luis Rey, 1993. Display of the traditional *maños* and *metates* grinding tools. Photo: E. Kryder-Reid.

who by stretching his wings causes the phases of the moon."[9] The second account was written in 1769 by a Spanish Franciscan, Father Juan Crespi, who landed on the Santa Barbara coast, not far from Santa Inés. In his journal he recorded the landscape he found: "We went over land that was all of it level, dark and friable, well covered with fine grasses." Nearing Point Conception Father Crespi went on to describe: "in sight of the shore, over some low rolling tablelands . . . [was] very good dark friable soil and fine dry grasses. . . . It was all flat land, excepting only some short descents into a few dry creeks. If it can be dry-farmed, all the soil could be cultivated."[10]

The view represented in the story recounted by María Solares reveals a cosmology or ideology of the universe and the landscape on which the Chumash resided that is quite different from a Western paradigm. Chumash stories map a concept of a closed universe composed of three flat circular worlds suspended in a great abyss and supported by powerful supernatural beings. The Chumash lived at the geographic center of the middle world, and moving from that center meant being met with increasing danger. The Chumash tales speak of a personalized universe where "plants, animals and birds, celestial bodies, and various natural forces are all part of the social universe," where kinship was extended to creatures, plants, and supernatural beings.[11] It was a world in which objects and beings were mutable, where forms could change, and beings could be transformed. The negotiation or avoidance of those transformations was one of the challenges of existing in a dangerous universe. Navigating places of transformation such as passages, caves, bodies of water, and darkness required prudence, personal power, and fluency in the relationships that bound the world together. It was a worldview in which Cartesian dichotomies of mind/body and nature/culture seem to have had little place.

In contrast, in Crespi's Catholic belief system the landscape was part of a natural world created by God for the purposes of mankind.[12] Crespi's eighteenth-century education imbued him with the belief that observation and knowledge of the natural world were hallmarks of human civilization—the culture that set humans apart from nature. Crespi also articulated the premise of his capitalist worldview that considered land "property" to be owned, presumably by the Spanish crown, and a resource to be improved. That it was arable implied it could be farmed, potentially producing not only life-sustaining food but also surplus that could be sold at local markets or exported. Land, in this economic system, required labor to make it productive—to improve it—and one labor source was clearly the indigenous population of California.

The stories of the founding of missions are illustrative of this Spanish ideology of landscape. The accounts, idealized and filtered through predominantly Catholic-produced histories, may more properly be called origin myths.[13] They present a codified narrative of possessing the land—name the place (always after a saint), dedicate it for God and for Spain, raise a cross, ring a bell, erect a shelter, and the mission is founded. The first missions were vernacular one-story adobe buildings with thatched roofs. The early buildings were expanded to create substantial churches and surrounding complexes generally in quadrangular or linear form. These mission institutions were far more than the church structures that now stand as the centerpieces of historic sites; they were extensive agricultural plantations and ranches claiming hundreds of acres. Even the core of the mission complex contained many components: the church, the residential areas for the priests and for the neophytes (as the baptized Indians were called)[14] including separate quarters for the unmarried girls; dedicated work areas such as tanneries, mills, and *lavandarias* (laundries) water systems with cisterns, reservoirs, and channels, surrounding agricultural areas such as orchards and fields; and of course the cemetery. The missions served many functions: school, workshop, hospital, plantation, prison, and church. In each aspect the landscape was a means by which the Spanish padres attempted to convert and control the native peoples and a means for resisting that imposition of power—in particular, the partitioning of space and the control of vision.

The mission landscape may be read, in one version, as a stage of colonialism on which the native peoples were removed from their villages, denied access to traditional hunting and fishing areas, and displaced from their sacred locales. The claim of the land by Serra and the Franciscans in the name of the Spanish crown inaugurated processes that within eighty years ended the millennia-old ways of life of the indigenous peoples in the region. In more particular ways, the Spanish shaping of the landscape was an instrument in their act of conquest. The Spanish organization of space and the ways in which vision was controlled were regulatory practices that helped to impose the will of the few Spanish over the many native peoples.

The Spanish ordered the landscape into zones of specialized functions, particularly areas of field, orchards, vineyards, groves, and walled courtyards, thereby implementing traditional boundedness.[15] For the Chumash who had supported complex chiefdoms and semi-sedentary settlement patterns by harvesting the abundant and stable resources of the coastal waters and woodlands, subsistence meant mapping oneself to the land—literally following the resources as they came into their seasonal harvesting times, whether migrating sea mammals or ripening acorns.[16] The collision of these ways of living off the land meant that the Spanish ordering of a productive pastoral and agricultural landscape created a landscape of exclusion that not only dislocated the native populations from their villages, but also from access to traditional resources. Furthermore, for those who came to live at the missions it also introduced a foreign structure on their habitus—their way of being in and of the land.

The impact of the Native Americans' transformed relationship with the land was not lost on the Spanish. In fact, teaching agricultural practices was one of the hallmarks of "civilizing" the Indians, along with teaching them to read, sing choral music, and recite the catechism.[17] A striking personification of this metaphor is revealed in an 1855 lithograph (fig. 9.5) depicting the California Indian as classified into three stages: wild on the right, partly civilized in the center and "civilized and employed" at left. Particularly telling is the treatment of the ground in which the domestication of plants parallels the civilization of the Indian. Native plants grow at the feet of the uncivilized Indian while the civilized chief is separated by a ridge of soil suggesting a garden furrow.

On a daily basis this process of civilizing, at least in its ideal form, may be seen as a series of disciplining exercises—classic examples of the methods historian Michel Foucault has identified as timetables, collective training, exercises, total and detailed surveillance.[18] An example of how these routines structured the day, much as they did monastic life itself, is recorded in a 1786 account by the Comte de La Pérouse, a member of the first French expedition to California, who described the daily regime of Mission San Carlos in Carmel (fig. 9.6):

> the Indians . . . rise with the sun, and immediately go to prayers and mass, which lasts for
> an hour. During this time three large boilers are set on the fire for cooking a kind of soup,
> made of barley meal. . . . Each hut sends for the allowance of all its inhabitants. . . .

Figure 9.5. *Three Stages of Civilization*, from *The Annals of San Francisco* by Frank Soulé, John H. Gihon, M.D., and James Nisbet, 1855. The equation of "savagery" with wild "nature" is illustrated in this engraving. Courtesy: Herman B. Wells Library, Indiana University, Bloomington.

There is neither confusion nor disorder in the distribution; and when the boilers are nearly emptied, the thicker portion at the bottom is distributed to those children who have said their catechism the best . . . after [the meal] . . . they all go to work, some to till the ground with oxen, some to dig the garden, while others are employed in domestic occupations, and all under the eye of one or two missionaries. . . . At noon the bells give notice of the time of dinner. . . . They resume work from two until four or five o'clock, when they repair to the evening prayer, which continues for nearly an hour, and is followed by a distribution of the atole, the same as at breakfast.[19]

Figure 9.6. Fr. Jose Cardero, *1786 Reception of Jean-François de La Pérouse at Mission Carmel*, 1791–1792. Disciplined formation is represented in this depiction. Courtesy: The Bancroft Library, University of California, Berkeley.

La Pérouse's account clearly describes multiple exercises of control from timetables to collective training, but for our discussion of vision and power in the landscape the most important are the creation of focal points in the landscape, the infrastructure and regulation of surveillance, and the iconography of vision

John Stilgoe, historian of the American landscape, has written about the creation of *landschafts*—prominent features in the landscape such as steeples, lighthouses, and columns that not only create focal points visible at a distance, but also features that mark a central place, and signifiers of a civilized locus in the midst of wilderness.[20] Rather than architectural *landschafts*, Native American cosmologies appear to privilege prominent peaks as symbolically charged locations, points in which the spheres of the world met, and places of sacred power.[21] The scale of architecture in these native traditions, however, was no larger than the domed nuclear and extended family Chumash dwellings. In contrast, the construction of missions, with their imposing facades, *campanarios* (walls with niches or piercings for bells), *espadañas* (ornamental false fronts), and bell towers, represented a scale of architecture unlike any in Alta California before that time. Accounts of approaches to the missions, such as Alfred Robinson's description of Santa Clara, note the impact of their profile visible for miles rising out of the distant plains.[22] San Juan Capistrano's church, begun in 1796, was built of stone with a 180-foot long nave, vaulted ceiling, seven domes, and a bell tower that was reportedly visible for ten miles. The facade of Mission Santa Barbara was visible from the harbor and must have been, for the Chumash, unlike any frame of reference outside of the natural landforms. The degree of transference of notions of the power of prominence between natural and architectural elements is not articulated in any written records, but the reception of these mission *landschafts* suggest an intersection not merely of displays of wealth (the "rule by ostentation" model),[23] but also the alignment of human and natural forces.

These mission facades also offered platforms for surveying the surrounding landscape and looking into the central plazas of the missions. The design of the mission quadrangles also offered opportunities for detailed surveillance. As noted in La Pérouse's description, much of the communal activity took place in a central plaza that was surrounded by four buildings, generally of adobe, with interior *corredors*. The quadrangle plan has a long tradition within monastic, Mediterranean, and Roman architecture, and a number of its design principles have made it an effective architecture of surveillance in each case. The padres' private and communal rooms, the girls' sleeping quarters, and many of the activity areas were located in the quadrangle. In the dormitories and some of the other activity areas the only passage between rooms was outside through the arched colonnade. The buildings' many windows and doors opened onto the interior mainly, with restricted access to the outside only through the *convento*, the church, and one or two cart passages in the walls.[24] These openings and their quadrangle arrangement lent themselves to at least the potential for internal surveillance of the plaza and the colonnade. In the principle of surveillance it is less important that someone be constantly watching than that there is the constant possibility of someone watching.

There is another vivid image of the missions in which resides a powerful convergence of both *landschaft* and surveillance. In two known executed examples, at Santa Clara and San Miguel, are found a symbol known as the "All-Seeing-Eye-of-God." An unsigned, undated drawing in the Santa Barbara archives provides a third example. Within doctrinal iconography this eye in a triangle represented the Trinity, and in each case was placed in a prominent, elevated position within the decorative program. At Santa Clara, the Eye of God was painted on the facade at the peak of the roofline. Descriptions of visitors approaching Santa Clara across a flat plain, report this facade was visible for miles (fig. 9.7). At San Miguel the "All-Seeing-Eye-of-God" has been restored as it was realized in three-dimensional form, jutting out above the altar. While this symbol is not unique to the California missions, within the mission context it appears linked to the surveillance principles of the mission architecture and the authority of the mission priests. Placed in its central, elevated position, this eye was a symbol of the omnipotence and omniscience of the All-Seeing God. Its location implies that the authority of the image was translated in some way to the priests who commissioned the paintings, led the liturgy beneath them, and presented themselves as God's representatives on earth.

The dynamics of the imposition of colonial power in Alta California clearly go beyond the control of sight in the landscape. Military forces at the regional presidios, the prolonged drought that stressed traditional subsistence resources, the diseases and plants introduced by Europeans, the introduction of new goods and their radical impact on native trade and distribution networks—all these factors had a profound influence on the Spanish colonial incursion into California. And yet, on a daily basis the missions functioned with apparent stability and relatively minimal explicit violence—either in the service of Spanish domination or Native American resistance. The control of vision appears to be one of the technologies employed in that daily imposition of power.

Figure 9.7. James P. Ford, interior courtyard, Mission Santa Clara, daguerreotype, c. 1854. This is the earliest known photograph of Mission Santa Clara and, although faint, depicts the "Eye of God" image at the top of the facade. Courtesy: Santa Clara University Archives.

Another perspective on the landscape is how the land might have been per-ceived by the Chumash and what role vision and landscape might have played in the Chumash experience of and resistance to the imposition of Spanish rule. From this subaltern perspective, vision in the landscape may have served as the inverse of surveillance—a means to cloak, mask, and shield from view. It is the physical corol-lary of what James Scott has called the "hidden transcript," that expression of resist-ance to the discourse of dominant ideology.[25]

One regulatory technique or discipline at the missions was the organization of movement through the landscape. Foucault wrote, "A discipline fixes; it arrests or regulates movements; it clears up confusion; it dissipates compact groupings of indi-viduals wandering about the country in unpredictable ways; it establishes calculated distributions."[26] Certainly the introduction of the permanent, year-round mission complexes to groups who had semi-nomadic settlement patterns was this sort of dis-cipline writ large. Traditional environmental management techniques were also thwarted by Spanish authorities; intentional, controlled burning, which had been a vital tool for managing wildfires and for prompting growth of favored plants and basket-making materials, was banned.[27] Other forms of control at a smaller scale—the formations for visitors and forced marching, the assembly of Indians at the ringing of the bell, the synchronized movements of standing and kneeling at the Mass, and the presence of locked doors and barred windows—were all forms of discipline designed to mold the neophytes into docile subjects. But resistance to this regulation and re-striction of movement is also widely documented. The most dramatic evidence is of isolated but quite violent revolts, but there is also evidence of runaways and even rela-tively permeable boundaries of the mission where neophytes continued to participate in kinship networks, practice traditional subsistence practices, and return periodically to native villages. There are also numerous references to the persistence of activities such as gambling and dancing which were not condoned by the missionaries.[28]

The missions went far beyond the confines of the present sites, and this broader view of the landscape suggests that the operations of surveillance and the control of movement were negotiable to those who knew the land well. Beyond the immediate vicinity of the missions were outlying pastures, fields, orchards and even more distant ranches that operated almost as satellite missions with their own supervisors, labor force, and sometimes chapels. In the highly varied geography of California, with its valleys and ranges, the distance of even a few miles can make a large difference in temperature, rainfall, and the seasonal availability of resources. A *diseño*, or pictorial map, of a ranchero of Mission San Antonio de Padua reveals the diverse catchment areas that were exploited at these outposts. The key to a map of the ranchero identifies, among other features, land under cultivation, irrigable land, deer hills, sheep folds, springs, as well as roads to other missions and settlements.[29] Native peoples working and living at the rancheros inhabited traditional lands, even if employing new techniques of agriculture and pastoralism. This exploitation of the traditional resources is further documented by excavations of neophyte barracks indicating that Indians at the missions continued to supplement mission diets with traditional foods and maintain traditional trade networks.[30]

Recent studies by archaeologists and geographers including John Johnson, Julia Costello, and David Hornbeck have combined climatic reconstructions with statistics from mission censuses, and the patterns suggest that the mission population changed seasonally as Indians took advantage of the stable rations and clothing supplies during certain times of the year while returning to their own settlements at other times. These authors have concluded that given the deterioration of traditional resource bases due to drought and sea temperature changes, and given the profound impact of Spanish settlement on indigenous social, economic, and political structures, the decision to join the mission system was one of "risk management." In other words, joining a mission was one of the best options presented to a people in the midst of extreme demographic and environmental stress.[31]

The more permeable boundaries presented by such reconstructions suggest that far from being a walled compound equated visually with classic panoptic plans of a cloistered monastic community or a prison with a central exercise yard, the missions were, at least in some places and times, residential communities with relatively porous boundaries. The decision to join a mission was irrevocable from a Franciscan perspective, but the strictures imposed clearly could be negotiated and resisted. The visual landscapes that the mission Indians inhabited, therefore, were far from bounded by the walls, cactus hedges, and quadrangles of the Spanish, but instead included their traditional lands with the spiritual significance that resonated in them.

ELIZABETH KRYDER-REID

On a smaller scale, the architecture of the missions reveals an element of resistance to control through surveillance—forms of symbolic violence, to use Pierre Bourdieu's phrase— literally inscribed on the walls. Many of the mission churches had elaborately painted walls and ceilings. Norman Neuerburg has been one of the few architectural historians who has studied mission church interiors and worked on several of their restorations. He has identified a number of the designers of the decorative programs and has also identified portions of the wall paintings likely executed by mission Indians.[32] More interesting for this discussion, Neuerburg identified several examples of "graffiti" by Native Americans. These images, one obviously a human form and the other as yet unidentified, were found on the bottom portion of a column in the nave of San Miguel. The circumstances of these anonymous, presumably clandestine images is not known, but their direct contradiction to the European-derived, Christian imagery that they literally overwrite suggests the active practice of traditional iconography and, perhaps, traditional belief systems. The execution of that belief in visible form on the very walls of the church nave points to a subtle yet enduring sign of resistance.[33]

One aspect of control exerted at the missions was to impose hierarchy and to attempt to eliminate or dilute the ties that bound people within their traditional communities. It is a classic principle of regulation or disciplines familiar to military bases, correctional prisons, schools, and, in this case, missions.[34] The hierarchy of Spanish society, particularly within the military and church institutions that were spearheading the colonization, was inculcated in the Indian population. Indian "leaders" called *alcaldes* or *caciques* were chosen and, according to one observer, their function was to "maintain there an air of good order and contemplation."[35] The neophytes were also trained to specialize in various occupations. Where before the social organization had been based on kinship, gender roles, and the political leadership of a chief and shaman, in the mission system, the Indians were partitioned into weavers, masons, carpenters, soap makers, blacksmiths, and tanners.[36] These roles were also aligned with Spanish notions of gender-appropriate labor mediated by the pragmatics of agricultural seasonal demands that required the combined efforts of the labor force to bring in the harvest or process the crops. At the missions, the partitioning of space and the creation of visually segmented landscapes reinforced these divisions. Girls were separated from their nuclear families, work areas were isolated, and housing was regimented into long blocks of rooms.

Despite these techniques, there are suggestions in the documentary record and in the landscape that horizontal solidarity persisted among the mission Indians. A significant aspect of this resistance is the continued agency of native women. Although only beginning to be explored by scholars, indigenous systems of gender and sexuality were "antithetical to a patriarchal ideology in which gender hierarchy, male domination, and heterosexuality were the exclusive organizing principles of desire, sexuality, marriage, and family."[37] While critical facets of the Spanish efforts to "civilize" were the control of sexuality and the imposition of Western ideologies of gender roles, the records of punishments and repeated exhortations suggest that defiance of the rules persisted.[38] Furthermore, the spatial segregation that was to protect the chastity of native women actually facilitated the solidarity of women's networks. For instance, segregation of women in separate dormitories, while devastating for formations of nuclear family bonds, also reinforced women's agency and community. Similarly, the *lavandería* at Mission San Luis Rey, which was located in what was called the sunken garden, a relatively secluded and visually shielded area, provided a venue for unguarded interactions.

Mission landscapes have played the role of tourist sites in California since the late nineteenth century. Each of the missions has a unique expression of its particular history and each has a unique set of constituencies, whether seminarians, local parishioners, students, those living on an Indian reservation, park rangers, or docents from the town, but the missions are also conceived as a corpus, sharing a common heritage and linked physically in a "chain" stretching from San Diego to north of San Francisco. This notion of each site as a link in the chain of missions has been present since their founding along the El Camino Real when they were sited to be approximately a day's ride apart, now approximately the equivalent of an hour's drive.

This conceptualization as a series of destinations has been a major factor in their history following the mission period. Since their secularization in 1834 and particularly following statehood in 1850, the missions have captured the popular imagination of travelers and artists who saw their crumbling walls and decaying roofs as picturesque ruins and artifacts of a romanticized past. The missions were some of the first sites in the West actively marketed as rustic retreats appealing both to tourists and to Californians seeking to escape from the increasing crowds of burgeoning cities like Los Angeles. The notion of the missions as a series of destinations fell squarely into the interests of the emerging car industry in California as well. The Inyo Roads Club sponsored tours of the missions and simultaneously argued for improved roads and transportation infrastructure. Popular magazines such as *Land of Sunshine* and *Sunset* published numerous articles on the missions with titles such as "A Southwest Sleepy Hollow" that embedded them in a mythic past and "Motoring Among the Missions: A Real Joy Ride Through the Cathedral Towns of California" that emphasized the tourist experience of consuming the site.[39] The articles, however, also consistently minimized the sites' active use by the Catholic priests who served the local parishes, the tenant farmers who leased buildings for agricultural purposes, or the native peoples in the communities who were descendants of those buried within the mission lands. Photos accompanying the article rarely included these residents of the sites, but instead depicted the tourists or photographers posed in front of the "empty" and "ruined" buildings as a record and commemoration of their visit.

The paradox of the presentation of these sites is obvious even in the early preservation efforts spearheaded by civic leaders and businessmen. Mission advocates such as Charles Lummis and others who sponsored restorations through The Landmarks Club balanced the tension in their preservation decisions between needing to stabilize the adobe buildings and wanting to preserve the picturesque charm and ancient patina of the sites. Recounting a visit to Mission San Diego for the *Pacific Mutual News*, a monthly publication by the life insurance company of the same name, the travel writer noted, "Would it not be a fine thing were there some way to preserve these ruins just as they are, so much more romantic and suggestive of past greatness are they than any effort at restoration can ever make them? But adobe bricks disintegrate rapidly when exposed to the weather, and unless the buildings are restored, what little remains of many of the Missions will soon have vanished."[40] Another visitor put it even more baldly. At San Luis Rey she noted, "The church building has been fairly well restored, and it would be hard to say just why the exterior is not more pleasing, but certainly robbed of that something wherein lies the charm of these lovely old missions at their best. For one thing, her make-up is unquestionably on the vivid side for one her age."[41]

The resonance of the mission sites with a romanticized past continued through the twentieth century, and the notion of traveling to see and experience the site in person, a pilgrimage to these historic shrines, became an iconic element of the California experience. Following the mission trail became a codified journey in the consumption of historic memory. Marked by uniform road signs along the El Camino Real and by the ubiquitous mission bell, tourists could travel to the destinations "in the footsteps of the padres." In her account *With a Sketch Book Along the Old Mission Trail*, Maude Robson Gunthorp exalted the experience of "seeing" instead of just touring.

> If one still has left to him the exciting adventure of visiting California for the first time, how fortunate is he if he comes with a mind conditioned to bear him beyond the sign-boards of a marvelous, modern commonwealth to the fast-fading background of California's romantic past . . . . It is indeed one thing to tour California and another to *see* her and to know her in her most fascinating aspects. It is to know her thus that we cherish what remains of the chain of old missions, the last crumbling relics of the most picturesque and romantic era in the history of the West—simple reminders of "the tender grace of the day that is dead."[42]

Such constructions of the past were reinforced by visual media that propagated the missions as both romantic oases and tourist destinations. As early as the 1870s, photographs of the missions were sold as local souvenirs.[43] Artists such as Alexander Harmer and photographers such as members of the amateur Pasadena Camera Club traveled to the sites to capture them as artistic subjects. Their work has left a rich visual record from this period, and it is telling that their composition of views consistently privileges the landscapes as empty, ruined spaces. Their framing of the abandoned buildings and eroding adobe not only bespeaks the nineteenth-century preference for the picturesque, but also the reception of these sites as "relics of a by-gone era." William Henry Hudson, who published a series of sketches of the missions, eulogized the experience of visiting these refuges of the modern world.

The missions of California passed away leaving behind them nothing but a memory. . . .
A tender sentiment clings about them—in their enclosures we breathe a drowsy old-
world atmosphere of peace. To linger within their walls or to muse in their graveyards
is to step out of the noisy present into the silence of departed years where everything is
of yesterday and whose marvelous natural beauty is but rarely touched by the associations of history or the charms of romance. These things have a subtle and peculiar
power—a magic not to be resisted by any one who turns from the highways of the modern world to dream among the scenes where the old padres toiled and died.[44]

Among the most famous of these photographers is Carleton Watkins.[45] One of
the pioneers of photography in the West, he included the missions as one of his few
subjects from the built environment, and his photographs are classic examples of
framing vision as a means of constructing the past. The composition of Watkins's
mission images, such as San Juan Capistrano and San Carlos, are similar to his photographs of the natural landscapes of the West; the texture of the buildings and the
undulating mounds of eroded and collapsed adobe recall the textures, patterns, and
forms of his geological subjects. Existing in splendid isolation, the missions Watkins
presents are generally devoid of any evidence of humans. This convention of missions
as abandoned ruins was further disseminated in publications such as William Henry
Jackson's *Ancient Missions and Churches of America* (1894). In the photographs, such
as "Mission San Juan Capistrano" (fig. 9.8), both the original occupants and the con-
temporaneous settlers are erased from the scenes and only the muted tones, eroding
surfaces, and repeating patterns of arches of the buildings' shells remain. Their time-
lessness and their faded glory signify the nostalgic romanticism surrounding these
remnants of another era while at the same time conveniently dispossessing, or at least
bypassing, those who continued to lay claim to the properties.

This representation of the missions was not merely a marketing ploy to lure
travelers to the sites. The romanticization of the past and nostalgic impulse for sim-
pler times were expressions of the place of the missions in the historical memory of
the emerging California state identity. Grade school curricula, popular press, and
widely available images disseminated the same presentation of the sites to the public
as "picturesque ruins" that privileged the Franciscans, minimized the darker sides of

Figure 9.8. Mission San Juan Capistrano, from William Henry Jackson, *Ancient Missions and Churches of America*, 1894. Courtesy: The Huntington Library.

colonialism, and largely erased the diverse peoples who had lived at the missions in the previous 120 years. A 1949 California history textbook opens the chapter on missions with "The mission fathers were happy. Father Serra was the happiest of all. To build missions in California and teach the Indians were what he had dreamed of doing for many years. The mission fathers made friends with the Indians."[46] The guidebooks and articles similarly discounted not only the realities of the Native American past at the site, but also the various settlers, many of them Mexican Americans, who had lived at the sites and continued to use them. These selective historical narratives celebrated the "padres" above all else, particularly the founding leader Serra. They generally skipped the inconvenient Mexican interlude in the history and simultaneously either removed the Native Americans altogether or reduced them to the status of docile pupil and eager neophyte.

It is in this crucible that the mission garden itself was born and the stage set for a different rendition of the visual consumption of the mission landscape. The garden was a key mediator in this tension between architectural restoration and the preservation of the patina of age by introducing "timeless" plantings, fountains, and other garden elements that evoked an "old world" origin and a pan-Mediterranean aesthetic.

At their most basic level, the mission gardens represent the patios and courtyards as ornamental spaces. They are dedicated to the pleasure of sight, smell, and sound. They are designed to attract visitors with their beauty, color, and artistry. They are intended, above all, to enhance the visitor's experience of the missions. Yet, these beautiful oases are not merely the product of neutral aesthetic choices; they contradict in fundamental and naturalizing ways the historical functions of the plazas and patios as work spaces devoted to producing life-sustaining and profit-making products and food. The gardens remove a people from the mission past and mask the life that they knew. They deny the traditional relationships with the land. And they erase the fundamental exercises of power inherent in the utilization of the Native Americans as a labor force to produce food and profit. Furthermore, they perform that erasure using many of the same visual instruments of control used by the padres to subjugate the mission Indians. They control movement, they direct the gaze to emphasize some elements of the sites and screen others, and they present a narrative of the past that is profoundly difficult to penetrate because it is inscribed in nature itself.

One of the prominent ways the sites are framed as tourist space is through the control of movement through the creation of prescribed paths. These structured experiences are less strictly choreographed than at more densely visited sites such as Mount Vernon or the Taj Mahal,[47] but they are sequenced to various degrees. All the missions have some sort of orientation experience, generally including a formal ticketing process and passage into a gathering space that often includes a display or interpretive area. This display space may utilize traditional museum cases and panels or it may be a shop with an array of religious objects and mission-related souvenirs. The museum displays have varying degrees of professionalism in their presentations, but most have artifacts associated with the mission history and religious devotion. Most of the narratives in these museum exhibits outline the history of the missions and celebrate particular achievements of illustrious persons associated with the missions. Some of the missions take a decidedly architectural track in their interpretations, while others present of a social history of the missions. As might be expected, these narratives are constructed from the perspective of the current proprietor, which is the Catholic Church in all but two instances. Deconstructing the narratives of these interpretations is a larger subject than can be addressed here, but the key themes are the courage and sanctity of the founding padres, the success and productivity of the missions at their height, and the valiant efforts of the church over the years to maintain and restore the sites. It is also interesting to note that, in contrast to the guidebooks and popular published literature, the interpretive narratives at the missions often highlight the local parish histories and current activities.

Rather than formal tours, the visitor's experience at the California missions is almost entirely self-guided, with the exception of school tours. There is relatively little signage and almost no guided or human-mediated interactions at most sites, although most missions have some sort of guidebook or brochure available. The routes and sequence of the tour experience are shaped almost entirely by the built environment itself, and visitors generally follow a prescribed pattern. Following the orientation experience, the visitor usually exits into an inner courtyard of the site where generally three choices are presented: to walk the corridors and visit whatever rooms are open for viewing, to explore the ornamental gardens in the center of the courtyard (or exterior forecourts, depending on the mission), or to visit the church. A few sites, such as Santa Barbara, restrict access into the garden itself although visitors can look into the garden (fig. 9.9). The proscribed route culminating in the sacred space conveys a sense of gaining access to an inner sanctum at the missions. The impression of privileged entry into a sacred space is reinforced by signs indicating the bounds of the public areas and by the generally subdued comportment of other visitors exhibiting the appropriate contemplative postures of the mission tourist. The atmosphere of these spaces is charged with a combined reverence for the historic and the religious.

While there is essentially free choice on the route and sequence of the experience at most of the missions, clear highlights of the visit are designed by their positions of prominence. Iconic artifacts include the mission bells and wooden crosses reminiscent of the original crosses. In the guidebooks, each mission has an epithet, such as "Queen of the Missions" or "Pride of the Missions," which personifies its per-

Figure 9.9. Courtyard garden, Mission Santa Barbara, 1992. Photo: E. Kryder-Reid.

sonality along the mission chain. Each is also known for one or more iconic features —particularly striking architectural elements such at the *campanarios* at San Antonio de Pala or unique botanical specimens such as a pepper tree at San Luis Rey. At some missions with more extensive grounds, there are also opportunities to stroll the areas around the mission buildings. Here one may encounter the local variations on the mission garden theme—an intriguing range of folk art, spaces for parish functions, evidence of the parish's political concerns and outreach, scout projects, demonstration gardens, native plant and botanical specimen gardens, and whatever excavated remains of the mission complex have survived.

What is less visible, either because of its complete absence, misinterpretation, or peripheral placement, is the presence of Native Americans on the landscape. With the exception of the cemeteries, some of which contain thousands of Indian burials, the representation of these Indian residents and workers at the mission is minimized. The neophyte barracks-style housing has rarely survived and has not been deemed a priority for reconstruction. Where direct remnants of the Indians' role as laborers survive, the interpretations generally range from absent to euphemistic. A smelting furnace at San Juan Capistrano is labeled not as a place where Native peoples worked, but as the "first industrial site in Orange County." Even when the labor of the Indians is acknowledged, such as their role in building the missions, they are generally posited as "helpers." Artifacts associated with the Native American ways of life are sometimes presented as part of the "before" portion of the story explaining the traditional lives prior to the coming of the Spanish. In other cases, representations of native ways of life appear decontextualized, such as the *maños* and *metates* noted earlier at San Fernando.[48]

One of the more telling examples of the contested nature of representing the native past at the missions is the reconstruction of traditional dwellings. At San Juan Capistrano a domed house sits in the forecourt of the mission in the midst of a rose garden, with minimal interpretive signage. At Santa Barbara, a similar reconstruction is even more marginally placed in a side parking lot behind a chain-link fence (fig. 9.10).[49] On the fence hangs a hand-lettered sign that reads, "This Chumash traditional house was built May, 1997 by Chumash Indian descendants Joaqun Robles Whiteoak and Nashun Hoate. It depicts the type of house originally built by local Indians. By the early 1800s a village of larger adobe houses was built (over 200 homes) where the parking lot is currently located."

Figure 9.10. Joaqun Robles Whiteoak and Nashun Hoate, Chumash dwelling, reconstruction, Mission Santa Barbara parking lot, 1997. Photo: E. Kryder-Reid.

Along with the control of movement, one of the other fundamental aspects structuring the tourist experience is the control of sight. The approach to the missions varies depending on their location, but many of those more oriented to the tourist visitor have carefully crafted the approach to the site for the maximal visual impact. Foundation plantings soften the massive fronts, while verdant lawns and dark green junipers and cedars contrast with the white facades. In an arid climate lawns are maintained with great effort, and the extent to which they are legitimizing contemporary water politics by embedding the greensward in California's early history is a point for debate. In many of the missions, this approach is complemented by staged photo opportunities where the quintessential shot can be taken through the arch or in front of the cascading vines, or reflected in the quiet surface of the pools. Some of

211

these images are deeply ingrained in the received history of the missions through their appearances in popular media and as advertising illustrations on fruit crates and canned goods. Other images can be traced more specifically to the texts that helped inform the design of the mission gardens in the early twentieth century. Popularizers of Mediterranean landscapes such as Byne and Byne's 1924 *Spanish Gardens and Patios* influenced the residential landscape nationally, but within California the style was seized upon as a perfect fit for the climate and the resort culture it aspired to.[50] California adopters of the Mediterranean revival gardens could also look to the missions as local landmarks echoing the aesthetic while gardeners at the missions were simultaneously echoing popular trends of the day.[51] Within the mission landscapes, the play of shadow and light along the corridors similarly alludes to the Mediterranean aesthetic praised by the earlier travel books. All of these sights are, of course, available for tourists to capture and possess with their own cameras, or available for purchase when they exit through the gift shop—tokens of their own authentic and historic experience.

If the exercises of power through the control of vision and movement in the landscape are similar in missions' colonizing landscapes and their tourist destination landscapes, what then might be the forms of resistance in the tourist experience? Missions have been picketed over the canonization of Junípero Serra, who represents to some the founder of Catholicism in California and to others the author of their people's genocide, but to date no one has protested the planting of marigolds or the building of an intentionally antiqued fountain.[52] The heated pitch of academic and political debates over the role of the missions in the conquest of California has largely bypassed the decision-making processes shaping the contemporary landscapes of these missions. Complicating potential reinterpretations at the sites is the fact that the church stands as both the historically accused and the current occupant. Furthermore, as at Williamsburg and other colonial revival sites, the gardens have become historic landscapes in their own right. In the midst of the controversial canonization process of Junípero Serra and accusations of genocide, debates over whether to replace a bed of roses with a dusty courtyard seem small stakes indeed. But the same power of landscape to naturalize relationships of power, reify romanticized images of the past, and erase a legacy of oppression is also the potential to create a landscape of reconciliation—one that makes conscious the subtexts of vision, landscape, and the interests they serve.

FOUR VIEWS, THREE OF THEM

THROUGH GLASS

Sandy Isenstadt

> Glass helped put the world in a frame: it made it possible to see certain elements of re-
> ality more clearly: and it focused attention on a sharply defined field—namely, that
> which was bounded by the frame.
>
> Lewis Mumford, *Technics and Civilization*, 1934

FROM AN AERIAL POINT OF VIEW BOUNDED ONLY BY THE HORIZON, THE POST-
war suburb was a spreading monotony of mass-produced houses on featureless streets,
which seemed to co me as a surprise to architects and planners. "If I only had known
how it would look later . . ." ran the caption to one such view, appearing in 1952 in
the inaugural issue of *House and Home*, expressing dismay and regret but implying
at the same time that it was supposed to have looked better (fig. 10.1). The reality of
the postwar suburb, in other words, seen more or less objectively in plan, was at odds

Figure 10.1. "Case for the Wider Lot," from *House and Home*, January 1952, 162. Evident from the planner's point of view, looking down from above, the suburb failed to meet the ideal that motivated it. Photo: Sandy Isenstadt.

with the image of the suburb. That image, however, was usually seen from the prospective homeowner's point of view—from the inside looking out, through glass, to a private landscape—and had for over a century been pictured in popular magazines and trade journals, encouraged by professional designers and by government, promoted by manufacturers, measured by appraisers of real estate, adjudicated by courts of law, and effectively internalized as a cultural ideal. Across a broad swath of postwar American life, the suburban home was imagined at the vertex of a beautiful view, and however many came to share that view, not one of them would ever overlook another like-minded citizen (fig. 10.2). Although not a common scene on most suburban sites, such a view was shared imaginatively. In fact, the leading resource for and symbol of domestic character was the view, although it was utterly immaterial. The postwar emphasis on private landscape views existed within a longer trajectory of domestic vision that includes also hearths, television, and the automobile; the American landscape became modern not through any particular formal motifs but by being seen routinely through glass.

Figure 10.2. Home of Dr. and Mrs. Robert Stockton, Gates Mills, Ohio. Ernst Payer, architect. The visual ideal of the suburb involved a view from inside the home out toward an expansive and private landscape. Photo: Fuller, Smith and Ross, August 1954. Courtesy: Libby-Owens-Ford Glass Company Records, MSS-066, Ward M. Canaday Center for Special Collections, University of Toledo.

The view's ascendance is all the more surprising given that the domestic icon the view most clearly displaced was the hearth — the spatial, mechanical, social, and structural solid core of the house (fig. 10.3). Prior to the advent of mechanical systems in the home, the hearth was the chief source of heat, of cooked food, and of light, often occupying a large proportion of wall and usually the most expensive part of the house to build. The hearth was central to the production of meals and comfort. It consumed fuel and labor, provided a setting for work, rest, and social exchange, and, through its continuous presence throughout family life, acquired a kind of domestic authority. Nineteenth-century advances in mechanical sources of heat and light, increasing reliance on the use of store-bought goods, and greater differentiation of interior spaces changed all that. In many ways, progress in the domestic sphere was measured through the nineteenth century by independence from the hearth.

That the hearth had become by the century's end technologically obsolete only seemed to increase its symbolic power. Reasons and occasions for coming together as a family around the hearth had to be invented once it was no longer necessary for warmth or light. The hearth then was fairly deified, with the whole house seeming, as Ruskin put it, "a temple of the hearth watched over by Household Gods." In the center of the family parlor, supplemented by its mantels and overmantels, framed by souvenirs of distant lands and pictures of absent faces and past events, and often with a mirror reflecting back an image of the family gathered there, the hearth became the primary place of self-conscious representation for the Victorian family. Prominent in the private home's most public space, the hearth organized the presentation of a family's best virtues and values. A visual essay on civility in that part of the private home given to social contact, the hearth was at the same time the setting and sign for self-sufficiency. Rising directly from the land and built from locally made brick, the hearth, according to Herman Melville, held also a "fertilizing charm," and its heat, in turn, made the soil directly around the home more fertile. The whole hearth-centered compound was one with divine creation: "Nature, and but nature, house and all." The hearth had become central not only to the individual family but to an aggregate of families, a nation. Especially after the American centennial, concepts of national identity were tied to the steady, centering power of the hearth. Reverend William G. Eliot remarked, "The corner-stone of our republic is the hearth-stone."[1] By the end

SANDY ISENSTADT

Figure 10.3. Henry Hudson Holly, *Modern Dwellings in Town and Country* (New York: Harper and Bros., 1878), 192. History is held by the hearth, legible in its light and transmitted with its warmth for generations to come. Photo: Sandy Isenstadt.

of the nineteenth century, as its former functions were being replaced by centralized heating, electric lights, and new cooking appliances, the hearth was appreciated more for the values it could represent than any crucial functions it could perform.

But Andrew Jackson Downing had said in 1842 that there were two elements necessary to assure domestic character, especially for modest homes: windows and chimneys were "the two most essential and characteristic features of dwelling-houses."[2] The chimney, as an extension of the hearth, was a visible sign to the larger world of a family gathered round its base; the window expressed that family's confident relationship with the environment surrounding it. From the outside, both externalized the merits of the interior—the hearth's material accommodation of somatic needs and the window's service to light and view and, so, to visual pleasure. Although in service to the same goal of domestic character, from inside the house, hearth and window led in opposite directions. One encouraged an inward and centralizing view while the other was aimed outward; one view terminated in a well-formed mass while the other view passed through glass and did not so much end as dissolve into the distance (fig 10.4). In the nineteenth century, the conflict between hearth and window was a minor one. Henry Hudson Holly, for instance, thought the two might be combined, and recommended the unusual arrangement of a window over a hearth in order to provide two

Figure 10.4. "Look Out, Not In," from E. C. Gardner, *Homes and How to Make Them*, (Boston: J. R. Osgood and Company, 1874), 154. This illustration registers a growing tension between window and hearth. Photo: Sandy Isenstadt.

views, with a landscape motif painted onto sliding shutters so that on dreary days the effect of a double view would not be lost.[3]

The tension became more grievous, however, as glass became more common in the home. In 1863, when Holly made his remarks, American-made window glass was scarce and poor in quality compared with European glass. By the 1880s, though, American production was said to be approaching that of the French, both in quality and quantity. With new fuels and technological innovations, and corporate partnerships that attracted greater investment in the capital-intensive industry (and despite several antitrust investigations resulting from corporate collusion), glass production skyrocketed in the last quarter of the century. Between 1880 and 1890, for instance, plate-glass production doubled from 93 to 188 million square feet.[4] Holly revealed his delight with this trend in his next book, amused by the story of a houseguest who injured himself trying to walk through an otherwise invisible window. Among its merits, Holly noted, the improved quality of plate glass also improved the view: "From the interior, plate-glass is so absolutely translucent, that no obstruction seems offered to the view; so that, in case of a window glazed with a single light, it is often supposed that the sash must be open, which is the acme of the effect to be produced." Although a prominent advocate of Queen Anne Revival, Holly criticized the unquestioning use of small panes of glass, which is one of the style's distinctive features: "for us to go back to the use of small panes, only because they belong to the style, would be ridiculous. We should not only injure our view by cutting it up with these little checkered squares, but would miss the brilliant effect that we might obtain from that most beautiful of modern inventions, plate-glass." Small panes, and a complete rendering of Queen Anne, were only acceptable to Holly when no good view was available.[5]

Holly, however, was rare in his embrace of larger windows; most architects offered reasons not to admire them. For one, they led to excessive heat loss and increased the likelihood of leaks. These were technical matters that only experts were expected to know, which was, according to one such professional in 1909, "why architects object to the very windows which their clients too often insist upon having. . . . Do not look upon this matter as trivial. There has been a craze for windows unduly large." Even if they were relatively weathertight, large windows simply looked cold. *Harper's Weekly* reported in 1864 that a Mr. Rogers got sick thinking he had dined by an open window; it was only plate glass but "such was the force of imagination, that he actually caught cold." Edith Wharton and Ogden Codman explained thirty years later that plate glass "gives a sense of coolness and the impression of being out of doors, [and] becomes for these very reasons a disadvantage in cold weather."[6]

More significantly, large windows shattered the sense of enclosure necessary for the creation of domestic character. Ruby Goodnow, author of the 1914 book *The Honest House*, noted with alarm: "People demand windows everywhere! Each room must have two and often three." She then explained to her readers that domestic character evaporates with bigger windows: "The offense doesn't lie in the fact that the windows are of *plate* glass, but in the hideousness of an unbroken expanse of glass. . . . If your architect insists on huge sheets of glass, instead of begging you to consider small panes, there is something wrong with him." By overrating their views and enlarging their windows, Goodnow said, clients trifled with the very container of domesticity and their guarantee of privacy. Large windows had become such a fad, Goodnow wrote, that a truly "radical idea" would be a house with "broad wall spaces and few windows." With a continuous enclosure, homeowners could find domestic tranquility and at the same time express their aesthetic independence.[7] With reciprocity well established between a home's architectural character and the moral character of its occupants, large windows also threatened an individual's personal development. Blurring the difference between inside and out diminished the spatial resources for developing one's own intimate and social sides. With both architecture and selfhood similarly resting on a clear demarcation between inside and out, a large window was a lost opportunity for spatial and psychic articulation.

Further, large windows suggested to architects more of a commercial rather than a domestic character. They were common to shops and encouraged exposure rather than privacy. And even for shops they produced an "unarchitectural effect," according to Russell Sturgis. An English travel writer contrasted small latticed windows with large windows of plate glass by remarking that small windows enclosed space, but, "the modern plate glass window suggests to me but a glazed void; so perfect is plate glass that it might be solidified air."[8] Solidified air might be a triumph of technology over nature, but it left a home without atmosphere. By making a glazed void, the modern window had a hollowness at its heart, representing a nonhuman sphere of industrial refinement. Mechanization and the perfectly transparent object posed a threat to a reflective, interiorized, and many-chambered self. In contrast to the privacy-loving English, Americans had become diseased by commercial culture, according to landscape architect Caroline Klingensmith who, in 1913, wrote that Americans were constitutionally given over to display. This was the only explanation she found for houses designed like shop fronts, filled with "hideous and unbroken expanses of glass." This illness, "bred in the bone," was all she could come up with to explain the common American desire "to see out": "It is hard to understand why most people insist upon 'seeing out,'" especially in domestic settings where the focus should be inward, Klingensmith wrote. Worse, any outward glance seemed to satisfy. She related her own experience when a client took her to his promising hilltop home site and, turning toward town and away from the natural scenes that lay about in abundance, declared: "'If we clear away the trees, . . . we shall be able to see out.'" She presented him with several alternatives to "seeing out" and ended up losing the job.[9]

Determining the openings in a facade was an activity central to professional practice, so their alteration on the part of clients untutored in niceties like proportion was an insult to disciplinary knowledge. While architects believed that clients displayed their faults in a variety of ways, exaggerating the view was especially irksome, and the complaint was only aggravated by the fact that, with the increasing separation between work and home, many house clients were women, while the profession remained steadfastly a male enterprise. One English architect, R. A. Briggs, addressed his book to "dear madam" and suggested ways to "preclude many wearisome conversations." He began by discrediting several "fallacious legends," which included the naive belief that unbroken expanses of glass were warranted by a good view. For Briggs, a client was blind to art if she insisted on maximum transparency to a view, for relinquishing the boundary between inside and out was to abandon architecture altogether: "Why cry against the bars in sash windows? Why? The reason usually is— 'Oh! they spoil the view.' If the bars spoil the view, then the window—or rather the walls all round the window—spoil the view. Therefore, if you must see the view in full, you must have either a glass front to your House, or you should go outside."[10] In this rendering, a wall of glass was both the logical outcome of insisting on a view and manifestly ridiculous, subverting as it did so many principles of fine planning, good taste, and circumspect manner. The preposterousness that such an inversion of sound values might even be entertained seemingly justified Briggs's tone of haughty derision. A fleeting thought that such a thing might actually come to pass perhaps accounts for an underlying note of anxiety. After all, the author's irony regarding glass fronts would in a few years be architectural orthodoxy. His mocking tone reveals that before the wall of glass was a modernist dream it was an Edwardian nightmare.

However parochial, architects' complaints regarding their clients' taste for views registers the growing place of real estate among the financial assets of the middle-class American family. With industrialization, the link between acreage and wealth had come undone, but the middle class seemed only to covet land all the more. Examining this seeming paradox, economist Thorstein Veblen distinguished productive "industry" from "business," which stimulated consumption and had tapped into the

Figure 10.5. "This Picture" *Los Angeles Times*, April 27, 1919, 116; "This View," *Los Angeles Times*, May 11, 1919, 111. Photos: Sandy Isenstadt.

middle-class "propensity for emulation." The middle class needed a visual "code of reputability," Veblen argued, and "an accredited line of conspicuous consumption" from which to draw. It needed artistic, that is, noneconomic, forms that were associated with higher social classes but reproducible on the cheap. Land, even a modest suburban plot, was a leading form of conspicuous consumption because it was both relatively costly and, in its visible uselessness, remote from economic concerns. The suburban yard, Veblen wrote, combined a "studious exhibition of expensiveness coupled with a make-believe of simplicity."[11] In a consumer society, its removal from productive activity was precisely what linked the suburban yard with the larger economy. Thus, ringed by a viewable landscape, a house in a country-like setting was the bull's-eye of upward mobility.

In the early twentieth century, as real estate transactions increased and markets for real estate formed, brokers learned that views motivated buyers (fig. 10.5). More and more, house lots were described as "sightly," along with being convenient to transit lines. However motivating, though, brokers were unable to actually charge for a view since, as it was commonly understood, a view was a gift of nature, or God. More to the point, it was immaterial, and it was off the site.

As the real estate appraisal industry formed in the early twentieth century, such an intangible factor did not lend itself to the emerging ideals of scientific appraisal. Early appraisal manuals in fact admonished appraisers to focus on measurable aspects of the home and consider intangible aspects only in general terms.[12]

Writings on landscape design had been grappling with the same problem: how to take advantage of a view that lay on someone else's property, that is, how to visually appropriate the neighbor's yard (fig. 10.6). For those large picturesque estates that were models for suburban yards, views were commensurate with the vast acreage a family owned. Designers of middle-class sites put a premium on the symbolic affects of a large estate, but they had far fewer acres on which to achieve them. How to achieve stately views on smaller sites thus became a key aesthetic problem in the design of suburban landscapes, with various strategies proposed, ranging from cooperating with neighbors to keep open view corridors, to trees colored to accord with atmospheric perspective, to varying views from specific windows, and so on. Frank J. Scott, for instance, claimed that an unfenced belt of lawn composed of adjacent yards would provide "a genteel air to the neighborhood" and so attract "a class of refined people of small means" who would recognize the environmental aesthetic to which they aspired.[13]

Against the opening of the house to the outside, the hearth began to appear less its own center of gravity than as one term of a polarity about which domestic space was thought to be organized. John Taylor Boyd Jr., an architect and a frequent contributor to *Architectural Record*, wrote a series of articles concerning the design of small houses—those of greatest concern to the middle class. The architect needed to strike a balance between the home's two opposing spatial standards, he said: "One principle is the separation of rooms to preserve individuality and privacy; and the other is the throwing of them open in order to gain that effect of ease and spaciousness which is so desirable."[14] One principle, in other words, connoted identity formation and restraint while the other implied enjoyment and desire, or more diagrammatically, one was a principle of ego, the other the id. These principles operated at both a perceptual and a psychological level, and hearth and view were their architectural correlates. To resolve the tension, architects suggested, for example, that patterns of occupation could vary seasonally, with the hearth a feature for winter and an outdoor orientation more suited to the summer. In most scenarios, oversized windows over-

The Starks
seem to live in a
vast tree-studded lawn,
but their prop-
erty line is just 50 feet
from the house.
The country club takes
care of the grass;
they look at
it.

HOW TO ENJOY LAND YOU DON'T OWN

Man has long been concerned with keeping exuberant nature and his various enemies out of his garden. Once his foes included wild beasts; today we struggle with gophers, beetles, and an occasional locust.

In mediaeval times, palisades, thorn thickets, and moats were some of the protective devices used.

Then came more benevolent times and man longed to see the landscape around him and to participate in it.

28   MR. & MRS. WILLIAM STARK, FRESNO 1950   DESIGNER: HARRY HUNTER   PHOTOGRAPHER: MAYNARD PARKER

Figure 10.6. "How to Enjoy Land You Don't Own," Thomas Church, *Gardens Are for People* (New York: Reinhold Pub. Corp, 1955), 28. Photo: Sandy Isenstadt.

looking open landscapes were tempered by the steadying mass of the hearth and enough enclosure to preserve the reassuring presence of finitude.

With the arrival from Europe of a "fenestrated architecture," as Thomas Tallmadge saw it in 1928, large windows were given a theoretical rationale along with a formal palette of flat roofs, cubic forms, and smooth surfaces devoid of applied ornament. As Henry-Russell Hitchcock and Philip Johnson, curators of the International Style Exhibition held at the Museum of Modern Art in 1932, explained, modern architecture really had no windows at all, just walls that appeared in one of two states, transparent or opaque. For Hitchcock and Johnson, glass walls made aesthetic sense of progress in the material sphere. Bigger glass certainly improved views to the outdoors, but in the two best-known examples of early domestic modernism, views through glass were not the main point. Le Corbusier placed the largest glass wall in his Villa Savoye to face not the outside but an interior court, itself enclosed by a screen wall, while the glass wall at Mies van der Rohe's Tugendhat house rolls out of the way to draw in fresh air along with the view. Mies's courthouse designs likewise feature glass walls but these face onto clearly demarcated interior courts. Glass in the 1930s was quickly embraced in the United States as an icon of modernity in the home, although this may have had less to do with architectural discourse than with the fact that use of glass in the home had been increasing for decades. Moreover, through technological innovations, glass had become a topos of uninterrupted scientific progress; it was the miracle material of the Depression.

By the late 1940s, landscape views had come to dominate many discussions of house design. Indeed, it is hard to find a single issue of a popular or professional house design journal from the 1940s and 1950s that does not at some point describe a house situated at the apex of a fabulous view. Even for very private places like bathrooms and bedrooms, designs often included a view. Other aspects of house design, which had formerly enjoyed more or less independent value, now began to be incorporated within a prevailing logic of the view. Mirrors for example, began to be placed opposite views to reflect them deep within the house; exterior lighting was directed toward the landscape to extend views beyond dusk; elaborate indoor gardens sprouted. Even manufacturers of goods for the home captured in their advertisements the idea of transparent relations with nature from the point of view of consuming homeowners, that is, as an unmediated relation with the outdoors. The open planning that characterized many postwar homes also came to rely on a view, which drew the eye outdoors and so legitimated the fundamental proposition of spatial continuity. An open plan meant little in a closed setting. Even the government directed home buyers' attention to their views, as some argued that a glass-walled "American style" would prove significant in the coming contest between freedom and totalitarianism.[15]

For some designers, the view seemed to define the very idea of the house, transforming even the most fundamental archetypes: Marcel Breuer's houses, for instance, were labeled "observation posts" and were compared both in function and appearance to cameras, with the architect described as "the man behind the camera" (fig 10.7). The view could likewise become the foundation of the design process: houses were described as being organized or "built around" a view, or "reversed" or "elevated" for one. William Wurster proposed glass walls as the answer to his question "When is a small house large?" and in one stroke redefined an American building type. With no small delight in the contradiction, his architectural style would be characterized as "the large small house."[16] The view was also one of the chief reasons offered to justify the reorientation of the house from the street to the private backyard. In the process, longstanding distinctions like "facade" and "rear" were redesignated in countless publications as "street side," "blind side," and "view side." The glass wall itself was valued less as a visible sign of the technical mastery of new materials and construction methods, as it had been for modernists in the 1920s, than as a technologically facilitated access to nature, which was conceived as a deep and unpopulated vista.

Glass walls worked best with extensive sites but they were championed as a means to democratize the experience of nature for a suburban middle class. A view could satisfy the postwar cliché of "bring the outdoors indoors" but without making the private public. The wall of glass required modern materials but it was promoted as a means to compensate for having to live in a technological society. The "large window," a diminutive version of the glass wall, was said to be "modern architecture's most important contribution to house design." But it was the first, and only, modern architectural element openly used on traditional or "Cape Cod" houses. It was "dear to the heart of the conservative as well as the modernist," *Architectural Forum* said in

Figure 10.7. Marcel Breuer, Clark House, Orange, Connecticut, 1949, from Marcel Breuer, *Sun and Shadow: The Philosophy of an Architect* (New York: Dodd, Mead, 1955), 32. Photo: Sandy Isenstadt.

1942. Coupled with the fact that they did not have to be owned to be enjoyed, views were seen as a discounted version of a formerly aristocratic pleasure. Finally, once the house was, as *Architectural Forum* wrote in 1948, "freed from the vertical axis of the chimney stack," the whole house could extend outward.[17] By recapitulating popular notions of spatial expansion, views were seen to emerge from the same frontier conditions that had shaped the American national character. As a representation of the historical landscape, seen from the altitude of the 1950s, a view could serve as a daily reminder of a national narrative that was still in the making, with middle-class suburbanites, especially those with a taste for modern design, often referred to as the new pioneers.

Although overshadowed by the view, the hearth was no less popular a home feature in the 1950s than it had been earlier. But it was incorporated within a different constellation of domestic values. As often as not, the hearth supplemented the view and assumed, in countless floor plans, significant axial relations with the view. In numerous houses fireplaces were placed next to a view window so that "the view and the cheery fire can be enjoyed simultaneously."[18] Typically, the fireplace was the quiet counterpoint to a dramatic view. *Architectural Forum*'s discussion of a 1943 house in Hollywood by Richard Neutra is characteristic. The house is presented as commanding "a fine view" and opening up "through a wide sliding door onto an outdoor sitting space confronting this fine panorama," while "the fireplace is at the center, opposite the main view, and has a comfortable sitting corner."[19] The fireplace was opposite in character, too. A modernist "drive toward experiment," associated both with open minds and open walls, was often described "in contrast to the warm joy of security at the fireplace." And the architect was often called upon to synthesize these equally important but "most contrasting elements of our nature," as Marcel Breuer put it.[20] Breuer made a habit in his house designs of placing the hearth directly in front of the view. If a conflict of visual interest emerged, which was usually the case, it was the hearth that started to erode. Breuer actually seemed to reenact this process by first placing the hearth in front of a wall of glass and then, in Peter Blake's description of Breuer's 1949 Clark House, "to prevent [the] fireplace from obstructing [the] view too much, it has been perforated in several places."[21] Like the hearth that it replaced, the view, too, opened onto a wider world. Sylvan scenes behind glass walls, like pictures and mementos around the fireplace, established within the private home a relationship with some other place and organized domestic space around that relationship.

"Character," a leading evaluative term for domestic architecture in the nineteenth century, had been threatened by large windows. In telling a truth about the industrialized processes on which the act of building was based, windows drained character from the interior by dissolving the enclosure in which the act of dwelling occurred.[22] Large windows came to be accepted by buyers of both modern and traditional styles, however, not because of any technical rationalization regarding materials but because for many Americans character itself had moved outdoors. Character no longer inhered in secure enclosures or the centripetal pull of the hearth; instead, the representative form of a modern dwelling was an open and friendly relation to landscape. The view, in other words, expressed the modern form of domestic character: it was evidence of a natural orientation; it visibly registered physical distance from work; it was an analog of freedom and lack of restraint; it provided therapeutic opportunities for those made anxious in the city or otherwise in need of psychic calm; and it was purchased, that is to say, its aesthetic and therapeutic benefits came at a price determined by the market, just as other goods formerly homemade had been replaced by manufactured goods. Moreover, because it did not necessarily depend on actual land owned at the site or the client's ability to pay, a landscape view was no longer restricted to the wealthy. Large windows overlooking landscape can thus be understood as a bid to disseminate and multiply encounters with nature in a rapidly urbanizing society. Rather than being cozy within four walls, the modern measure of domestic joy was openness to a landscape, where even slight impediments to viewing were thought to disturb the viewer's newly intimate relationship with the outdoors. In this way, having a view was analogous to having at the family fireside an uninvited and silent stranger. Wall could dissolve to window because the landscape itself had been domesticated, that is, drawn into the *domus*, the circle of human inhabitation.

As before, hearth and view served contradictory impulses of human nature, signifying, respectively, introspection and extroversion. However, rather than the former repository and matrix for the display of family values, the hearth was usually understood as a kind of agreeable compromise with one's vestigial neanderthal Other. As a Museum of Modern Art publication put it in 1946: "Man retains his primitive need for cave-like security even while he delights in unlimited light and space, and the best modern houses, give both."[23] The hearth had become a refuge from the view in the same way that the house was a refuge from the larger world. Older notions of the house as a system of discrete rooms with determinate character and within a definite enclosure gave way before this idea of an alternation of prospect and refuge, which was literalized by the view and the hearth. Interior domestic space literally took on a landscape conception: the hearth is a harbor in a sea of movement both physical and visual, it anchors a landscape of circulation.

With views, or expectations of views, being built into so many dwellings, it was not long before they were given more precise values in real estate and greater protection in legal circles. In other words, with so much personal identity riding on visual relations to the outdoors, those relations were gradually codified by law and commodified by real estate appraisers who made it their business to pinpoint the price for a private panorama. Sometime in the early 1940s the term "view" first appeared as a line item on appraisal forms. By 1951, the *National Real Estate and Building Journal* asserted that "rule number one" of planning a home was to focus on the site. This was less a matter of square footage than it was of finding the view and then fixing it in a house plan. Also in 1951, the *Appraisal Journal*, leading organ of the appraisal industry, published its first full-length article on "The Value of View." In this article, a professional appraiser noted that views had become especially important lately because houses had become so characterless. In an era of standardization in housing design, the view, even an "artificial view" or a "prefabricated view," gave a house its individuality. Other appraisers also began to argue that banks should take views into account since such "intangible amenities" made for more attractive homes in the event of default or a soft market.[24]

With a view's economic value more amenable to measurement, it became increasingly subject to adjudication. The 1954 Supreme Court decision in *Berman v. Parker* validated the idea of a "scenic easement," that is, a right to look at, but not to tread upon, a landscape. A number of cases following the Court's decision went on to seek monetary damages for ruined views. The fact that one was not legally entitled to step on the landscape that was so central to a house's design was celebrated the following year by the landscape architect Thomas Church. Church diagramed, at the level of the small home site, an everyday truth: the size of the viewpoint is immaterial to the scope of the view, as any camera or keyhole made clear. Church illustrated how a sunken fence, or "ha-ha," marked the boundary between properties without marring the view, and so made the most of scenic easements. If architectural dreams of sylvan scenes descended from such picturesque-era landscape meditations, they were perpetuated by explicit adaptation for middle-class consumption. Based on the creation of visual space borrowed from distant vistas, Church retained the ideological scope of a landscape view while reducing the actual size and cost of the land overlooked.[25]

Despite all the discussion of the view, it was soon displaced as a domestic focus. By the end of the 1950s, families gathered around the television more frequently and more earnestly than around a view. Advertisements for home products, which during the 1940s and 1950s had borrowed heavily from view imagery, also turned more and more to television for their marketing cues. As it turned out, the view was an intermediate stage between a Victorian domesticity, represented by the hearth, and the postwar reorientation of domestic space around television, the "electronic hearth."

But television was absorbed within the home in accordance with a logic of looking pioneered by the view. The fascination with viewing distant vistas without leaving home is common to both. The TV was described as a "looking glass" and as the "biggest window." Early books on television, like Thomas Hutchinson's *Here is Television, Your Window on the World* made the connection explicit. Competition between the hearth, the view, and television grew fierce. Though the hearth had made a provisional peace, its "position," Ray Faulkner wrote, was "being challenged by window walls and television" and consequently, once a sober requirement, the hearth was rendered "a delightful extravagance."[26] In turn, when *Architectural Forum* asked "Will the television set replace the fireplace—or, how soon will it replace the fireplace?" it surmised that television, similarly competing with views out, would lead to fewer and smaller windows to prevent glare or distract attention. In addition, the editors insisted that screens would get larger, contrary to the consensus of engineers, basing their contrarian claim not on faith in technical progress but on their assessment of the visual culture of the house in the 1950s: no one would be satisfied in their own home with "a last-row balcony view of the world." Television was incorporated within the home during the 1950s precisely by seizing upon the rhetoric of the view. Bruno Funaro, who had earlier coauthored a history of the use of glass in modern architecture, wrote in 1957 that with technology already replacing other window functions with mechanical ventilation and artificial illumination, even outward views might be replaced by a "TV window." *House Beautiful* claimed: "The walls of today's home are as wide as the world. You can savor the earth and the fullness thereof from a seat in your living room," referencing not a glass-walled prospect but the television, a glass-screened scene.[27] If the hearth had focused vision inward, and the view led the eye toward the periphery, the television managed to do both: to give vision a center of gravity made up of views taken from the periphery. In a sense, television centralized vision but peripheralized attention.

If there was a single moment of peaceful coexistence in this Cold War of domestic representation, it had to be September 1954 (fig 10.8). At that time, *House and Home* perspicuously observed, "Nowadays, most living rooms have three views—two of them inside, one of them outdoors": the television, the fireplace, and a landscape view. "In a good living room you do not have to move the furniture around . . . these three views are all visible within a 90-degree arc from wherever you sit." From the comfort of one's own couch, three visual axes spanning cultural objects whose origins lay in different centuries conveniently converged in one great sweep of visual delight. The primary reason they came together was that the home had a new role to play in society. Samuel Paul wrote, "The home of today has a new function: visual recreation," and whatever served that need might logically be linked together. In accordance with the reigning consumer philosophy of the day, no object, no single set of values, no implied pattern of spatial arrangement could be so incompatible with another as to prevent happy harmony in the family living room. This reorientation in the home was indicative of a more sweeping reformulation of life in the modern age. Raymond McGrath and A. C. Frost, in their 1937 history of glass in architecture, related modern house design to these larger patterns, "At its simplest it may be stated as the shifting of the focus from the fireplace to the window, or rather the change from a local secluded interest to a distributed active interest."[28] And, in fact, with Pearl

GOOD LIVING ROOMS MUST SOLVE SPECIAL PROBLEMS

Nowadays, most living rooms have three views—two of them inside, one of them outdoors:

first, a view of the TV set;   second, a view of the fireplace;   and third, a view of the garden through a glass wall

In a good living room you do not have to move the furniture around (and thus scar the floor and wear out the carpet) every time you want to look at your favorite TV program, or watch the fire, or look out of the window. In a good living room, these three views are all visible within a 90° arc from wherever you sit.

The Terra Linda development in California (W. J. Severin, designer; see also p. 154) is a good example. The principal seating area surveys all three major views: the TV set, the fireplace and the garden. It would be very difficult to furnish this room badly—especially if the model house shows how to get the most out of it by furnishing it right.

Figure 10.8. "Three Views," *House and Home* 6 (September 1954), 138. Photo: Sandy Isenstadt.

Harbor just four years later decisively ending their isolationist streak, Americans may well have taken a broader and more "distributed" interest in the world.

Judging by the discussion in 1954, however, it does not appear to have been an especially active one. Indeed, *House and Home*'s "Three Views" are premised on a sedentary observer. Far from being an anomaly, however, such motionlessness had long been an adjunct to views through glass. In writings on the picturesque, seeing a landscape and moving through it were mutually reinforcing. Richard Payne Knight abjured the sedentary view, noting that "few persons ever look for compositions when within doors." Humphry Repton had distinguished the landscape painter's fixed views from those of the gardener, who must plan for the viewer's movement through the scenes he composes. Views from windows were, like paintings, fixed, and so lacked the variety and surprise that accumulate when walking. Just as land was acquired by commercial activities, views were obtained by physical activity; walking in a landscape rehearsed its initial appropriation, with weariness a somatic register of successful acquisition and the viewpoint confirmation of the social status attained.[29]

With viewing and ownership linked in picturesque theory, it took a long time for the sedentary view to become acceptable. Fifty years after Repton, Henry Winthrop Sargent, one of Downing's admirers and amateur designer of his own estate, was cited in regard to Americans' neglect of outdoor activities in contrast with English traditions. In America, "we have always thought it highly desirable not to tell our whole story from the house. . . . We cannot well imagine anything more dreary than those country-places where there is no motive to go out, because everything is gathered and crowded around the house, and can be seen from the windows." In the 1880s, naturalist John Burroughs thought it was not enough to see nature "from parlor windows and through gilt-edged poems," while architect Charles Hooper reasoned similarly in 1913: "If we get all the effect of the outside from the more or less close confines of the interior, there is less incentive to stir out of doors." Alfred Hopkins likewise recalled that clients lobbied their architects for larger windows, the "better to see something beautiful." But he cautioned that they discouraged mobility: "If there *is* a view, those who wish to see it will enjoy going to see it. . . . Remember that human beings can walk about to see what they wish to see. Their bodies do not remain stationary.

It is only their minds which sometimes indicate this lack of progress." It would be foolish "to reverse the wise and proper course of building, merely to be able to see from within what may be seen better from without."[30]

In fact, the only cases where views through glass were actually recommended were for those who had trouble moving. An 1840 issue of the *American Journal of Insanity*, for instance, recommended extra-large windows for those who had to be restrained, while the Massachusetts State Housing Board wrote a century later that views to the outdoors were best suited for those who were most sedentary, due to age or infirmity. Only for the frail and unstable should "seeing out" substitute for going out. Indeed, some of the best views around were found in picturesque cemeteries, with the inevitable contrast between, on the one hand, mobile life and collective views, and on the other hand, motionless death, serving as an object lesson in the peril of inaction. By the twentieth century, however, the sedentary view was cause for celebration. Homeowners frequently described the uniquely modern pleasure of visual immersion in nature without motion or discomfort. A client of architect John Johanson confirmed the effect: "I have to remind myself to go for walks, as the outside view comes in so much that I don't feel the need to go out to see the countryside," he explained. Glass manufacturers promised windows that would "actually bring your favorite view right in front of your easy chair" and so provide "restful comfort."[31] Visual variety and bodily stasis were routinely aligned in advertisements for a range of products for the home as an emblem of the diminished labor new appliances promised. Nearly always, vision encompassed continual change while comfort was registered as somatic stability. In other words, repose did not just take place *in* a landscape—it was visualized *as* a landscape.

Mobility made a great leap forward with the automobile. Cars consolidated themes that had long been present in landscape design: the abrogation of topographical limits, leisurely movement through a landscape, fascination with changing points of view, and a pleasurable paradox between movement and stasis. From the moment one first sat in the car, the body was still but mobility was maximized to an extent choreographers of landscape strolls could only have dreamed of. Even the unaccustomed speed of the car brought with it rapid juxtapositions, providing the variety and surprise prescribed in the picturesque system of visual values, but now with greater aesthetic emphasis on the speed of visual variation than on the specific merits of any one scene. Moving views were increasingly obtained through glass (figs. 10.9 and 10.10): windshields became commonplace, wipers were invented and then automated, and, in the 1920s, enclosed sedans became prevalent. By the 1920s the vast majority of flat glass in the United States went either to homebuilders or to Detroit. Ford Motors created notable advances in the mechanization of flat glass production, to the benefit of both houses and cars. As car makers learned how to incorporate more glass into their designs, driving became even more an experience of the periphery, which may account for how it came to represent a kind of independence. "See for yourself" was the advertising theme of General Motors' new "panoramic windshield" in the 1950s, praised for making parking easier and driving safer and, not least, for its delivery of views.

The connection between big windows in the home, the car, and visual pleasure in landscape was seen early on. Charles Sumner Greene, who, with his brother Henry Greene, installed some of the largest domestic windows of their time (including a rollup window in the 1911 Cordelia Culbertson house), noted in 1915 that "between the automobile mania and the bungalow bias, there seems to be a psychic affinity. They have developed side by side and they seem to be the expression of the same need and desire, to be free from the commonplace of convention." Even Repton's nineteenth-century observations regarding the tension between a home's orientation on a site and available views were made while he rode in a carriage; he noted that simply by turning away from the "unpleasant glitter" of obscuring raindrops on the windows he could take in the view clearly. More directly, cars opened up vast new tracts of land for small houses to sit on. The drive to move to the suburbs was facilitated by a new ease of access to city peripheries, with macadam roads cheaper to construct than transit lines. And suburban sites were always more promising for landscape: "It is becoming more and more usual, when selecting the site for the new house, to regard picturesque location and favorable natural environment as of great importance. The auto has immeasurably broadened horizons in this respect," wrote Florence Taft Eaton in 1921.[32] Automakers frequently depicted their latest models alongside a modest home and a happy family in a picturesque setting.

THE EFFICIENT LUXURY OF MODERN DINING — In Lincoln, you find the most dramatic fabrics and fittings on wheels — but every detail is magnificently efficient. There is an amazing view — thanks to 3,721 square inches of glass. The down-sweep hood permits a view of the road directly ahead. And beneath it is the new Lincoln overhead valve V-8, premium product of the world's most experienced builders of V-8 engines.

Figure 10.9. "Efficient Luxury of Modern Dining," *House and Garden*, August–September 1952, 9. Photo: Sandy Isenstadt. The view opens onto the new car while ad copy discusses the view from the windshield.

Just as the advent of mechanical systems of comfort altered the architect's consideration of the home's exposure to weather, so did the car change ideas about the site. Landscape writers lamented that homeowners usually overrated their views and made poor siting decisions. They advised therefore a balance between view, which improved with greater elevation, and convenience, which was satisfied by proximity to roads, usually low-lying. Hillside homes in the nineteenth century were, because

SAFETY <u>PLATE</u> GLASS WINDOWS IN YOUR CAR

...*beauty at your side*

Because of the added comfort and enjoyment it brings to motoring, and the touch of distinction it lends to today's smart motor car designs, many manufacturers now completely equip their cars with Safety Glass made of the finest polished PLATE Glass.

This finer glass, which is first carefully ground, then painstakingly polished to a mirror-like brilliance, eliminates the waviness and accompanying distortion characteristic of Safety Glass made of ordinary window glass. Consequently Safety PLATE Glass minimizes eyestrain and fatigue, and makes every window in the car a pleasing

frame for the unfolding panorama of the open country and the swiftly changing scenes of city life. Furthermore, the recognized higher quality of this ground and polished glass gives you the very personal satisfaction of knowing that your car is correct to the last detail.

Since so many manufacturers now install Safety PLATE Glass in their cars at no extra cost, look for the Hallmark of Higher Quality on every window when considering the purchase of a new car.

• • •

PLATE GLASS MANUFACTURERS OF AMERICA, PITTSBURGH, PA.

FOR GREATER MOTORING COMFORT FROM YOUR NEW CAR AND
A MORE LASTING SATISFACTION IN ITS APPEARANCE, LOOK
FOR THIS MARK OF HIGHER QUALITY IN <u>ALL</u> ITS WINDOWS.

Figure 10.10. "Beauty at Your Side," Plate Glass Manufacturers of America. "Advertising Scrapbook," 1937. Physical comfort and visual enjoyment are aligned through the safety plate glass windows of a car. Courtesy: Libbey-Owens-Ford Glass Company Records, MSS-066, Ward Canaday Center for Special Collections, University of Toledo.

of the expense of construction and access, usually reserved for the wealthy. Cars rode over this constraint on viewing; they put hillsides within commuting distance of city centers and cleared slopes for middle class houses. By the 1930s, urban planner Carol Aronovici noted that due to construction innovations and the car, "some of the so-called natural objectionable conditions in land due to slope which make it undesirable for certain uses have been capitalized as assets, particularly in luxury housing." Hillsides, once uneconomic to develop had become quite popular, he noted. "Not only have these lands become useful as residential areas, but in many cities they have attained values undreamed of before." Along with the car, this development was the result of "progress in the design of hillside homes," which included greater sensitivity to view. According to a 1951 article in *Holiday*, modernism had made all the difference: modern houses were of two sorts, one on flat land and easily accessed and the other a remote "mountaintop or hillside house," which involved "the view, and the chance for comparative inaccessibility," a pairing cemented by the car. More often than not, the number one reason for choosing a hillside house was "the view";[33] for getting to a hillside house, the number one means was the car. Automobiles, in short, facilitated the search for view-worthy sites, which to some as-of-yet-uncharted extent helped bring about suburban sprawl. In turn, suburban construction only increased demand for cars, affecting many other aspects of American life. Refrigerators, to take only one example, improved food storage and so made sites remote from city markets more feasible, and were, for a few years in the postwar era, themselves advertised as food landscapes.[34]

Four views—the hearth, the idealized private landscape, the television, and the view from a moving car—have at varying points served as representational icons that have embodied domestic values as much as they have altered spatial relations within homes and between them. Each implies different spatial relations for architecture, for the family, and for larger patterns of settlement. Each connotes a whole range of social relations and may, by finding a resonant formal expression of social values, serve to stabilize those relations or, possibly, open them to new challenges. The absorption of landscape imagery within this sequence of shifting domestic representations and the corresponding effort to build settlements that correspond with that imagery, including its economic valuation and legal protection, reveal that the long diffusion of picturesque ideals that helped determine the form of American suburbs did not just change the look of landscape; it changed how we look at landscape. Whatever the formal innovations of landscape architects, seeing it through glass must also be counted as one of the ways the landscape became modern.

CLEAN AND BRIGHT AND

EVERYONE WHITE

Dianne Harris

Seeing the Postwar Domestic Environment in the United States

VISUAL REPRESENTATIONS OF POSTWAR LANDSCAPES AND INTERIORS HAVE A
surprisingly uniform appearance that typically features pastel colors and favors the
perspective or axonometric view, biomorphic garden forms, and depictions of well-
dressed and neatly coiffed women in high-heeled shoes. It is a graphic style we have
come to readily associate with the 1950s, images that sometimes seem comical now
for their contrivance and naiveté. If modes of depiction stylize and formulate modes
of viewing, then the consistent quality of these images allows us to consider them as
contributions to the formation of a "habit of perception"—a way of seeing the world
that contributes to a mode of cognition—or to what Michael Baxandall called "the
period eye."[1]

Every age has its habits of perception, but in the United States at mid-century, a perceptual habit coalesced that contributed to a consumerist vision intended to appeal to an overwhelmingly white, middle-class majority of new or soon-to-be first-time homeowners. The anthropologist Karen Brodkin has written of the development of a "public iconography of white nuclear family bliss" in this period, and images of the postwar house contributed significantly to this representational system. An essential aspect of these images was their depiction of racial and class distinctions. More than many others in American history, the 1950s were a truly anomalous period of racial and ethnic reassignment and class mobility—a time in which, to use Brodkin's terms, "Jews became white folks" and, as numerous sociologists and economic historians have indicated, vast numbers of Americans joined the middle class, constituting a new middle-majority.[2] The insecurities that resulted from these shifts in ethnic, racial, or class identities could be considerable in a time of mass societal conformity and assimilation. The stakes—and the resultant anxiety—were quite high, as some images from *Ebony* magazine reveal. An image from 1955 for example, showed a "white" family in Florida that suffered a sheriff's racist policies: their children were barred from public school when they were accused of actually being black. Another article in a 1955 issue of *Ebony* illustrated the difficulties mixed-race couples encountered in the housing market.[3] To be identified as white and to be among the middle-majority was to benefit from a range of societal privileges that included access to housing through Federal Housing Administration (FHA) loans. To be identified as nonwhite was to have that access, among many others liberties, denied. Thus the GI Bill, along with FHA and Veterans Administration (VA) mortgages, were essentially a set of racial privileges reserved for whites.[4] In the economy of prestige that emerged in the postwar United States, whites possessed economic and social fluidity that was denied to others. The zealous nature of postwar housing segregation was such that a mere rumor that blacks might move into an area was enough to trigger a riot in a Chicago neighborhood bordering the so-called "black belt" in the late 1940s.[5] Although the U.S. Supreme Court's 1948 decision in *Shelley v. Kramer* rendered restrictive covenants legally unenforceable, little changed in practice for decades to follow.

Surprisingly, this aspect of postwar history has to date received relatively little focused attention from those who study architecture and landscape (though a more extensive bibliography on the topic exists for urban history and geography).[6] Perhaps this is to the credit of those amazingly consistent representations of mid-century spaces. It is, after all, easy to overlook much that they include and easier still not to notice what is missing from them and the anxious times they represent. Conspicuously absent from the drawings are significations and images that represented anything *other* than white, middle, or upper-class environments. All others are excluded—completely erased or controlled through selective omission. Popular representations of the postwar house and garden that appeared in shelter and women's magazines (which are among the essential archives for such a project) contributed to an ideology of architectural exclusion—one that helped consumers see and desire environments designed for the white middle-majority. The magazine images are especially significant because of the wide audience they reached; an estimated 50 million Americans read these magazines each month during the postwar era.[7]

Richard Dyer has noted that representations deeply affect our feelings, thoughts, and cognition of and about that which is represented.[8] In this way, popular representations of houses and gardens confirmed accepted norms associated with racial and class status and provided subtle lessons for new and aspiring first-time homeowners, who may also have been newly identified as "white" or middle class. The drawings provided a kind of promise depicting spaces that, if emulated in built form, could also help to strengthen the identity and status many viewers and homeowners had so recently attained. These popular representations of spaces were a lens through which notions of class and race were established or reaffirmed. Such renderings were not, however, uniformly received. Indeed, there is little evidence concerning the reception of such images. Instead, these drawings facilitated the implementation of a uniform set of practices that created the framework for a mode of viewing among the magazine-reading public, and they likewise reflected and contributed to a set of dominant cultural values.

If critical race theorists and cultural, political, and economic historians have too rarely examined space and the built environment as a critical agent in the formation of their narratives, architectural and landscape historians have too seldom considered race. Especially in studies of domestic environments in the postwar era—a period when racial politics dominated national news—it is hard to imagine leaving racial conflict out of the inquiry, even if it is never actually depicted in any representations of domesticity from the period. However, it is this very absence that is so significant.

Of course, all architectural renderings, whether presented to an individual patron or to a mass audience in a serial publication, are intended to explicate and persuade —as architects are fully aware. The architect produces drawings or models that will most clearly convey his or her ideas, incorporated with the client's needs and desires, and that will persuade the client to proceed with the project. This is nearly always done in the most time- and cost-efficient manner possible, so that embellishments surrounding the project—such as human figures, artifacts of material culture, pets, neighbors, and even plantings—are generally kept to a minimum and carefully selected. Architectural renderings derive their persuasive powers, in part, from their apparently guileless nature and because they appear as though strictly documentary, so that any ideological content remains largely hidden. In this way, they are very like maps and some forms of landscape representation.[9]

Architectural and landscape drawings are a specific form of two-dimensional representation. Unlike an artist's painting or drawing, which may engage the emotions, the viewer of an architectural drawing is meant to imagine the spaces of the rendered home and garden as if she or he were its inhabitant—a mental projection that is seldom dispassionate or disconnected from desire. The drawings require a mental projection on the part of the viewer that is at once spatial and acquisitive. The eyes cannot simply play across the surface of the page (which holds little or no interest), nor does looking at or into the image necessarily reveal an artistic agenda, because artistic goals of self-expression are suppressed in favor of a particularized mode of descriptive mapping. Instead, one enters a cognitive realm that is in equal parts map and dream world. We imagine ourselves, our family members, our neighbors, and a newly acquired and idealized life that is completely dependent upon an image of a space and its surroundings. Inclusion and exclusion of people and things are implicit in the dream as we mentally envision a desired environment. It is nearly impossible to "shop" for house plans without projecting a hoped-for life and lifestyle. As the eye moves over the plan, the imagination conjures and catalogs the space, and desire takes hold (fig. 11.1).

A $25,000 Pace-Setter House

proves that ideas—not dollars—make better living

HOUSE KEEPS WINDS OFF TERRACE

TERRACE GETS EARLY AFTERNOON AND MORNING SUN

Here is the second of this year's 3 Pace-Setter houses.

It shows that, even in the ready-built field,

you can get a lot of good living at moderate cost—

if you know what to look for and won't take less

Figure 11.1. "A Cautious Pace-Setter," *House Beautiful*, September 1950, 95. Photo: ©The Hearst Corporation. All Rights Reserved.

Advertisers might simply call this the development of "eye appeal"—the simple act of determining and implementing those aspects of the built environment that appeal to the consumer's eye. But in the process of crafting eye appeal, postwar architects and architectural draftsmen produced drawings that "crafted white settings," hoping to sell attractive houses to Americans who were eager to gain entrée to the white middle-majority.[10] As historian Annie Coleman's analysis of the visual culture of skiing has shown, house and garden representations "idealized a particular construction of whiteness . . . that [drew] attention to itself and placed people of color on the periphery" through total exclusion.[11] In addition to depicting the form of domestic worlds, the drawings are also images of a white culture that privileged spaciousness, cleanliness, order, leisure, and the fashionable appeal of aesthetic modernity. Not only did the drawings make house and garden attractive—they also subtly persuaded the purchase of a culturally constructed white identity.[12] Images of modern homes were therefore equally about containing and eliminating the signs of ethnic difference and attaining class status. The look is remarkably homogenous: clean, tidy, orderly, shiny, and bright, they broadcasted the symbolism of sameness, safety, and assimilation (fig. 11.2). The descriptions are likewise tremendously consistent. Words like informality, casual lifestyle, leisure, individuality, privacy, and cleanliness, served as code words for an identity that was clearly white, clearly middle class.

The housing advertisements that appeared in shelter and women's magazines of the period never depicted people of color—everything was displayed in the homes of and surrounded by white families. It is probably true that nearly all architectural renderings (then and now) have a "whiteness" to them since they are mostly produced by white male architects for actual or imagined white patrons.[13] But this takes on new poignancy in the postwar period, in which the absence of architectural features in black magazines speaks eloquently of their limited place in the burgeoning housing market. For the entire decade of the 1950s, women's magazines, shelter magazines, and even popular serials like *Life, Look,* and *Popular Mechanics* published regular features on housing developments, house design, do-it-yourself housing, and stock plans that could be purchased from the magazine for as little as five dollars. Indeed, there are few issues in which housing is not featured in some manner. But in *Ebony* magazine during the 1950s, there are very few articles on houses or housing and no housing sections or special features. Between 1954 and 1956, for example, the magazine featured only one house, the elaborate and costly modern residence of a successful black physician—an example that was well outside the reach of the vast majority of its readership.[14] *Ebony*, which began publication in November 1945, was dedicated to promoting a positive image of black lifestyles in America, or as the editors put it, "to mirror the brighter side of Negro life," and included mostly images of blacks

who had accepted white codes of behavior, appearance, and status.[15] In order to focus on black achievements, the housing question would have to be largely ignored. Although African American suburbs and housing tracts developed in specific settings and circumstances, such as those surrounding historically black university campuses, they were nonetheless rare, and obtaining decent housing remained a primary concern for nonwhites in the postwar era.[16]

What then, did draftsmen and architects do to obscure blue-collar or ethnic roots? Using a system of signs or representational techniques to create an atmosphere of desirable domesticity, architectural renderers produced drawings for publication that allowed the American Dream to be captured or encapsulated using a series of simple ideograms and graphic formulas.

Many magazine features on postwar houses included drawings rather than photographs because they could be more selective, and because they frequently depicted unbuilt designs (fig. 11.3). Photography was preferred for displaying built works, particularly high-style or architect-designed houses, but it doesn't lend itself well to the representation of ordinary, small houses and gardens. Whereas the interiors of 1,000-square-foot houses were particularly difficult to portray to advantage through photography, drawings permitted a degree of spatial distortion and a sense of spaciousness in which credibility and fantasy could coexist. Aerial perspectives and axonometric views were ideal. Plans and blueprints are notoriously difficult to read, especially for those not well acquainted with architectural or visual culture.[17] But aerial views portray space with the illusion of dimensionality and are easier to decipher. They provide the supposed realism of a constructed model, yet can be made even more persuasive due to the inherent possibility for manipulation. In addition, aerial views signal privilege and authority, since they provide a commanding view from above.[18] In this case, they provided potential consumers with a visual language of freedom in which the eye is unconstrained by either a single viewpoint or any boundary other than the edge of the page. Moreover, the aerial perspective assumes a universal viewer for whom vision is monolithically and homogenously conceived. No viewer is defined or specified, because the assumed viewer is white and middle class, an assumption of unitary/collective identity that suppresses alternatives (fig. 11.4).

The drawings conveyed the key principles of a design to a mass audience, and modernity was one of the most important aspects of a scheme. Despite the fact that aesthetic preferences among the majority of Americans favored traditional architectural forms and styles, and despite the fact that the FHA made it difficult or impossible to receive home loans for houses that were nontraditional in form and appearance, most of the magazines promoted at least "soft-modern" house styles.[19] The renderings therefore conveyed a sense of the new, the exciting, and the comfortably modern. Yves-Alain Bois has clarified the possible ideologies of axonometry facilitated by the abolition of the fixed viewpoint of perspective renderings. Bois points out that axonometric drawings are useful tools for seeing the modern because there is "no limit or

Figure 11.3. Drawing for three-bedroom, two-bath Greenbriar custom-line home, National Homes Corporation, 1955. Photo: Dianne Harris.

stopping point of space," resulting in a feeling of visual "liberation."[20] The overhead, hovering axonometric or aerial view grants the viewer the perceptual command of space, which implicitly in the drawings, and explicitly in the everyday life of the pre–civil rights era 1950s, was a privilege reserved primarily for whites. Unrestricted movement, whether of the eye or the body, was implicitly linked to whiteness and class identity, so that axonometric representations not only conveyed aesthetic and architectural modernity but also subtly reinforced racial constructs, as did the very aesthetic of modernity with its emphasis on cleanliness, spaciousness, and lack of clutter.

In the renderings, the fence is the property boundary and empty space surrounds the dwelling. Neighbors are rarely depicted, in part because the focus of the rendering is the single-family dwelling, and because too-close neighbors could recall prewar apartment living.[21] In reality, postwar suburban houses were constructed very close together on small lots. But in the 1950s culture of containment, neighbors were to be kept at bay, on the other side of a fence that ensured family privacy and insularity, reinforcing the period cult of nuclear family togetherness and its counterpart, exclusion of outsiders.[22] The house and garden are therefore never depicted as part of a neighborhood or shown in any sort of broader physical context (fig. 11.5). A front view of the house is sometimes included, since that was the view intended for the evaluative gaze of neighbors and passing strangers.

The representations themselves are clean and bright, rendered carefully with ink line drawings or with appealing pastel and color washes. Ironically, if the houses and representations could affirm racial whiteness, the drawings, like the houses themselves, frequently contained great numbers of brightly colored products and surfaces. The whitewall aesthetic of high modernism seldom appeared in ordinary postwar domestic settings, where instead bright colors conveyed attributes such as hygiene, novelty, sophistication, and individual distinction. The parts of the drawings are often clearly displayed and labeled for consumption to avoid confusion: Everything is impeccably neat. Nothing is out of place, as though every house is occupied by an obsessively tidy owner, an attribute made more visible by the careful placement of a single child, playing with a single toy; a parent taking care of the lawn with a single tool; nothing is ever lying about, overgrown, or out of place. The houses and gardens are portrayed as clutter-free environments, when in actuality they were jammed full of new consumer goods, causing storage to become one of the primary design considerations for ordinary small houses from 1945 onward (fig. 11.6). Cluttered and untidy environments signaled lower class and ethnic identity for the occupants and so the reality and the ideal were at odds with each other. As geographer David Sibley has noted, "Exclusionary discourse draws particularly on colour, disease, animals, sexuality, and nature, but they all come back to the idea of dirt as a signifier of imperfection and inferiority, the reference point being the white, often male, physically and mentally able person. . . . In the same system of values, whiteness is a symbol of purity, virtue and goodness and a colour which is easily polluted . . . thus white may be connected with . . . an urge to clean, to expel dirt and resist pollution, whether whiteness is attributed to people or to material objects."[23]

Moreover, as Jenna Weissman Joselit has noted, Jewish social reformers from the first half of the twentieth century attempted to establish "the parameters of domesticity" for new immigrants by concentrating primarily on "issues of personal and environmental cleanliness . . . [and they] focused almost exclusively on the cultural ramifications of dirt. As they understood it, the elimination of dirt was by no means an exclusively physical act but one fraught with profound social and cultural meaning, intrinsic to the process of integration. When seen from this perspective, housekeeping itself was nothing less than civic virtue." The taste-making and housekeeping literature therefore advised Jewish immigrants to "keep decoration to a minimum" and to aim for simplicity in home design and decor. These were reactions against the typical tenement, which was "replete with colored wallpaper, brightly patterned linoleum, and yards of lace and fabric trimmings."[24]

In 1958, a study by University of Chicago sociologist James Davis revealed the pervasive association of dirt and disorder with class and racial identities. Davis asked a sample group of middle-class housewives to examine a set of photographs of four different living rooms. Overwhelmingly, the women identified the photographs of untidy, disheveled and cramped spaces as those belonging to the uneducated, the slovenly, the impoverished, and the nonwhite.[25] In contrast, clutter-free and clean environments were perceived as belonging to middle-class, white occupants (although if the room contained elements of high-style modernism or too many books, it was sometimes identified as belonging to Jewish occupants).

An article from a 1950s *Better Homes and Gardens Gardening Guide* reinforces the point. Essentially a twelve-point lesson in home maintenance, the feature was

Figure 11.6. "A Window Overlooking a Play Area from Kitchen," *Window Planning Principles*, Small Homes Council, University of Illinois, September 1954, 8. Courtesy: The University of Illinois at Urbana-Champaign Archives.

intended to help suburban homeowners keep the proper appearance of cleanliness and order.[26] In an aerial perspective, the illustration shows the kind of chaos and clutter that can result from an ill-kept yard: overgrown shrubs, trash receptacles on display, lawn and garden equipment lying about, lawn chairs tipped over, children's toys distributed randomly over the site, and laundry drying on the line for all to see (fig. 11.7). The article asks its readers, "Does your lot and setting make a nice picture for you?" and urges that a well kept, tidy home reflects the "spirit of wholesome family life and reflects . . . the people in it. Others (that are not well kept) tell us that within and around there is insensitiveness and indifference." Litter and untidiness signaled unwholesome, and therefore lower-class living. Trash and its containers were to be hidden, along with laundry lines and many other signs of everyday, active family life.

Figure 11.7. "Ever Really Look at Your Place?" *Better Homes and Gardens Gardening Guide*, c. 1950s. Courtesy: Doug Baylis Collection [1999–4], Office Records/Clippings, Environmental Design Archives, University of California, Berkeley.

The pervasiveness of this association in the popular literature attests to its significance. An article in *Ebony* from 1956 featured a Gary, Indiana, black developer, who noted that he "envisioned someday building blocks of homes that could not be identified as Negro by the familiar signs of shoddy construction and cramped home-sites."[27] Kevin Fox Gotham's study of race and the development of Kansas City likewise details the terms real estate agents drew on to create a vocabulary of exclusion that was linked to cleanliness and order.[28] So ubiquitously recognized was the iconography of race that even *Ebony*'s writers and readers acknowledged and affirmed it: shoddy or untidy and cramped living spaces were universally recognized as spatial and visual signs of blackness. In another *Ebony* article of 1956 titled "I Live in a Negro Neighborhood," the white author, Leon Paul, assured readers that "Ours is a happy, vibrant neighborhood. Any outsider would be impressed with the neatness of the gardens and the attractive appearance of the houses. Our block looks good because the people who live there are always working in their gardens and on their lawns, improving the look of their houses and driveways and generally keeping their homes in good shape."[29] Mr. Paul clearly understood that these were the visual clues to ethnic or racial identity that resided in the domestic sphere—neatness chief among them—and he wanted to assure his readers that his black neighbors could make their neighborhood appear as clean and bright, and therefore as white, as any other, despite the contrary prevailing stereotypes.

Mary and Russel Wright's *Guide to Easier Living* (first published in 1950) provides an example of the postwar obsession with cleanliness in the domestic sphere and its links to race and class distinction. Books that instruct housewives on etiquette, domestic efficiency, and taste have a deep and significant history, in large part because they were used "to reinforce simultaneously both class and race ideals."[30] Although scholars have examined it primarily as a design handbook, the Wrights' *Guide to Easier Living*, which was widely read and published in multiple editions, equally served to teach first-time homeowners how to live as white, middle-majority members. It carefully instructs housewives on how to clean their houses as white-collar professionals and how to distinguish themselves from their lower-class or ethnic servants. In fact, the book is dedicated to the Wrights' former housekeeper, Dorcas Hollingsworth, and, as the Wrights noted, to "the whole present generation, who will never have a Dorcas Hollingsworth." As a guide intended to help families learn to cope in the postwar world of homeownership without servants, the book contains a chapter on "The Housewife-Engineer," which includes time and motion studies, and appendices and charts on cleaning routines and products, providing lessons on how to appear solidly middle class by keeping the house spotlessly clean. Again, they drew on a range of well-known precedents, but as leading participants in the production of the all-white majority culture that constituted mid-century homeownership, the Wrights responded to the implicit concerns of their audience.

Indeed, the *Guide to Easier Living* focused to a large extent on eliminating household disorder, and the Wrights wrote that bedrooms should be kept functional to avoid the following scene in "the cold light of morning: Bedcovers cascade to the floor, and lamp shades hang askew; the housewife must stumble over assorted shoes, slippers, and oddments of clothing that litter the carpet. Drawers and closets are open-mouthed, mute witness of the frantic hunt just made within their disordered depths. The elegant dressing table lewdly bares its skinny legs, and lint is a dingy film over everything. From coast to coast, in rich homes and poor, the American bedroom at 8:00 AM looks the same . . . like an Okie camp."[31]

The message was clear: if you don't keep an uncluttered house, you look like an "Okie," a Depression-era image most Americans desperately wanted to escape or avoid.[32] Okies were imagined as not quite "white" in the same way that "white trash" is configured as a tainted form of whiteness. The book therefore provided a wealth of diagrams for appropriately designed rooms, closets, and storage spaces.[33]

Their time and motion studies of household efficiency were designed, like the well-known precedents they drew from, to make house and garden work a white-collar endeavor for the generation that had no hired help. Like the trend in postwar kitchen design that dictated inclusion of a kitchen desk so that housewives could comport themselves like white-collar executives or engineers controlling the household, the Wrights advised women to "Sit down to work whenever possible . . . Have chairs or stools of the right height for your various tasks." When scraping and polishing absolutely had to be done, they recommended hiring someone for the job.[34] Likewise, if maids no longer helped inside the house, hired gardeners, also typically nonwhite and from the lower economic classes, were no longer a common part of the outdoor, middle-class suburban scene. Instead, suburban gardeners used new and expensive power tools to provide the required maintenance. As Virginia Scott Jenkins has pointed out, the names of 1950s lawn mowers, such as "Dandy Boy," "Lawn Boy," and "Lazy Boy" appealed to racial stereotypes held by many white Americans, since they may have conjured associations with, for example, a Filipino "house boy" or an African American "yard boy."[35] The "Black Sambo" lawn sprinkler advertised in a 1958 issue of *Popular Mechanics* clarifies the currency enjoyed by such stereotypes in the minds of many middle-class, white Americans during the postwar era. The advertisement for the sprinkler included an illustration in which white homeowners (a father and son) stood watching as a mechanized "black" servant watered the yard. Although the magazine would not provide permission to reproduce the image, the

Figure 11.8. Sambo Lawn Sprinkler, Hillsdale Barn Antiques, Hillsdale, N.Y., 1936. Courtesy: Frank and Rose Marie Francis.

artifact itself appears here in figure 11.8. The "Black Sambo" lawn sprinkler allowed its owners to maintain the notion that black servants toiled happily so that whites could continue a life of leisured privilege. As Maurice Manring has shown in his analysis of Aunt Jemima products, purchase of these artifacts allowed the consumer to appropriate "a life of leisure with racial and sexual harmony, seemingly more free but inherently dependent on a black laborer." With the growing absence of servants in postwar America, the Black Sambo lawn sprinkler "was sold with the promise that the buyer could appropriate the leisure, beauty, and racial and class status of the plantation South."[36]

Keeping dust and dirt from infiltrating the home and maintaining order were also partially about maintaining whiteness. Many nonwhite and lower-economic-class Americans did not have equal access to home and personal sanitation in this period, and the stereotype of the dirty nonwhite was pervasively held.[37] To be white and middle class was to be clean, clean, clean. Even in the garden, the Wrights' primary rule for design or selection of things for the outdoors was "to ask yourself whether you can wash them with a hose." Outdoor floors were to be hard-surfaced and supplied with a drain, wall coverings were to be washable with a garden hose, rubberized "raincoats" placed over furniture, and "whisk brooms tied to the furniture for a quick brush-off."[38] For especially fastidious Americans, a 1953 issue of *Life* magazine recommended the implementation of washable rooms that could be hosed down on cleaning day, thereby minimizing the housewife's labor.[39]

If tidiness was a key sign of middle-class, white identity, the illusion of spaciousness was equally important. Just as cramped and crowded living conditions signaled ethnic origins and reminded Americans of a Depression-era past, so too a cramped and crowded suburban house and garden appeared undesirable. Landscape architects grappled with this problem in a variety of ways. For example, one of the period's most successful landscape architects, Thomas Church, recommended moving plantings to the lot lines, away from the foundation of the house, a design trick that, as he stated, "greatly expands the apparent spaciousness by pulling the eye away from the house to see the distant view."[40] In the drawings, the aerial perspective could be manipulated to great advantage, giving an impression of a large lot instead of the more diminutive reality, whether or not the designer followed a formula like Church's. No matter what their actual dimensions, all the houses and gardens seem ample, stretching out on the page, unconfined by the realities of lot lines or budgets.

Although they may appear somewhat formulaic to us today, architects and draftsmen took care to produce designs that appeared distinctive within the framework of acceptable homogeneity. The drawing and appearance of the garden was especially important as a means for creating distinguished environments in otherwise monotonous suburbs. Readers of magazines such as *Popular Mechanics* and *LIFE* understood that the images portrayed were of houses whose plans could usually be purchased or easily replicated. To have a house that looked exactly like the neighbors' could be comforting for its assurance of belonging, but look-alike houses were also stigmatized, especially by the high-style design critics and magazine editors who associated the "ticky-tacky" houses all in a row (as in the Malvina Reynolds song) with lower-class or ethnic occupants. A telling illustration of this association between house form and racial stereotypes of conformity appears in Elizabeth Mock's 1946 publication, *If You Want to Build a House*. Mock wrote: "the real basis for house planning should be the individual, not the group" and she illustrated her assertion with a cartoon captioned "undifferentiated Indians entering an undifferentiated tepee."[41] For Mock, the tepee was a vernacular and therefore lower form of architecture, one tepee indistinguishable from the next, and thus a perfect illustration of the lower-economic-class housing her readers hoped to avoid by designing or selecting houses and gardens that were inflected with individual character. The renderings of gardens helped to banish subdivision monotony through the depiction of modernistic settings containing families engaged in leisure activities that conveyed a distinguishing identity.

The uniformity of these clean images is most starkly illuminated by an exception: Arne Kartwold's eccentric drawings (fig. 11.9). A Bay Area architect and draftsman who worked in the firm of Wurster, Bernardi and Emmons from 1944 to 1946 and served as illustrator for at least one popular publication on home buying and construction, Kartwold's renderings include vegetation that seems to have been irradiated to grow to enormous and threatening proportions.[42] Homeowners lounge about reading newspapers that they carelessly cast aside and scatter around, their peculiar possessions crowd the space and clamor for attention, and their dog seems constantly to be doing something strange and almost subversive. The owners, oddly enough, are depicted as "hayseeds" who spray each other or the dog with the garden hose and loudly announce their presence. They look like the kind of neighbors who would prompt fence building. Kartwold even depicted rain clouds over some of his otherwise perfect domestic worlds. Little is known so far about Arne Kartwold's career, but these renderings are remarkable for their wonderfully comic departure from drafting conventions. Yet the very deviance of Kartwold's drawings points to the rigidity of architectural drawings generally, and of postwar house depictions specifically. Although these drawings are not outlandishly different, their subtle variations from convention attract our attention because they are so rare.

Despite the eccentricity of Kartwold's garden inhabitants, it is important to note that they doze in the garden rather than work, and play with the garden hose rather than toil in the soil. A class issue emerges here, for if immigrant and blue-collar Americans were in gardens before 1945, they were likely working in them instead of lounging—making productive vegetable gardens of their own, working in Victory gardens, or weeding, hoeing, pruning, fertilizing, mowing, and clipping for someone else. Even those Americans who made productive Victory gardens during the war wanted them gone or hidden once the war was over, since they symbolized an era of scarcity, apartment living, and pre-middle-majority lifestyles.[43] For lower-income blacks and minorities, garden work often recalled unpleasant past associations and was considered something to be left behind as quickly as possible. Therefore, any image that implied physical labor was banished entirely from postwar garden renderings, located

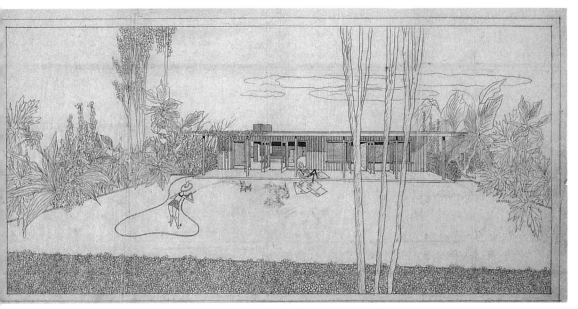

Figure 11.9. Arne Kartwold, "Design for a Suburban House," drawing, c. 1950s. Courtesy: Arne and Lois Kartwold Collection, Environmental Design Archive, Berkeley.

at the periphery of the image, or hidden away in a discreet corner of the designed space.

Postwar gardens, after all, were distinctly *not* about work. One of the distinguishing features of postwar gardens was that they were designed to require as little maintenance as possible so that they could be sites for the so-called "new leisure," and the prescriptive literature of the period uniformly described the means to attain gardens that required little or no labor.[44] The static garden was the ideal: one that was paved, terraced, contained a limited number of plant species that were either evergreen or self-regenerating, a lawn that could be easily mowed with the use of a power mower, and shrubs that could be easily trimmed with power tools. In part, the postwar garden was designed to promote leisure in order to cultivate the individuality prescribed by social critics who feared societal overconformity.[45] Articles in *House Beautiful* provided tips on how to obtain "The Most Beautiful Garden for the Least Work" and encouraged readers to plant slow-growing shrubs and ground covers, garden with gravel, incorporate large areas of paving to avoid maintenance, and design the garden for maintenance with power tools, whose expense and novelty made them status-conferring objects.[46] Any obligatory garden work would be done with expensive power tools, the operator standing upright—never bent over—much as the white, middle-class housewife would perform her labor in the house with the aid of the new electrical appliances, outfitted in a dress, heels, and pearls to indicate her white-collar status.

Because the garden was to be strictly for leisure, and to further obscure associations of labor with garden spaces, many drawings make the garden appear to be an extension of the living room of the house—an additional room, albeit outdoors, for lounging about, reading the paper, or sipping martinis. Terrace paving, therefore, was the equivalent of an outdoor carpet. If women were at work in the home, men were depicted at leisure in the garden. Images of backyard barbecues and of relaxed living predominate in the renderings; people swim, chat, and lounge while wives serve drinks on trays and husbands tend to steaks on the grill. In a *Popular Mechanics* article of 1959, entitled "Unusual and Modern Ideas for Living Outdoors," the author provided ideas for "converting your backyard into an open-air 'room' where you can bask, dine, and spend the summer in true lazy-man style."[47] An illustration for the piece appropriately depicted a barbecue in progress, with a grinning "dad" holding his cooking implement aloft and a scene of active entertainment in the background. The outdoor furniture industry prospered under this conception of the garden, and furniture outdoors—especially the ubiquitously placed chaise lounge—became a potent symbol of a leisured class. To be in a garden designed exclusively for ease and comfort was a white and upper-class concept and image (one with a long history), as was the very idea of outdoor living, which was so persuasively publicized in the postwar era. But this was outdoor living for the backyard only, as far away as possible from the front stoop culture of inner-city ethnic neighborhoods.

Both Stuart Hall and Paul Gilroy have pointed out (separately) that "race is the modality in which class is lived" and "gender is the modality in which race is lived," and we have to consider them as inextricably linked when considering house form.[48] In the postwar era, the house, more than any other possession, stood as an unmistakable cipher in the landscape, signaling membership in the modernized middle-majority. The house and its representations served as the site for struggles with and expressions of class and racial anxiety because in the domestic environment they could be controlled and manipulated, unlike the exterior world, which was otherwise structured by powerful and often oppressive forces. It was through the mechanism of the house that anxious Americans from a range of economic and cultural backgrounds learned "the ways of whiteness" with the help of radio, television, and magazine images.[49]

When they looked in popular magazines shopping for the small houses they might one day afford, postwar Americans saw plans that fulfilled dreams. But as they looked at the housing features with their enticing drawings, they equally looked to the house to confirm identities, images of the self, and perhaps most subtly, racial assignment. The man pausing by his car in one image or working in the garden as a leisure or hobby activity in another, or an efficient and contented mother serving beverages in the garden from a tray, or the family swimming in the backyard pool are all part of this system of representing a classed world. The drawings contained images of whiteness that became enshrined in the magazines in which they appeared, but also enshrined within the actual houses. As such, the drawings were, in Valerie Babb's words, "in actuality part of a multifaceted cultural matrix that was diagramming and urging conformity to a white ideal."[50] The distinctive styling of the houses and gardens joined a constellation of images in mid-century visual culture to become yet another marker of class and racial distinction. By employing an iconography of whiteness, combined with the viewing mechanism of the architectural drawing, popular publications in the 1940s and especially the 1950s attempted to capture the broadest possible consumer audience through the development of "eye appeal" that targeted the middle-majority readership to the exclusion of nonwhite viewers. The drawings therefore do not merely reflect the virtual absence of a black middle class in the mid-century residential world, but also contributed to the construction of that condition through continual reinforcement.

Although historians have focused on architectural modernism's innovations in this period, we have to remember that for all their emphasis on formal and spatial novelty, most modern architects persisted in imagining within the social box—one that implicitly accepted racially restricting covenants and the pre-civil rights era social armature. Given the visual codes described herein and their persistence in popular representations of the home, the taste-making and design literature from the postwar era onward must be viewed in an entirely new light—one that considers race and class as embedded subjects in discourses on the built environment.

Chapter 1: Landscape and Vision

1. W. J. T. Mitchell, "Showing Seeing: A Critique of Visual Culture," *Journal of Visual Culture* 1, no. 2 (2002): 171. Mitchell connects this to what Norman Bryson has called "the Natural Attitude," in which all sight is assumed unmediated by cultural production. See Bryson, *Vision and Painting: The Logic of the Gaze* (New Haven: Yale University Press, 1983), 1–12.

2. Denis Cosgrove, *Social Formation and Symbolic Landscape* (Madison: University of Wisconsin Press, 1998), 1.

3. Frédéric Pousin, "Visuality as Politics: The Example of Urban Landscape," in *Deterritorializations . . . Revisioning Landscape and Politics*, ed. Mark Dorrian and Gillian Rose (London: Black Dog Publishing, 2003), 161. On etymology see Anne van Erp-Houtepen, "The Etymological Origin of the Garden," *Journal of Garden History* 6, no. 3 (1986): 227–31.

4. Jacques Derrida, "Parergon," in *The Truth in Painting*, trans. G. Bennington and I. McLeod (Chicago: University of Chicago Press, 1987), esp. 37–92.

5. Keith Moxey, "Motivating History," *Art Bulletin* 77 (1995): 392–401.

6. See for example: Hal Foster, ed., *Vision and Visuality* (Seattle: Bay Press, 1988); Norman Bryson, *Vision and Painting: The Logic of the Gaze* (New Haven: Yale University Press, 1983); Jonathan Crary, *The Techniques of the Observer: On Vision and Modernity in the Nineteenth Century* (Cambridge, Mass.: MIT Press, 1990); Stephen Melville and Bill Readings, eds., *Vision and Textuality* (Durham: Duke University Press, 1995); Martin Jay, *Downcast Eyes* (Berkeley: University of California Press, 1994); David M. Levin, ed., *Modernity and the Hegemony of Vision* (Berkeley: University of California Press, 1993); Teresa Brennan and Martin Jay, eds. *Vision in Context: Historical and Contemporary Perspectives on Sight* (New York: Routledge,

1996); Michael Ann Holly, *Past Looking: Historical Imagination and the Rhetoric of the Image* (Ithaca: Cornell University Press, 1996); Margaret Miles, *Image as Insight: Visual Understanding in Western Christianity and Secular Culture* (Boston: Beacon Press, 1985); and Nicholas Green and Frank Mort, "Visual Representation and Cultural Politics," *Block* 7 (1982): 59–68.

7. On such connections, see Dell Upton, "Speaking Self and Hearing Race in the Antebellum City," *Landscape Journal* 26, no. 1 (Spring 2007), guest edited by Dianne Harris.

8. The symposium organized by Paul Groth at the University of California, Berkeley, in 1990 entitled "Vision, Culture, and Landscape," and the resulting publication, took cultural landscape studies as the primary focus, but vision served as a secondary theme for about half of the symposium speakers. In particular, see Catherine Howett, "Where the One-Eyed Man is King: The Tyranny of Visual and Formalist Values in Evaluating Landscapes," 85–98; Anthony D. King, "The Politics of Vision," 134–44; Dell Upton, "Seen, Unseen, and Scene," 174–79; and Robert Riley, "The Visible, the Visual, and the Vicarious: Questions About Vision, Landscape, and Experience," 200–210 in *Understanding Ordinary Landscapes*, ed. Paul Groth and Todd W. Bressi (New Haven: Yale University Press, 1997). See also Elizabeth Kryder-Reid, "The Archaeology of Vision in Eighteenth-Century Chesapeake Gardens," *Journal of Garden History* 14 (1994): 42–54 (and the entire special issue, guest edited by D. Fairchild Ruggles and Elizabeth Kryder-Reid); D. Fairchild Ruggles, *Gardens, Landscape and Vision in the Palaces of Islamic Spain* (University Park: The Pennsylvania State University Press, 2000); Mark P. Leone, "Rule by Ostentation: The Relationship Between Space and Sight in Eighteenth-Century Landscape Architecture in the Chesapeake Region of Maryland," in *Method and Theory for Activity Area Research*, ed. Susan Kent (New York: Columbia University Press, 1987), 604–63.

9. On the Claude Glass and mirror, see Deborah Jean Warner, "The Landscape Mirror and Glass," *Antiques* 105 (1974): 158–59. See also John Dixon Hunt, *Gardens and the Picturesque: Studies in the History of Landscape Architecture* (Cambridge, Mass.: MIT Press, 1992), 174–75. On the stereoscope, see Crary, *Techniques of the Observer*, 116–36.

10. Ann Reynolds, "Enantiomorphic Models," in *Robert Smithson*, ed. Eugene Tsai with Cornelia Butler (Berkeley: University of California Press, 2004), 139. Indeed, Smithson's career was marked by an ongoing concern for vision and modes of visuality, as with his "Eliminator" project that aimed to make the viewer "see sight" by creating a state of temporary blindness. As Thomas Crow has recently noted, Smithson's Nonsites can also be read as "Nonsights," that evoke the notion that there is nothing to see. Crow situates this as a parody of the Modernist obsession with looking. On the "Eliminator" project, see Eugenie Tsai, "Robert Smithson: Plotting a Line from Passaic, New Jersey to Amarillo, Texas," in *Robert Smithson*, 19. For Crow's contribution, see "Cosmic Exile: Prophetic Turns in the Life and Art of Robert Smithson," *Robert Smithson*, 53.

11. Mitchell, "Showing Seeing," 166.

12. J. B. Jackson published many essays and books, but two classics that make the point are *Discovering the Vernacular Landscape* (New Haven: Yale University Press, 1984) and *The Necessity for Ruins and Other Topics* (Amherst: University of Massachusetts Press, 1980). But

see also Kathryn Gleason and D. Fairchild Ruggles, "Revisiting the Gardens of Rome and the Alhambra: New Research on Perception and Experience," in *1999 ASLA Annual Meeting Proceedings* (Washington, D.C.: American Society of Landscape Architects, 1999), 241–43, where the authors remark that what we see today at historic sites is not necessarily historically accurate, an important concept that can be difficult for designers to grasp when they look at landscapes. See also James Borchert, "Visual Landscapes of a Streetcar Suburb," in Groth and Bressi, *Understanding Ordinary Landscapes*, 25–43.

13. Jay Appleton, *The Experience of Landscape* (London: John Wiley and Son, 1986), chaps. 1–4.

14. These ideas owe a considerable debt to a paper delivered by Dell Upton at the University of Illinois, Urbana-Champaign, March 2004; see his "Speaking Self."

15. See Michel Conan, ed., *Landscape Design and the Experience of Motion*, Dumbarton Oaks Colloquium on the History of Landscape Architecture 24 (Washington, D.C.: Dumbarton Oaks Research Library and Collection, 2003), excerpt available online at http://www.doaks.org/Motion/11Motion.pdf. Kate Soper asserts that despite the persuasive arguments for landscape studies that examine a range of sensorial experiences, multi-perceptual studies must still address the central question of landscape as aesthetic experience, in "Privileged Gazes and Ordinary Affections: Reflections on the Politics of Landscape and the Scope of the Nature Aesthetic," in Dorrian and Rose, *Deterritorializations*, 340.

16. Upton, "Seen, Unseen, and Scene," 239n1. Upton is currently developing an urban history that explores not only sight but the full sensory spectrum as a means for understanding the disposition and use of antebellum urban spaces. See *Another City: American Urban Life and Urban Spaces, 1790–1850* (New Haven: Yale University Press, 2008).

17. Kate Soper, "Privileged Gazes," 345–46. In this same vein, W. J. T. Mitchell has written that "Vision has played the role of the sovereign sense since God looked at his own creation and saw that it was good. . . . The notion of vision as hegemonic or non-hegemonic is simply too blunt an instrument to produce much in the way of historical or critical differentiation." See Mitchell, "Showing Seeing," 174.

18. On the multisource approach, see Tom Williamson, "Garden History and Systematic Survey," in *Garden History: Issues, Approaches, Methods*, ed. John Dixon Hunt (Washington, D.C.: Dumbarton Oaks Research Library and Collection, 1992), 59–78; also Dianne Harris, *The Nature of Authority: Villa Culture, Landscape, and Representation in Eighteenth-Century Lombardy* (University Park: Pennsylvania State University Press, 2003).

19. Marshall Hodgson, "In the Center of the Map," in *Rethinking World History*, ed. Edmund Burke III (Cambridge: Cambridge University Press, 1993), 29–34; J. B. Harley, "Silences and Secrecy: The Hidden Agenda of Cartography in Early Modern Europe," *Imago Mundi* 40 (1988): 57–76; J. B. Harley, "Deconstructing the Map," *Cartographica* 26, no. 2 (1989): 1–19.

20. Michel Foucault, "Space, Knowledge, Power" (interview by Paul Rabinow), in *The Foucault Reader* (New York: Pantheon, 1984); Michel de Certeau, *The Practice of Everyday Life*, trans. S. F. Rendall (Berkeley: University of California Press, c. 1984).

21. Laura Mulvey, "Visual Pleasure and Narrative Cinema," in *Visual and Other Pleasures* (Bloomington: Indiana University Press, 1989), 14–26; Griselda Pollock, "Beholding Art History: Vision, Place, and Power," in Melville and Readings, *Vision and Textuality*, 38–66; Rosalyn Deutsche, *Evictions: Art and Spatial Politics* (Chicago: Graham Foundation for Advanced Studies in the Fine Arts; Cambridge, Mass.: MIT Press, 1996) esp. "Boystown," 203–44.

22. Edward Soja, *Thirdspace: Journeys to Los Angeles and Other Real-and-Imagined Places* (Cambridge, Mass.: Blackwell, 1996). In contrast, John Tagg insists on the spatial situatedness of cultural politics, emphasizing the importance of the "where" and "when" of social practices, all the while acknowledging that that very space is a contested area of displacement and difference. John Tagg, "Introduction/Opening," in *Grounds of Dispute* (Minneapolis: University of Minnesota Press, 1992), 1–39.

23. As Raymond Williams pointed out, definitions of nature are among the most complex in the English language. See Williams, *Keywords* (New York: Oxford University Press, 1976; repr., 1983), 219–24. Citations are to the 1983 edition. We confine our analysis to "landscape" alone and therefore refer the reader to the extensive literature dealing with the history of ideas about nature.

24. Many scholars have grappled with the concept of desire in the visual realm. Freud and Lacan are well summarized in Kaja Silverman, *The Subject of Semiotics* (New York: Oxford University Press, 1983). See also Jacques Derrida, "The Double Session," in *Dissemination*, trans. Barbara Johnson (Chicago: University of Chicago Press, 1981), 175–286; Peter Brunette and David Wills, "An Interview with Jacques Derrida," in *Deconstruction and the Visual Arts* (Cambridge: Cambridge University Press, 1994), 15–18; and Jean Baudrillard, "The Precession of Simulacra," in *Simulations*, trans. P. Foss, P. Patton, and P. Beitchman (New York: Semiotext(e), 1983), 3–47. Norman Bryson explains "the Real" in semiotic terms as the difference between connotative and denotative levels of the sign. *Vision and Painting*, 56–65.

25. John Tagg, personal communication with authors, August 25, 2005, quoted with permission.

26. Tagg, "Introduction/Opening," 1–39; Jacques Derrida, "Parergon," in *Truth in Painting*, 15–147; in a landscape context, see D. Fairchild Ruggles, "The Eye of Sovereignty: Poetry and Vision in the Alhambra's Lindaraja Mirador," *Gesta* 36 (1997): 182–91.

27. Derrida, *Truth in Painting*, 64.

28. Michel Foucault, "What is an Author?" in *The Foucault Reader*, 101–20; Roland Barthes, "The Death of the Author," in *Image, Music, Text*, trans. S. Heath (New York: Hill and Wang, 1977), 142–48; Jacques Derrida, "Signature Event Context," in *Margins of Philosophy*, trans. Alan Bass (Chicago: University of Chicago Press, 1982), 309–30; Derrida, "Double Session," in *Dissemination*, 175–286.

29. Derrida, "Signature Event Context," 309–30.

30. Upton, "Seen, Unseen, and Scene," 176. On the question of meaning, see also Marc Treib, "Must Landscapes Mean? Approaches to Significance in Recent Landscape Architecture," *Landscape Journal* 14, no. 1 (1995): 47–62.

31. Upton, "Seen, Unseen, and Scene," 176.

32. A notable exception is Marvin Trachtenberg, *Dominion of the Eye: Urbanism, Art, and Power in Early Modern Florence* (Cambridge: Cambridge University Press, 1997).

33. Michael Baxandall, *Painting and Experience in Fifteenth-Century Italy* (Oxford: Oxford University Press, 1972; repr., 1988).

34. On reception theory see Robert Holub, *Reception Theory: A Critical Introduction* (New York: Methuen, 1984); and Elizabeth Freund, *The Return of the Reader: Reader, Reception, Criticism* (New York: Methuen, 1987).

35. Baxandall, *Painting and Experience*, chap. 2. Nicholas Green likewise postulated the similar notion of a "structure of spectatorship" in "Looking at the Landscape: Class Formation and the Visual," in *The Anthropology of Landscape: Perspectives on Place and Space*, ed. Eric Hirsch and Michael O'Hanlon (New York: Oxford University Press, 1997), 31–42. A recent addition to this line of inquiry includes Renzo Dubbini, *Geography of the Gaze: Urban and Rural Vision in Early Modern Europe*, trans. Lydia G. Cochrane (Chicago: University of Chicago Press, 2002).

36. Trachtenberg, *Dominion of the Eye*.

37. Denis Cosgrove, "Prospect, Perspective and the Evolution of the Landscape Idea," *Transactions of the Institute of British Geographers* 10 (1985): 47, cited in Gillian Rose, "Geography as a Science of Observation," in *Human Geography: An Essential Anthology*, ed. John Agnew, David Livingstone, and Alisdair Rogers (Cambridge: Blackwell, 1996), 344.

38. Indra Kagis McEwen, "Housing Frame: In the Tuscan Villa of Pliny the Younger," *Res* 27 (Spring 1995): 11–24.

39. David Freedberg, *The Eye of the Lynx: Galileo, His Friends, and the Beginnings of Modern Natural History* (Chicago: University of Chicago Press, 2002). It should be noted that Mirka Beneš presented an excellent paper, entitled "In the Eye of the Beholder: Perception and Reception of Villas and Landscapes in Galileo Galilei's Rome," on the Lincaen Academy and the seventeenth-century Roman landscape at the Landscape and Vision symposium, University of Illinois, Urbana-Champaign, fall 2002.

40. Smithson's mirror projects, as previously noted, are the best example of this. Turrell's famed Roden Crater in the Arizona desert is intended as a massive and precisely formulated device for viewing the sky; Irwin's "Two Running Violet V Forms" on the University of California, San Diego, campus, is a good example of his engagement with landscape art and vision. On Turrell, see Robert Knight and Debra Hopkins, eds. *James Turrell, Infinite Light* (Scottsdale: Scottsdale Museum of Contemporary Art, 2001). On Irwin, see Robert Irwin, *Being and Circumstance: Notes Toward a Conditional Art* (Larkspur, CA: The Lapis Press, 1985); and Lawrence Weschler, *Seeing is Forgetting the Name of the Thing One Sees* (Berkeley: University of California Press, 1982).

41. John Rachjman, "Foucault's Art of Seeing," *October* 14 (1988): 103.

42. Terrence Epperson, "Panoptic Plantations: The Garden Sights of Thomas Jefferson and George Mason," in *Lines that Divide: Historical Archaeologies of Race, Class, and Gender*,

ed. James A. Delle, S. A. Mrozowski, and R. Paynter (Knoxville: University of Tennessee Press, 2000), 58–77.

43. This corpus of literature is becoming extensive, but as a starting point, see Raymond Williams, *The Country and the City* (New York: Oxford University Press, 1973); Steven Daniels, *Fields of Vision: Landscape Imagery and National Identity in England and the United States* (Princeton: Princeton University Press, 1993); Anne Bermingham, *Landscape and Ideology: The English Rustic Tradition, 1740–1860* (Berkeley: University of California Press, 1986); John Barrell, *The Dark Side of the Landscape: The Rural Poor in English Painting, 1730–1840* (New York: Cambridge University Press, 1989).

44. Owen J. Dwyer and John Paul Jones III, "White Socio-spatial Epistemology," in *Social and Cultural Geography* 1, no. 2 (2000): 209–22.

45. Hubert Damisch, *The Origin of Perspective*, trans. John Goodman (Cambridge, Mass.: MIT Press, 2000), xvii–xviii.

46. Dwyer and Jones, "White Socio-spatial Epistemology," 212.

47. See George P. Rawick, *From Sundown to Sunup* (Westport, Conn.: Greenwood, 1972), 110; Dell Upton, "White and Black Landscapes in Eighteenth-century Virginia," in *Material Life in America, 1600–1860*, ed. Robert Blair St. George (Boston: Northeastern University Press, 1988), 357–69; Terrence Epperson, "Race and Disciplines of the Plantation," *Historical Archaeology* 24 (1990): 29–36.

48. Deutsche, *Evictions*, 208–9.

49. Valerie Babb, *Whiteness Visible: The Meaning of Whiteness in American Literature and Culture* (New York: New York University Press, 1998), 8.

50. John Passmore, *Man's Responsibility for Nature*, 2nd ed. (London: Duckworth, 1980), 28–32.

51. S. Kaplan and R. Kaplan, *The Experience of Nature* (Cambridge: Cambridge University Press, 1989); William C. Sullivan, "The Savanna and the City: Nature at Home," in *Urban Place: Reconnections with the Natural World*, ed. P. Barlett (Atlanta: Academic Exchange, 2003), 55–63; Frances Kuo, M. Bacaicoa, and W. C. Sullivan, "Transforming Inner-city Landscapes: Trees, Sense of Safety, and Preference," *Environment and Behavior* 30, no. 1 (1998): 28–59; and Clare Cooper Marcus and M. Barnes, *Healing Gardens: Therapeutic Benefits and Design Recommendations* (John Wiley and Sons, 1999).

52. Gillian Rose, "Geography as a Science of Observation: The Landscape, the Gaze and Masculinity," in *Nature and Science: Essays in the History of Geographical Knowledge*, History of Geography Research Series 28 (Lancaster, UK: Historical Geography Research Group of the Institute of British Geographers, 1992), 8–18; reprinted in J. Agnew, D. Livingstone, and A. Rogers, eds., *Human Geography: An Essential Anthology* (Cambridge, Mass.: Blackwell, 1996), 341–50. See also Mulvey, "Visual Pleasure."

53. On the analytical premises of art history, see Georges Didi-Huberman, *Confronting Images: Questioning the Ends of a Certain History of Art*, trans. John Goodman (University Park: Pennsylvania State University Press, c. 2005), especially chaps. 2 and 3.

54. Stephen Daniels and Denis Cosgrove, "Introduction: Iconography and Landscape," in *The Iconography of Landscape* (Cambridge: Cambridge University Press, 1988), 1–10.

55. De Certeau, "Walking in the City," in *Practice of Everyday Life*, 91–110.

56. F. Hamilton Hazlehurst, *Gardens of Illusion: The Genius of André Le Nôtre* (Nashville: Vanderbilt University Press, 1980).

57. The theatricality of gardens was explicit, for many of the early French formal gardens served as settings for theatrical entertainments such as the water spectacles staged at Fontainebleau, while later gardens such as André Le Nôtre's plan for the Tuileries were designed expressly as outdoor theaters. Seventeenth-century viewers were fascinated by illusions, both optical and scenic, and it is no coincidence that as garden designers were experimenting with trompe l'oeil effects in the gardens at Versailles and Vaux-le-Vicomte, architects were also perfecting the perspectival organization of the baroque stage.

58. Lucia Nuti, "The Perspective Plan in the Sixteenth Century: The Invention of a Representational Language," *Art Bulletin* 76 (1994): 105–28; Denis Cosgrove, *Apollo's Eye: A Cartographic Genealogy of the Earth in the Western Imagination* (Baltimore: Johns Hopkins University Press, 2001).

59. Williams, *Country and the City*, 32, 46, 125, 179.

60. Michel Foucault, *Discipline and Punish: The Birth of the Prison*, trans. Alan Sheridan (New York: Pantheon Books, 1977).

61. Foucault, *Discipline and Punish*, 221–23.

62. John Tagg, "A Means of Surveillance," in *The Burden of Representation* (Minneapolis: University of Minnesota Press, 1993), 66–102.

63. Web sites on the Surveillance Camera Players and their works include: http://www.notbored.org/the-scp.html and http://www.joannaelizabeth.com/Amnesia.html. We are grateful to Nicholas Brown for introducing us to this work.

64. Ruggles, *Gardens, Landscape, and Vision*.

65. James L. Wescoat Jr., "Water in Landscape Heritage Conservation & Design: Lessons from the Taj Mahal," (paper presented at the California Water Colloquium, University of California at Berkeley, March 11, 2003).

66. Dell Upton, *Architecture in the United States* (Oxford: Oxford University Press, 1998), 20–39.

Chapter 2: Landscape and Invisibility

This material appeared in an expanded and revised version as "Christo's Gates and Gilo's Wall" in *Critical Inquiry* 32, no. 4 (Summer 2006): 587–601.

1. George Berkeley, *An Essay towards a New Theory of Vision* (1709) in *Berkeley's Philosophical Writings*, ed. David Armstrong (New York: Macmillan, 1965), 344–45.

2. Ernst Gombrich, *Art and Illusion: A Study in the Psychology of Pictorial Representation* (Princeton: Princeton University Press, 1961), 7.

3. José Saramago, *Blindness* (New York: Harvest Books, 1999).

4. Jean-Paul Sartre, "The Look," in *Being and Nothingness* (New York: Philosophical Library, 1956; repr. 1999), 252–302.

5. Jacques Lacan, "The Split Between the Eye and the Gaze," in *The Four Fundamental Concepts of Psychoanalysis* (New York: Norton, 1978), chap. 6.

6. Ibid., 116.

7. Jay Appleton, *The Experience of Landscape*, rev. ed. (London: John Wiley and Sons, 1996).

8. I am grateful to Israeli artist Larry Abramson for introducing me to this remarkable piece of landscape art.

9. I regard the Warsaw Ghetto wall as more sinister than the Berlin Wall because the latter was "merely political." The walls currently being erected in Israel are racial, a symptom of ethnic cleansing in the landscape.

10. United Nations Office for the Coordination of Humanitarian Affairs (OCHA), OCHA Weekly Briefing Notes Update for oPt (28 January–10 February 2004), http://www.humanitarianinfo.org/opt/docs/UN/OCHA/WBN39.pdf.

11. Alexander Pope, "Windsor Forest" (1713), lines 11–14, in *Selected Poems of Alexander Pope*, ed. William K. Wimsatt Jr. (New York: Holt, Rinehart, and Winston, 1964), 42. See "Frederick Law Olmsted and the Dialectical Landscape," in *Robert Smithson: The Collected Writings*, ed. Jack Flam (Berkeley: University of California Press, 1996).

12. In fact the rooftop of the Metropolitan Museum was wrapped in orange construction sheets during the Christo installation, and thus seemed to become an unintended extension of the work.

Chapter 3: No State of Grace

1. It should be noted that the shift is not universal. Take, for example, the contrasting discussions of oxalis in two different gardening manuals (written for gardens in markedly different climates) in my library.

> You have real trouble if this weed is in your lawn. It resists 2,4-D (although repeated applications may get it). It seems to have roots all along its stems, so that pulling is next to impossible. It has been discouraged by heavy applications of ammonious sulfate, removing source of shade that it needs to survive, and by digging plants out early and burning them. Force lawn grasses to smother it. (*Sunset Western Gardening Book* [Menlo Park, Ca., 1957], 113).

> These are among the best of the indoor bulb plants. Not only are they easy to find and easy to grow, they have a long bloom period and come in a variety of colors. . . . The bulbs will have produced a pot full of small bulblets, and even the tiniest of them—no larger than the head of a corsage pin—will produce a small plant and some flowers. Eventually all

the little bulbs will grow to full size. So sift through the soil carefully, plant up all the bulbs, and you'll never have to buy another oxalis bulb." (James Underwood Crockett, *Crockett's Indoor Garden* [Boston: Little, Brown, 1978], 224–25).

Context is all.

2. W. J. T. Mitchell, "Imperial Landscape," in *Landscape and Power*, 2nd ed., ed. W. J. T. Mitchell (Chicago: University of Chicago Press, 2002), 29–30.

3. John Barrell, *The Dark Side of the Landscape: The Rural Poor in English Painting, 1730–1840* (Cambridge: Cambridge University Press, 1980).

4. For a general assessment of his work, see Peter Beilharz, ed., *Zygmunt Bauman: Dialectic of Modernity* (London: Sage, 2002).

5. Ernest Gellner, *Nations and Nationalism* (Ithaca: Cornell University Press, 1983), 50–52.

6. Zygmunt Bauman, *Legislators and Interpreters: On Modernity, Post-modernity and Intellectuals* (Oxford: Polity Press, in association with B. Blackwell, 1987), 52.

7. Zygmunt Bauman, *Modernity and the Holocaust* (Ithaca: Cornell University Press, 1989), 70.

8. Bauman, *Legislators and Interpreters*, 51.

9. R. W. Darré, "Marriage Laws and the Principles of Breeding," in *Nazi Ideology before 1933: A Documentation*, ed. and trans., Barbara Miller Lane and Leila J. Rupp (Austin: University of Texas Press, 1978), cited in Zygmunt Bauman, *Modernity and Ambivalence* (Ithaca: Cornell University Press, 1991), 27.

10. Bauman, *Modernity and Ambivalence*, 29.

11. See, for example, Amir Weiner, "Nature, Nurture, and Memory in a Socialist Utopia: Delineating the Soviet Socio-Ethnic Body in the Age of Socialism," *American Historical Review* 104, no. 4 (October 1999): 1116; Peter Holquist, "'Information is the Alpha and Omega of Our Work': Bolshevik Surveillance in its Pan-European Context," *Journal of Modern History* 69, no. 3 (September 1997): 417.

12. See, for example, Yehuda Bauer, *Rethinking the Holocaust* (New Haven: Yale University Press, 2001), chap. 4.

13. Michael Crozier, "*Inter putatorem et vastitatem*: The Ambivalence of the Garden Metaphor in Modernity," in *The Left in Search of a Center*, ed., Michael Crozier and Peter Murphy (Urbana: University of Illinois Press, 1996), 72.

14. Henri de Saint-Simon, cited in D. G. Charlton, *New Images of the Natural in France: A Study in European Cultural History, 1750–1800* (Cambridge: Cambridge University Press, 1984), 31. For a more extensive critique, see Chandra Mukerji, "Reading and Writing with Nature: Social Claims and the French Formal Garden," *Theory and Society* 19, no. 6 (December 1990). For a discussion of Cartesian perspectivalism, see Martin Jay, "Scopic Regimes of Modernity," in *Force Fields: Between Intellectual History and Cultural Critique* (New York: Routledge, 1993), 114–33.

15. J. Mordaunt Crook, "Between Art and Nature: Landscape as a Metaphor of Mind," review of *The History of Garden Design*, by Monique Mosser and Georges Teyssot, eds., *Times Literary Supplement*, July 5, 1991, 15.

16. Yi-Fu Tuan, *Dominance and Affection: The Making of Pets* (New Haven: Yale University Press 1984), 19–21.

17. Robert B. Riley, "Flowers, Power and Sex," in *The Meaning of Gardens: Idea, Place and Action*, ed. Mark Francis and Randolph T. Hester Jr. (Cambridge, Mass.: MIT Press, 1990), 62.

18. See John Dixon Hunt and Peter Willis, eds., *The Genius of the Place: The English Landscape Garden, 1620–1820* (Cambridge, Mass.: MIT Press, 1988). The French were later to pick up the trend, but it can be discerned in the last third of the eighteenth century there too. See Charlton, *New Images of the Natural in France*, chap. 2.

19. For a discussion of the interplay between landscape design and pictorial representations of gardens, see Roy Strong, *The Artist and the Garden* (New Haven: Published for the Paul Mellon Centre for Studies in British Art by Yale University Press, 2000).

20. Raymond Williams, *The Country and the City* (London: Chatto and Windus, 1973).

21. Arthur O. Lovejoy, "The Chinese Origin of a Romanticism," in *Essays in the History of Ideas* (Baltimore: The Johns Hopkins University Press, 1948; New York: Capricorn Books, 1960), chap. 7. He argues that the Chinese style of natural gardening was championed as early as the 1680s and in the writings of Sir William Temple, but that it only came into its own in the late eighteenth century. Ironically, its popularity was undermined by the excessive enthusiasm of Sir William Chambers, who claimed it went beyond imitating nature in its wild and imaginative irregularities. The later history of the Western interpretation of the Chinese garden is traced by Craig Clunas in "Nature and Ideology in Western Descriptions of the Chinese Garden," *Nature and Ideology: Natural Garden Design in the Twentieth Century*, ed. Joachim Wolschke-Bulmahn (Washington, D.C.: Dumbarton Oaks Research Library and Collection, 1997), 21–33. He shows that by the 1820s, Chinese gardens came to be attacked as the essence of artificiality, but then a century later, they were once again regarded as close to nature!

22. John Constable, *John Constable's Correspondence*, ed. R. B. Beckett, vol. VI (Suffolk Records Society 1962–68), 98. Cited in Keith Thomas, *Man and the Natural World: A History of the Modern Sensibility* (New York: Pantheon Books, 1983), 266.

23. Simon Schama, *Landscape and Memory* (New York: Knopf, 1995), 521; see Thomas, *Man and the Natural World*, 254–69.

24. Ann Bermingham, "System, Order and Abstraction: The Politics of English Landscape Drawing around 1795," in Mitchell, *Landscape and Power*, 77–101.

25. Edmund Burke, *Reflections on the Revolution in France*, ed. J. G. A. Pocock (Indianapolis: Hackett Publishing Co., 1987), 152.

26. Schama, *Landscape and Memory*, chap. 3.

27. The gamekeeper model contrasted by Bauman with modernist gardening was, of course, itself open to precisely this charge, as it involved a crucial distinction between those who were given the right to hunt and those prohibited from poaching.

28. Terry Eagleton, *The Ideology of the Aesthetic* (Oxford: Blackwell, 1990).

29. Mitchell, "Imperial Landscape," 9.

30. Willy Lange, *Gartengestaltung der Neuzeit* (Leipzig: J. J. Weber, 1907). His first essays appeared in 1900 and 1901 in the journal *Gartenwelt*.

31. Joachim Wolschke-Bulmahn and Gert Groening, "The Ideology of the Nature Garden. Nationalistic Trends in Garden Design in Germany during the Early Twentieth Century," *Journal of Garden History* 12, no. 1 (1992), 73–80; Joachim Wolschke-Bulmahn, "The 'Wild Garden' and the 'Nature Garden'—Aspects of the Garden Ideology of William Robinson and Willy Lange," *Journal of Garden History* 12, no. 3 (1992), 183–206; Gert Groening and Joachim Wolschke-Bulmahn, "Some Notes on the Mania for Native Plants in Germany," *Landscape Journal* 11, no. 2 (Fall 1992): 116–26; Gert Groening, "The Idea of Land Embellishment," *Journal of Garden History* 12, no. 3 (1992): 164–82; Joachim Wolschke-Bulmahn, "The Nationalization of Nature and the Naturalization of the German Nation: 'Teutonic' Trends in Early Twentieth-Century Landscape Design," in Wolschke-Bulmahn, *Nature and Ideology*, 187–219; Gert Groening, "Ideological Aspects of Nature Garden Concepts in Late Twentieth-Century Germany," in Wolschke-Bulmahn, *Nature and Ideology*, 221–48; and Joachim Wolschke-Bulmahn and Gert Groening, "The National Socialist Garden and Landscaping Ideal: *Bodenständigkeit* (Rootedness in the Soil)," in *Art, Culture and Media under the Third Reich*, ed. Richard A. Etlin (Chicago, University of Chicago Press, 2002), 73–97.

32. See, for example, Hans-Günter Zmarzlik, "Social Darwinism in Germany, Seen as a Historical Problem," in *Republic to Reich: The Making of the Nazi Revolution*, ed. Hajo Holborn (New York: Pantheon Books, 1972).

33. For a lucid and sympathetic discussion of the role of *Lichtung* in Heidegger, see Hubert L. Dreyfus, *Being-in-the-World: A Commentary on Heidegger's Being and Time, Division I* (Cambridge, Mass.: MIT Press, 1991), chap. 9.

34. Heinrich Friedrich Wiepking-Jürgensmann, cited in Wolschke-Bulmahn and Groening, "The National Socialist Garden and Landscaping Ideal," 82.

35. Siegfried Kracauer, *From Caligari to Hitler: A Psychological History of the German Film* (Princeton: Princeton University Press, 1947), 257–63.

36. Robert N. Proctor, *The Nazi War on Cancer* (Princeton: Princeton University Press, 1999).

37. Jim Robbins, "Native Grounds," *New York Times Magazine*, May 16, 2004, 68.

38. Kim Sorvig, "Natives and Nazis: An Imaginary Conspiracy in Ecological Design: Commentary on G. Groening and J. Wolschke-Bulmahn's 'Some Notes on the Mania for Native Plants in Germany,'" *Landscape Journal* 13, no. 1 (Spring 1994): 58–61. Groening and Wolschke-Bulmahn's unrepentant response is in the same issue: "If the Shoe Fits, Wear It," 62–63.

39. Sorvig, "Natives and Nazis," 59.

40. Mitchell, "Imperial Landscape," 10.

41. Jeffrey Herf, *Reactionary Modernism: Technology, Culture, and Politics in Weimar and the Third Reich* (Cambridge: Cambridge University Press, 1984).

42. Michel Foucault, "Of Other Spaces," *Diacritics* 16 (Spring 1986): 22–27.

43. Yi-Fu Tuan repeats the familiar association of landscaping and visuality when he claims that landscape painting and gardening were "forms of art that emphasized sight over the other senses. Sight commanded space—panoramic views and regions. One could envisage a potentate, most likely male, standing on a hill and casting his proprietary gaze over a large and handsomely landscaped domain." Yi-Fu Tuan, "Introduction: Cosmos Versus Hearth," in *Textures of Place: Exploring Humanist Geographies*, ed. Paul C. Adams, Steven Hoelscher, and Karen E. Till (Minneapolis: University of Minnesota Press, 2001), 321.

44. Martin Heidegger, "The Age of the World Picture," in *The Question Concerning Technology and Other Essays*, trans. William Lovitt (New York: Harper and Row, 1977), 115–54.

45. The complicated and multifaceted battle between "place" and "space" is vividly brought out in Edward S. Casey's learned and subtle history of *The Fate of Place: A Philosophical History* (Berkeley: University of California Press, 1997). Among his topics is the crucial role of place in Heidegger's philosophy. See also his rumination on "Body, Self, and Landscape: A Geophilosophical Inquiry into the Place-World," in Adams, Hoelscher, Till, *Textures of Place*, 403–25; and Kenneth R. Olwig, "Landscape as a Contested Topos of Place, Community, and Self," in Adams, Hoelscher, Till, *Textures of Place*, 93–117.

46. Marc Treib, "Power Plays: The Garden as Pet," in Francis and Hester, *Meaning of Gardens*, 93.

47. Thomas, *Man and the Natural World*, 256.

48. For a brilliant analysis of all the dimensions of this painting, see Louis Marin, "Toward a Theory of Reading in the Visual Arts: Poussin's *The Arcadian Shepherds*," in *Calligram: Essays in New Art History from France*, ed. Norman Bryson (Cambridge: Cambridge University Press, 1988).

49. Hannah Arendt, "On Violence," in *Crises of the Republic: Lying in Politics, Civil Disobedience on Violence, Thoughts on Politics, and Revolution* (New York: Harcourt, Brace, Jovanovich, 1972), 144.

Chapter 4: Moving the Eye

1. William M. Ivins Jr., *On the Rationalization of Sight* (New York: Metropolitan Museum of Modern Art, 1938; repr., New York: Da Capo Press, 1973). For commentary on Giotto's Arena Chapel in Padua, see John White, *The Birth and Rebirth of Pictorial Space* (Boston: Boston Art and Book Shop, 1967), esp. 57–71.

2. "Alberti's perspective scheme of 1435–36 . . . marked the effectual beginning of the substitution of visual for tactile space awareness, because its novel procedure of central projection and section not only automatically brought parallel lines together in logically determinable vanishing points, but provided a basis for the hitherto missing grammar or rules for securing both logical relations with the system of symbols employed and a reciprocal, or two-way, metrical correspondence between the pictorial representation of objects and the shapes of the objects as located in space." Ivins, *On the Rationalization of Sight*, 10.

3. Erwin Panofsky, *Perspective as Symbolic Form* (orig. 1925), trans. Christopher Wood (New York: Zone Books, 1997), 66. He adds: "For the modern vanishing-point construction distorts all widths, depths, heights inconstant proportion, and thus defines unequivocally the apparent size of any object, the size corresponding to its actual magnitude and its position with respect to the eye" (40).

4. Panofsky states that perspective: "negates the difference between front and back, between right and left, between bodies and intervening space ('empty' space), so that the sum of all the parts of space and all its contents are absorbed into a single 'quantum continuum.'" *Perspective as Symbolic Form*, 31.

5. See Richard Gregory, *Eye and Brain: The Psychology of Seeing* (New York: McGraw Hill), 1966.

6. William Ivins, *Prints and Visual Communication* (1953; repr. Cambridge, Mass.: MIT Press, 1978).

7. John Berger, *Ways of Seeing* (London: British Broadcasting Corporation and Penguin Books, 1972).

8. "Why vision and visuality, why these terms? Although vision suggests sight as a physical operation, and visuality as sight as a social fact, the two are not opposed as nature to culture: vision is social and historical too, and visuality involves the body and the psyche. Yet neither are they identical: here, the difference between the terms signals a difference within the visual—between the mechanism of sight and its historical techniques, between the datum of vision and its discursive determinations—a difference, many differences, among how we see, how we are able, allowed, or made to see, and how we see this seeing or the unseen therein." Hal Foster, "Preface," *Vision and Visuality* (Seattle: Bay Press, 1988), ix.

9. Gregory, *Eye and Brain*, 50–71.

10. Carl L. Franck, *The Villas of Frascati* (New York: Transatlantic Arts), 1966.

11. See Thierry Mariage, *The World of André le Nôtre*, trans. Graham Larkin (Philadelphia: University of Pennsylvania Press), 1999, 78–92.

12. This disconnect between château and park in some ways weakens the relationships so strongly stated in the plan. Vaux is much stronger in this regard because the axis swallows the château as the whale consumed Jonah. The bulge of the ovular salon acknowledges its position on the axis; no corresponding feature at Versailles makes this connection. Courtiers using cosmetics with a wax base are said to have detested this terrace. There was no shade and they were exposed to the mercy of the hot summer sun.

13. The château appeared in Androuet du Cerceau's noted anthology *Les plus excellents bastiments de France*. Cited in Nicole Garnier-Pelle, *André le Nôtre (1613–1700) et les jardins de Chantilly* (Paris: Somogy éditions, 2000), 18.

14. See Garnier-Pelle, *André le Nôtre*.

15. Horace Walpole sniped at the French in his essay on the development of the English landscape garden: "When a Frenchman reads of the garden of Eden, I do not doubt but he concludes it was something approaching that of Versailles, with clipt hedges, berceaus, and trellis work." See "On Modern Gardening" (1770; repr. London: Brentham Press, 1975), 4.

16. Alexander Pope, "An Epistle to Lord Burlington" (1731), lines 19–20, in *The Genius of the Place: The English Landscape Garden 1620–1820*, ed. John Dixon Hunt and Peter Willis (Cambridge, Mass.: MIT Press, 1988), 213.

17. On Stourhead, see Kenneth Woodbridge, *The Stourhead Landscape* (Wiltshire: The National Trust, 1986); on one of several interpretations see James Turner, "The Structure of Henry Hoare's Stourhead," *Art Bulletin* 21 (March 1979), 68–77.

18. Lancelot "Capability" Brown, quoted in Roger Turner, *Capability Brown and the Eighteenth-Century English Landscape* (London: Weidenfeld and Nicolson, 1985), 79.

19. "[T]hose [lines] composed of all the former [i.e., straight and geometric curves] together with an addition of the waving line, which is a line more productive of beauty than any of the former, as in flowers, and other forms of the ornamental kind; for which reason, we shall call it the line of beauty." William Hogarth, *The Analysis of Beauty* (1753; repr. Chicago: Reily and Lee, 1908), 72.

20. René de Girardin, *An Essay on Landscape* (orig. 1777), trans. Daniel Malthus (New York: Garland Publishing, 1982), 11, 3–4.

21. Girardin, *Essay on Landscape*, 53. "But in general, the great masses and the forest trees should be placed in front; for the stronger the fore-ground, and the more it is raised, the better will be the effect of the perspective" (100).

22. Note the relation to Alexander Pope's dictum that "all the rules of Gardening are reducible to three heads:—the contrasts, the management of surprises, and the concealment of bounds." Cited in Dorothy Stroud, *Capability Brown* (1950; repr. London: Faber and Faber, 1975), 157.

23. Girardin, *Essay on Landscape*, 150, 6.

24. Jean-Jacques Rousseau, *La Nouvelle Héloïse: Julie: or, The New Eloise* (orig. 1761), trans. Judith H. McDowell (University Park: Pennsylvania State University Press, 1968), 311; 305.

25. Jay Appleton, *The Experience of Landscape* (New York: John Wiley, 1975).

26. The Captain, for example, comments upon the functional placement of the existing house, a product of prior generations. But he notes: "'Food and drink taste better after a long walk than they would have tasted at home. We want variety and unfamiliar things . . . [A] building intended more for pleasure trips than as a house would be very well placed over there and during the fine seasons would afford us the most agreeable hours." Johann Wolfgang von Goethe, *Elective Affinities* (orig. 1809), trans. R. J. Hollingdale (Harmondsworth: Penguin, 1971).

27. Jane Austen, *Mansfield Park* (1814; repr. Harmondsworth: Penguin, 1966), 86, 119.

28. See Richard R. Brettell, "Richard Long's Circle: An Essay in Six Parts," in *Richard Long: Circles, Cycles, Mud, Stones* (Houston: Museum of Contemporary Art, 1996), 48–56.

29. Fearing undue influence by the European powers in general, and the Catholic Church in particular, the Tokugawa shoguns closed Japan to almost all outside traffic in 1638. The sole exception was a small and heavily monitored Dutch trading colony established on the artificial island of Dejima in Nagasaki Bay. See Edwin Reischauer, *Japan: The Story of a Nation* (Rutland, VT: Charles Tuttle, 1970), 93–117, and Johannes Laures, *The Catholic Church in Japan* (Rutland, VT: Charles Tuttle, 1954).

30. Henry D. Smith II, "The Problem of Perspective in Tokugawa Culture" (unpublished paper presented at the University of California, Berkeley, May 16, 1979).

31. David Slawson, *Secret Teachings in the Art of Japanese Gardens* (Tokyo: Kodansha International, 1987), 111–12.

32. See Marc Treib and Ron Herman, *A Guide to the Gardens of Kyoto*, rev. ed. (Tokyo: Kodansha International, 2003), 96–98; and Teiji Itoh, *The Japanese Garden: An Approach to Nature* (New Haven: Yale University Press, 1972), 142–57.

33. Teiji Itoh, *Space and Illusion in the Japanese Garden*, trans. Ralph Friedrich and Masajiro Shimamura (Tokyo: Weatherhill, 1973).

34. While generally credited to Enshu, the attribution has been questioned by some scholars.

35. For information on this mixing of formalities see Marc Treib, "Modes of Formality: The Distilled Complexity of Japanese Design," *Landscape Journal* 12, no. 1 (Spring 1993): 2–17.

36. Slawson, *Secret Teachings*, 114–15. Slawson offers two Western parallels to explain the intention of the garden makers. "The single-depth technique," he writes, "thus produces a relatively flat, two-dimensional effect reminiscent of Gauguin and the primitivists he admired." In addition, he cites monochrome as a choice "over full color in painting and photography" (115).

37. See Marc Treib, "Making the Edo Garden," *Landscape* 24, no. 1 (1980): 24–29.

38. During the eighteenth century, some English writers regarded this nonformal beauty as originating in China, coining the word "Sharawadgi" to express this particular quality. Horace Walpole, quoting Sir William Temple, stated: "[F]or there may be other forms wholly irregular, that may, for aught I know, have more beauty than any others; they must owe it to some extraordinary dispositions of nature in the seat, *or some great race of fancy or judgment in the contrivance*, which may reduce many disagreeing parts *into some figure*, which shall yet, upon the whole, be very agreeable. Something of this I have seen in some places, but heard more of it from others, who have lived much among the Chinese, a people whose way of thinking seems to lie as wide of ours in Europe, as their country does—Their greatest reach of imagination is employed in contriving figures, where the beauty shall be great and strike the eye, but without an order of disposition of parts that shall be commonly or easily observed." Horace Walpole, *On Modern Gardening* (1770; repr. London: Brentham Press, 1975), 17. Those more familiar with the gardens of China and Japan would tend to assign this characterization to the later rather than the former.

Chapter 5: Landscape and Global Vision

1. John Pickles, *A History of Spaces: Cartographic Reason, Mapping and the Geocoded World* (Routledge: London, 2004).

2. J. Corner, "Representation and Landscape. Drawing and Making in the Landscape Medium," *Word and Image* 8, no. 3 (1992): 243–75.

3. Edward S. Casey, *Representing Place: Landscape Painting and Maps* (Minneapolis: University of Minnesota Press, 2002).

4. Denis Cosgrove, *The Palladian Landscape: Geographical Change and its Cultural Representation in 16ᵗʰ Century Italy* (Leicester: Leicester University Press and University Park: Pennsylvania State University Press, 1993), esp. 163–87; Thierry Mariage, *The World of Andre Le Notre* (State College: University of Pennsylvania Press, 1998), 27–46.

5. Michael Charlesworth, "Thomas Sandby Climbs the Hoober Stand: The Politics of Panoramic Drawing in Eighteenth-century England," *Art History* 19, no. 2 (1996): 247–66.

6. Denis Cosgrove, "Eyeing Nature: Landscape and the European Sense of Sight," in *Handbook of Cultural Geography*, ed. K. Anderson, M. Domosh, S. Pile, N. Thrif (London: Sage, 2003), 249–68.

7. W. J. T. Mitchell, "Imperial Landscape," in *Landscape and Power*, 2nd ed., ed. W. J. T. Mitchell (Chicago: University of Chicago Press, 2002), 10.

8. The most sustained recent discussion of the connections between chorography and place in mapping and landscape painting is to be found in Edward Casey's *Representing Place*, esp. 213–30.

9. Denis Cosgrove, "Cosmography," in *The History of Cartography*, ed. D. Woodward, Vol. III "European Renaissance" (Chicago: University of Chicago Press, forthcoming).

10. Christopher S. Wood, *Albrecht Altdorfer and the Origins of Landscape* (London: Reaktion Books, 1993).

11. Walter S. Gibson, *"Mirror of the Earth": The World Landscape of the Sixteenth Century* (Princeton: Princeton University Press, 1989).

12. Denis Cosgrove, *Apollo's Eye: A Cartographic Genealogy of the Earth in the Western Imagination* (Baltimore: Johns Hopkins University Press, 2001), 257–62.

13. Abraham Ortelius, *Theatrum Orbis Terrarum* (Anversa: Aegidius Coppens van Diest, 1570), translated as *The Theatre of the Whole World* (London: John Norton, 1606), reproduced in facsimile and edited by R. A. Skelton (Amsterdam: Theatrum Orbis Terrarum Ltd., 1968). Citations are to the 1968 edition.

14. Ann Blair, *The Theater of Nature: Jean Bodin and Renaissance Science* (Princeton: Princeton University Press, 1997), 153–79.

15. Giorgio Mangani *Il "mondo" di Abramo Ortelio: mysticismo, geografia e collezionismo nel rinascimento dei Paesi Bassi* (Modena: Franco Cosimo Panini, 1998).

16. The epigrams read as follows:

Top left: "For man was given life that he might inhabit that sphere called Earth, which you see in the center of this temple" (Cicero).

Bottom left: "The purpose of the horse is for riding, of the ox for plowing, of the dog for hunting and keeping guard; the purpose of man alone is contemplating the world" (Cicero).

Bottom right: "I desire only that philosophy should appear before us in all her unity, just as the whole breadth of the firmament is spread before us to gaze upon" (Seneca).

"'Is this that pinpoint which is divided by sword and fire among so many nations? How ridiculous are the boundaries of mortals!" (Seneca).

17. Ortelius, Preface to "Parergon," in *Theatre*, n.p.

18. Susan Schulten, *The Geographical Imagination in America, 1880–1950* (Chicago: University of Chicago Press, 2001).

19. Archibald MacLeish, "The Image of Victory," In *Compass of the World. A Symposium on Political Geography*, ed. H. W. Weigert and V. Stephansson (London: Harrap, 1944), 3.

20. Richard Edes Harrison, *Look at the World: The Fortune World Atlas for World Strategy* (New York: Alfred Knopf, 1944).

21. Harrison's images are known largely through Schulten, *Geographical Imagination*, 214–28.

22. The quotation from *Touring Topics* is reprinted in J. Ott, "Landscapes of Consumption: Auto Tourism and Visual Culture in California, 1920–1940," in *Reading California: Art, Image, Identity*, ed. S. Brown, S. Bernstein, and I. S. Fort (Los Angeles: University of California Press 2000), 51–68 (quotation on 53).

Chapter 6: Ancient Rome through the Veil of Sight

1. Modern attempts at scientifically accurate cityscape reconstructions of Rome include large-scale models created in the last century by Paul Bigot (three versions) and Italo Gismondi. See François Hinard and Manuel Royo, eds., *Rome. L'espace urbain et ses représentations* (Paris: Presses de l'Université de Paris-Sorbonne, 1991); Philippe Fleury, "Le Plan de Rome," Centre for Research in Social Sciences (MRSH), http://www.unicaen.fr/rome/index.php. More recently, comic book artist Gilles Chaillet has published a large pictorial representation of the city. Gilles Chaillet, *La Rome des Césars* (Paris: Glenat, 2004). Filmic representations have tended to be only marginally accurate, often preferring to give the ancient city a Fascist gloss. Arthur J. Pomeroy, "The Vision of a Fascist Rome in *Gladiator*," in *Gladiator Film and History*, ed. Martin M. Winkler (Malden, Mass.: Blackwell, 2004), 111–23.

2. Digital reconstructions of large parts of the Imperial capital are under construction at Altair and UCLA's Cultural Virtual Reality Lab and Experiential Technology Center. See Altair, "Altair4 Multimedia," http://www.altair4.it; UCLA, "ETC.," http://www.etc.ucla.edu.

3. Poststructuralist developments led to the study of optic knowledge as applied to the totalizing gaze of an all-knowing subject. See, for example, Marisa Lazzari, "Archaeological Visions. Gender, Landscape and Optic Knowledge," *Journal of Social Archaeology* 3, no. 2 (2003): 194–222; David Fredrick, ed., *The Roman Gaze, Vision, Power, and the Body* (Baltimore: The Johns Hopkins University Press, 2002). See also John R. Clarke, *Looking at Lovemaking: Constructions of Sexuality in Roman Art, 100 B.C.–A.D. 250* (Berkeley: University of California, 2001), 106–7, 223–29.

4. On view-planning and visual alignment, see: Bettina Bergmann, "The Roman House as Memory Theater: The House of the Tragic Poet in Pompeii," *Art Bulletin*, 76, no. 2 (June 1994): 225–56; John R. Clarke, *The Houses of Roman Italy 100 B.C.–A.D. 250: Ritual Space and Decoration* (Berkeley: University of California, 1991); Lise Bek, *Towards Paradise on Earth:*

Space Conception in Architecture. A Creation of Renaissance Humanism (Odense: Odense University Press, 1980).

5. William L. MacDonald perceptively interprets viewing in Roman cities and provides an overview of urban images in Roman art in *The Architecture of the Roman Empire: An Urban Appraisal*, rev. ed. (New Haven: Yale University Press, 1986). At Pompeii, where the physical remains are extensive, initial studies of viewsheds have been undertaken. See S. J. R. Ellis, "The Distribution of Bars at Pompeii: Archaeological, Spatial and Viewshed analyses," *Journal of Roman Archaeology* 17 (2004): 371–84. For conceptual urban alignments in ancient Rome see: Penelope Davies, *Death and the Emperor: Roman Imperial Funerary Monuments, from Augustus to Marcus Aurelius* (Cambridge: Cambridge University Press, 2000); Hubert Cancik, "Rome as Sacred Landscape. Varro and the End of Republican Religion in Rome," *Visible Religion* IV/V (1985/86): 250–65.

6. The current definition of cityscape differs significantly from that of townscape. The latter term, which also appeared in the second half of the nineteenth century, initially defined an urban view. A century later, Gordon Cullen and others adopted the term to define a humanist reinterpretation of modernist design, leading to the insertion of townscape into the official planning lexicon of England. Robert Tavernor, "From Townscape to Skyscape," *Architectural Review* 215, no. 1285 (March 2004): 78–83. Paul Zanker used the term townscape when analyzing the interplay between history, function, and architecture in Pompeii in *Pompeii: Public and Private Life* (Cambridge, Mass.: Harvard University Press, 1998), 3–25.

7. Ptolemy, *Geographia*, 1.1, trans. Denis Cosgrove, "Mapping New Worlds, Culture and Cartography in Sixteenth-Century Venice," *Imago Mundi* 44 (1992): 66; see also Strabo, *Geography*, 1.1.1, trans. Horace L. Jones, Loeb Classical Library (Cambridge, Mass.: Harvard University Press, 1917); Vitruvius, *De architectura*, 8.2.6, trans. Frank Granger, Loeb Classical Library (Cambridge, Mass.: Harvard University Press, 1931); Edward S. Casey, *Representing Place. Landscape Painting and Maps* (Minneapolis: University of Minnesota Press, 2002), 158. On the possibility of a map being simultaneously chorographic and geographic see Claude Nicolet, *Space, Geography, and Politics in the Early Roman Empire*, trans. Hélène Leclerc (Ann Arbor: The University of Michigan Press, 1991), 100–101, 171–72, 184. La Rocca defines a third map type as topographic, representing a single place or adding topographical specificity to a chorographic image; Eugenio La Rocca, "L'affresco con veduto di città dal colle Oppio," in *Romanization and the City, Creation, Transformations, and Failures*, ed. E. Fentress (Portsmouth, R.I.: Journal of Roman Archaeology, 2000), 63.

8. Norman Bryson, "The Gaze in the Expanded Field," in *Vision and Visuality*, ed. Hal Foster (Seattle: New Press, 1988), 91–92. Most discussions of ancient visuality focus on sculpture, for example, R. S. Nelson, *Visuality Before and Beyond the Renaissance* (Cambridge: Cambridge University Press, 2000).

9. Michael Baxandall stresses that the period eye is also a class eye in *Painting and Experience in Fifteenth-Century Italy* (Oxford: Oxford University Press, 1986), 29–39. Unfortunately, the remaining documentary evidence from antiquity almost exclusively presents optic knowledge relating to the upper classes.

10. Pioneering work on viewing in relation to ancient architecture includes: Vincent Scully, *The Earth, the Temple and the Gods; Greek Sacred Architecture* (New Haven: Yale University Press, 1962); Constantinios Doxiadis, *Architectural Space in Ancient Greece*, trans. and ed. Jacqueline Tyrwhitt (Cambridge, Mass.: MIT Press, 1972); Lise Bek, "Venusta Species: A Hellenistic Rhetorical Concept as the Aesthetic Principle in Roman Townscape," *Analecta Romana Instituti Danici* 7 (1974): 139–48; Franz Jung, "Gebaute Bilder," *Antike Kunst* 27, no. 2 (1984): 71–122; Paul Zanker, "In Search of the Roman Viewer," in *The Interpretation of Architectural Sculpture in Greece and Rome*, ed. Diana Buitron-Oliver (Washington, D.C.: National Gallery of Art, 1997). See also Jaś Elsner, *Roman Eyes: Visuality and Subjectivity in Art and Text* (Princeton: Princeton University Press, 2007), which had not yet been published at the time of this writing.

11. Tower chambers, such as that mentioned in the house of the emperor Augustus, were associated with isolation and contemplation, though in 64 CE Nero allegedly watched the city burn from such an elevated position; Suetonius, *The Lives of the Caesars, Augustus*, 57.2 and *Nero*, 38, trans. John Rolfe, Loeb Classical Library (Cambridge, Mass.: Harvard University Press, 1914).

12. Vitruvius, *De architectura*, 2.8.17, 5.6.9, trans. Frank Granger, Loeb Classical Library (Cambridge, Mass.: Harvard University Press, 1931).

13. Alan Rodger, *Owners and Neighbours in Roman Law* (Oxford: Clarendon Press, 1972), 124–34.

14. Ulpian, *Digesta*, 8.2.15, in *The Digest of Justinian*, ed. Alan Watson (Philadelphia: University of Pennsylvania Press, 1985).

15. Javolenus, *Digesta*, 8.2.12; see also Pomponius and Sabinus, *Digesta*, 8.1.15; Ulpian, 43.8.12. Cicero refers to possible charges being leveled for spoiling the view of monument; *The Verrine Orations*, 4.79, trans. L. H. G. Greenwood, Loeb Classical Library (Cambridge, Mass.: Harvard University Press, 1935).

16. Cicero, *de Oratore*, 1.39.179–80, trans. E. W. Sutton, Loeb Classical Library (Cambridge, Mass.: Harvard University Press, 1942); Gaius, *Institutes*, 2.31, trans. W. M. Gordon and O. F. Robinson (Ithaca, N.Y.: Cornell University Press, 1988).

17. Pliny, *Letters*, 2.17, trans. William Melmoth, rev. W. M. L. Hutchinson, Loeb Classical Library (Cambridge, Mass.: Harvard University Press, 1961); see also Statius, *Silvae*, 2.2.63–97, trans. D. R. Shackleton Bailey, Loeb Classical Library (Cambridge, Mass.: Harvard University Press, 2003). Quintilian in the first century CE wrote, "beauty belongs to sea views, to plains, and to pleasant localities," conspicuously omitting cities and mountains; *The Orator's Education*, 3.7.27, trans. H. E. Butler, Loeb Classical Library (Cambridge, Mass.: Harvard University Press, 1953).

18. Pliny the Younger, *Natural History*, 35.117, trans. H. Rackham, Loeb Classical Library (Cambridge, Mass.: Harvard University Press, 1952); Vitruvius, *De architectura*, 7.5.2.

19. The majority of such scenes are from second-style wall painting. On the villa mania that gripped urban residents of Pompeii see Zanker, *Pompeii*, 145–55. Rome's residents also attempted to recreated the country in the city; see Pliny, *Natural History*, 19.19.59; Seneca the

Elder, *Declamations: Controversiae*, 2.1.13, trans. M. Winterbottom, Loeb Classical Library (Cambridge, Mass.: Harvard University Press, 1974); and Vitruvius, *De architectura*, 6.3.10.

20. Note the inclusion of seaside towns in Pliny's list of fresco subjects, *Naturalis historia*, 116–18. The binary opposition between the city as the place for work and the villa for leisure was a common trope in ancient literature, and appears pictorially on the Torlonia Avezzano relief juxtaposing an ordered, rigid grid city with a more relaxed rural setting. In truth, the analysis of economic data indicates that the separation was not so distinct. J. H. D'Arms, "Senators' Involvement in Commerce in the Late Republic: Some Ciceronian Evidence," *Memoirs of the American Academy in Rome* 36 (1980): 77–89.

21. Jimmy Dunn, "Pharos Lighthouse of Alexandria," Tour Egypt, http://touregypt.net/featurestories/pharoslighthouse.htm; Diane Favro, "The iconiCITY of ancient Rome," *Urban History* 33 no. 1 (2006): 20–38.

22. A late mosaic of the fifth century from Antioch is an exception, depicting the buildings passed on a walk through the city. Christine Kondoleon, *Antioch: The Lost Ancient City* (Princeton: Princeton University Press, 2001), 114–15.

23. Lionel Casson, *Travel in the Ancient World* (Baltimore: The Johns Hopkins University Press, 1974); Tony Perrottet, *Pagan Holiday: On the Trail of Ancient Roman Tourists* (New York: Random House, 2003).

24. Benet Salway, "Travel, *Itineraria* and *Tabellaria*," in *Travel and Geography in the Roman Empire*, ed. Colin Adams and Ray Laurence (London: Routledge, 2001), 22–66; Oswald A. W. Dilke, *Greek and Roman Maps* (London: Thames and Hudson, 1985), 113–20; Annalina and Mario Levi, *Itineraria picta, Contributo allo studio della Tabula Peutingeriana* (Rome: L'erma di Bretschneider, 1967).

25. Casson, *Travel*, 286–91. Coins with representations of famous statues, local monuments, and city images may also have been collected as tourist mementos. Martin Jessop Price and Bluma L. Trell, *Coins and Their Cities: Architecture on the Ancient Coins of Greece, Rome, and Palestine* (London: Vecchi, 1977); Marvin Tameanko, *Monumental Coins: Buildings and Structures on Ancient Coinage* (Iola, Wisc.: Krause Publications, Inc., 1999).

26. Ancient elevations or prospects of cities appear less frequently, usually in relation to cities seen across the water. On types of city representations see David Buisseret, ed., *Envisioning the City. Six Studies in Urban Cartography* (Chicago: University of Chicago Press 1998), ix–xi.

27. A single temple is also included. See Steven Ostrow, "The Topography of Puteoli and Baiae on the Eight Glass Flasks," *Puteoli. Studi Storia Antica* 3 (1979): 77–140; Dilke, *Maps*, 148; Paul Zanker, "The City as Symbol: Rome and the Creation of an Urban Image," in Fentress, *Romanization*, 40–41.

28. Regarding residential tours by Roman house owners see Bergmann, "Roman House," 249–54.

29. Hadrian apparently recreated buildings, not cityscapes; *Scriptores Historiae Augustae, Hadrian*, 23.7, trans. David Magie, Loeb Classical Library (Cambridge, Mass.: Harvard University Press, 1921).

30. Polybius, *Histories*, 10.10, trans. W. R. Patton, Loeb Classical Library (Cambridge, Mass.: Harvard University Press, 1925).

31. Seneca, *Epistles*, 51, trans. Richard M. Gummere, Loeb Classical Library (Cambridge, Mass.: Harvard University Press, 1917).

32. Livy, *Roman History*, 37.59, trans. B. O. Foster, Loeb Classical Library (Cambridge, Mass.: Harvard University Press, 1935); Sorcha Carey, *Pliny's Catalogue of Culture: Art and Empire in the Natural History* (Oxford: Oxford University Press, 2003), 62–63. The simulacra may have been paintings or physical models. The state also used public displays of maps to assert power. P. D. A. Harvey, *The History of Topographical Maps: Symbols, Pictures and Surveys* (London: Thames and Hudson, 1980), 126–27; Dilke, *Maps*, 96.

33. Jon Coulston, "The Architecture and Construction Scenes on Trajan's Column," in *Architecture and Architectural Sculpture in the Roman Empire*, ed. Martin Henig (Oxford: Oxford University Committee for Archaeology, 1990), 39–50.

34. The image of painted Italy was associated with the Temple of Tellus; Varro, *De re rustica*, 1.2.1, in *Cato and Varro on Agriculture*, trans. W. D. Hooper and H. B. Ash, Loeb Classical Library (Cambridge, Mass.: Harvard University Press, 1935).

35. La Rocca, "L'affresco." In 2005, further explorations in the area revealed mosaics with architectural elements, though apparently no cityscapes (personal communication of Euguenio La Rocca with the author, 2005).

36. Catharine Edwards, "Imaginaires de l'image de Rome ou comment (se) représenter Rome?" in *Images Romaines*, ed. Clara Auvray-Assays (Paris: Presses de l'Ecole normale supérieure, 1998), 235–45; Favro, "IconiCITY," 31–38.

37. Dionysius of Halicarnassus, *Roman Antiquities*, 4.13, trans. Earnest Cary, Loeb Classical Library (Cambridge, Mass.: Harvard University Press, 1939).

38. The populations of Alexandria and Antioch were approximately half that of Rome, with other cities being considerably smaller; Neville Molrley, *Metropolis and Hinterland, The City of Rome and the Italian Economy 200 B.C.–A.D. 200* (Cambridge: Cambridge University Press, 1996), 2.

39. Juvenal records that one could buy an excellent house in the country for the same price as the yearly rent of a dark garret apartment in Rome; *Satires* 3.223, trans. G. G. Ramsay Braund, Loeb Classical Library (Cambridge, Mass.: Harvard University Press, 1918).

40. On the smoke of Rome see Horace, *Odes*, 3.29.5, trans. C. E. Bennett, Loeb Classical Library (Cambridge, Mass.: Harvard University Press, 1914). Ironically, the public life was equated with the sun, yet pollution blocked sunlight in the city where such activity centered; J. P. V. D. Balsdon, *Life and Leisure in Ancient Rome* (New York: McGraw-Hill, 1969), 130–37.

41. During the Republic a guard was always posted on the Janiculum when the assembly (*comitia centuriata*) met in the Campus Martius; Dio Cassius, *Roman History*, 37.28, trans. Earnest Cary and Herbert B. Foster, Loeb Classical Library (Cambridge, Mass.: Harvard University Press, 1914).

42. Cicero, *de Officiis*, 3.16.66, trans. Walter Miller, Loeb Classical Library (Cambridge,

Mass.: Harvard University Press, 1913); Cancik, "Sacred Landscape," 252–53; Filippo Coarelli, *Il Foro Romano, Periodo Arcaico* (Roma: Quasar, 1983, 101–3.

43. Ovid, *Fasti* 2.684; 5.91–6, trans. J. G. Frazer, Loeb Classical Library (Cambridge, Mass.: Harvard University Press, 1931); see also Ovid, *Epistulae ex Ponto*, 2.1.23–24, trans. A. L. Wheeler, Loeb Classical Library (Cambridge, Mass.: Harvard University Press, 1924); Virgil, *Aeneid* 1.255, trans. H. Rushton Fairclough, Loeb Classical Library (Cambridge, Mass.: Harvard University Press, 1916). On written use of the capital city as metonym for *imperium* see Catharine Edwards, *Writing Rome: Textual Approaches to the City* (Cambridge: Cambridge University Press, 1996), 69–95.

44. Edmond Frézouls, "Rome Ville Ouverte. Réflexions sur les problémes de l'Expansion urbaine d'Auguste à Aurélien," in *L'Urbs. Espace urbain et histoire. Ier siècle avant J.C. III^{er} siècle après J.C., CÉFR* 98 (Rome: École Française de Rome, 1987), 381–82.

45. Also translated as *anno urbis conditae*, "the year of the city's foundation."

46. Cicero, *De finibus*, 5.2, trans. H. Rackham, Loeb Classical Library (Cambridge, Mass.: Harvard University Press, 1914).

47. Edwards, "Imaginaires," 235–45.

48. Plutarch, *Moralia*, 559a, trans. Benedict Einarson, Loeb Classical Library (Cambridge, Mass.: Harvard University Press, 1959).

49. One could argue that textual descriptions of Rome gave the reader a sense of ownership. Overall, however, Roman authors focused on Rome's intense and politically sophisticated street life and specific structures rather than on panoramic views. For written descriptions of the city see Edwards, *Writing Rome*; and Mary Jaeger, *Livy's Written Rome* (Ann Arbor: University of Michigan Press, 1997).

50. Notably, the divine view from on high tended to trivialize human urban activities, as portrayed in Lucian's *Ikaromenippos* and Varro's *Endymiones*.

51. Vitruvius, *De architectura*, 4.5.2. Significantly, the temple to Rome's premier god Jupiter stood atop the Capitoline Hill looking over developments to the south.

52. Aelius Aristides, *Orationes* 26 (*Speech to Rome*), 6–9; 61–62, trans. C. A. Behr (Leiden: Brill, 1981). Earlier, Horace, wrote "O quickening Sun (equated with Apollo) . . . Unaltered may thou never view a city greater on earth than Rome," Horace, *Carmen saeculare*, 9–12, trans. C. E. Bennett, Loeb Classical Library (Cambridge, Mass.: Harvard University Press, 1978). In the late Empire, Claudianus wrote of Rome, "Eye cannot match her extent, nor mind her glory, nor voice her praise," *De consulatu Stilichonis*, 1.3.65–70, see also 130–37, trans. M. Platnauer, Loeb Classical Library (Cambridge, Mass.: Harvard University Press, 1922).

53. Susan Matheson, *An Obsession with Fortune: Tyche in Greek and Roman Art*, exhibition catalog (New Haven: Yale University Art Gallery, 1994).

54. Carla Fayer, *Il culto della dea Roma, origine e diffusione nell'impero* (Pescara: Trimestre, 1976); Ronald Mellor, "The Goddess Roma," *Augstieg und Niedergang der römischen Welt* II (1981): 952–59.

55. Significantly, Dea Roma did not receive a temple or major festival in Rome until the

second century CE, when Hadrian exploited the cult and its association with the city to unify and stabilize the Empire. In the center of the capital he erected the great Temple of Venus and Roma, also called *templum urbis Romae* (Servius in *Aeniad*, 2.227, 351), and *templum urbis* (Scriptores Historiae Augustae, *Hadrian*, 19).

56. Diane Favro, "The Street Triumphant: The Urban Impact of Roman Triumphal Parades," in *Streets: Critical Perspectives on Public Space*, ed. Zeynep Çelik, Diane Favro, and Richard Ingersoll (Berkeley: University of California Press, 1994), 151–64.

57. The *genius loci* could also play a protective role. Rome, like other cities, had a *genius urbis*. Ettore de Ruggiero, ed., *Dizionario Epigrafico di antichità romane* (Rome: L'Erma, 1961), s.v. *Genius*.

58. Cicero, *de Finibus*, 5.2. Edwards stressed the link between knowing Roman history and customs and knowing the city. *Writing Rome*, 17–18.

59. Cicero, *Divinatio in Caecilium*, 16, trans. W. E. Heitland (Cambridge: Cambridge University Press, 1933). Similarly, after climbing atop the Column of Trajan in the sixth century, Cassiodorus described the Forum at his feet, rather than the city spreading in every direction; *Variae*, 7.6.1. Such elevated viewing platforms must have been used sparingly in conjunction with rituals, rather than for general viewing as advocated by Davies, *Death and the Emperor*, 130, 162–67.

60. Martial, *Epigrams*, 1.108, trans. By C. A. Ker, Loeb Classical Library (Cambridge, Mass.: Harvard University Press, 1919).

61. Strabo, *Geography*, 5.3.7–8.

62. Mario Torelli, *Typology and Structure of Roman Historical Reliefs* (Ann Arbor: University of Michigan Press, 1982).

63. Ferdinando Castagnoli, "Gli edifici rappresentati in un rilievo del sepolcro degli Haterii," *Bullettino della Commissione archeologica Comunale di Roma* 69 (1941): 59–69; James C. Anderson Jr., *Roman Architecture and Society* (Baltimore: The Johns Hopkins University Press, 2002), 111–12.

64. M. Livius Drusus, quoted in Velleius Paterculus, 2.14.3; see also Plutarch, *Moralia*, 800. Cicero records the doors of a house in Messina were left open so people could enter and view the art; *In Verrem* 4.3.6.

65. Susan Treggiari, "The Upper-class House as Symbol and Focus of Emotion in Cicero," *Journal of Roman Archaeology* 12 (1999): 41–56.

66. Cicero is referring here to the house of Drusus mentioned above, which he subsequently purchased; *De Domo suo*, 100. In the imperial period patricians had less power and the interest in being visible waned. In particular, emperors such as Domitian who feared assassination took great pains to avoid being easily seen. Suetonius, *Domitian*, 14.

67. John E. Stambaugh, *The Ancient Roman City* (Baltimore: The Johns Hopkins University Press, 1988), 175.

68. Martial, *Epigrams*, 1.108, 4.64.

69. Cicero, *De Domo suo*, 45.116.

70. Seneca, *Controversiae*, 5.5.

71. Suetonius, *Nero*, 31.

72. The distances from the capital to major cities throughout the Empire were inscribed on the Golden Milestone (Milliarium Aureum) in the Forum Romanum, situating Rome as the generating point of power; Plutarch, *Galba*, 24. By the third century a nearby monument, the Umbilicus Romae, marked the center of the city and empire.

Chapter 7: Making Vision Manifest

1. The issue of the view as a sign and the symbolic meaning of landscape is discussed in D. F. Ruggles, *Gardens, Landscape, and Vision in the Palaces of Islamic Spain* (University Park: Penn State University Press, 2000). The provision of windows in mosques is discussed in the chapter "The Here and Hereafter," in D. F. Ruggles, *Islamic Gardens and Landscapes* (Philadelphia: University of Pennsylvania Press, 2007).

2. D. F. Ruggles, "The Mirador in Abbasid and Hispano-Umayyad Garden Typology," *Muqarnas*, 7: (1990): 73–82; Ruggles, "The Gardens of the Alhambra and the Concept of the Garden in Islamic Spain," in *Al-Andalus: The Arts of Islamic Spain*, ed. Jerrilynn Dodds (New York: Metropolitan Museum, 1992), 162–71; the *jharoaka*, which is a common feature in Mughal palaces, is discussed in Catherine Asher, "Sub-Imperial Palaces: Power and Authority in Mughal India," *Ars Orientalis* 23 (1993): 281–302, and Gulru Necipoglu, "Framing the Gaze in Ottoman, Safavid, and Mughal Palaces," *Ars Orientalis* 23 (1993): 303–26.

3. Ernst Gombrich, *Art and Illusion: A Study in the Psychology of Pictorial Representation* (New York: Pantheon Books, 1960), 5, introduction, and chap. 1.

4. Martin Jay, "Scopic Regimes of Modernity," in *Vision and Visuality*, ed. Hal Foster (Seattle: Bay Press, 1988): 3–23.

5. Jacques Derrida, *Of Grammatology* (orig. 1967), trans. Gayatri Spivak (Baltimore; The Johns Hopkins University Press, 1976); Jean Baudrillard, "The Precession of Simulacra," in *Simulations* (New York: Semiotext(e), Inc., 1983), 3–47. Norman Bryson, in addition to his work on Western painting, wrote an unusual essay on Japanese painting and philosophy: Norman Bryson, "The Gaze in the Expanded Field," *Vision and Visuality*, ed. Hal Foster (Seattle: Bay Press, 1988), 87–108. While Bryson is very well known for *Vision and Painting: The Logic of the Gaze* (New Haven: Yale University Press, 1983), he is generally not known for his work on Japanese visual culture. Indeed, at a summer seminar on visual theory that I attended in 1998, the participants (primarily from the United States, Europe, New Zealand, and Australia) generally agreed that Bryson's analysis of Kitaro Nishida and Keiji Nishitani lacked relevance for art history because it explored a non-Western perception of history. However, I take the opposite view: the book/essay was provocative precisely because, in demonstrating the alternatives to Western concepts of Cartesian space and Hegelian time, it exposed those concepts as culturally produced.

6. The great and enduring exception is Alois Riegl, *Stilfragen* (orig. 1893), translated by

Evelyn Kain as *Problems of Style: Foundations for a History of Ornament* (Princeton: Princeton University, 1993); and Alois Riegl, *Spätrömische Kunstindustrie* (orig. 1927), translated by Rolf Winkes as *Late Roman Art Industry* (Rome: Giorgio Bretschneider, 1985).

7. Oleg Grabar, *The Formation of Islamic Art*, rev. ed. (New Haven: Yale University Press, 1987), chap. 3, pp. 43–71.

8. Marianna Shreve Simpson, *Sultan Ibrahim Mirza's Haft Awrang: A Princely Manuscript from Sixteenth-century Iran* (New York: Yale University Press, 1997); and Simpson, *Persian Poetry, Painting and Patronage: Illustrations from a Sixteenth-century Masterpiece* (Washington, D.C.: Freer Gallery of Art, 1998), esp. 9–13.

9. Ruggles, *Gardens, Landscape, and Vision*, esp. 86–109, 200–208.

10. Erwin Panofsky, *Perspective as Symbolic Form* (New York: Zone Books; Cambridge: MIT Press, 1991).

11. A. I. Sabra, trans., *The Optics of Ibn al-Haytham: Books I-III on Direct Vision*, 2 vols. (London: The Warburg Institute, 1989); and A. I. Sabra, "Ibn al-Haytham," in *Dictionary of Scientific Biography*, vol. 6 (New York: Scribner, 1972), 189–210.

12. For example, George Michell and Snehal Shah, eds., *Ahmadabad* (Bombay: Marg, 1988); Dominque Clévenot and G. Degeorge, *Décors d'Islam*, trans. *Splendors of Islam: Architecture, Decoration, and Design* (New York: Press, 2000); Christopher Tadgell, *History of Architecture in India* (London: Architecture, Design, and Technology Press, 1990); and even in the popular Lonely Planet guidebook, *India: A Travel Survival Kit*, 2nd ed. (South Yarra, Victoria: Lonely Planet, 1984).

13. On Champaner, see Bianca Maria Alfieri, *Islamic Architecture of the Indian Subcontinent* (London: Laurence King, 2000), 122–26; and H. Goetz, "Pawagadh-Champaner," *Journal of the Gujarat Research Society* 11, no. 2 (1949): 49–66. In conjunction with gaining status as a World Heritage Site, the city has been the focus of new studies on landscape interpretation and heritage management by the Heritage Trust of Baroda and the University of Illinois, Amita Sinha et al., including: *Champaner: Archaeological Park* (Champaign: Department of Landscape Architecture, University of Illinois at Urbana-Champaign, 2001); *Champaner-Pavagadh: Cultural Sanctuary* (Champaign: Department of Landscape Architecture, University of Illinois at Urbana-Champaign, 2003); and *Panch Yatras in the Cultural Heritage Landscape of Champaner-Pavagadh, Gujarat, India* (Champaign: Department of Landscape Architecture, University of Illinois at Urbana-Champaign, 2005).

14. Ruggles, *Gardens, Landscape, and Vision*, 200–208, and Ruggles, "The Eye of Sovereignty: Poetry and Vision in the Alhambra's Lindaraja Mirador," *Gesta* 36 (1997): 180–89.

15. Ebba Koch, "The Mughal Waterfront Garden," in *Gardens in the Time of the Great Muslim Empires: Theory and Design*, ed. Attilio Petruccioli, Muqarnas Supplements 7 (Leiden: E. J. Brill, 1997), 140–60.

16. For an explanation of Rajput origins and social and political roles, see G. H. R. Tillotson, *The Rajput Palaces: The Development of an Architectural Style, 1450–1750* (New Haven: Yale University Press, 1987), 1–4.

17. On the Amber Fort, see Oskar Reuther, *Indische Palaste und Wohnhäuser* (Berlin: L. Preiss, c. 1925); Tillotson, *Rajput Palaces*, 93–105; and Catherine Asher, *Architecture of Mughal India*. The New Cambridge History of India, I: 4 (Cambridge: Cambridge University Press, 1995), 246–49. On its gardens, see D. F. Ruggles, "Landscape and View in Islamic Spain and Mughal India," in *The Garden: Myth, Meaning, and Metaphor*, ed. Brian Day (Windsor: The University of Windsor, Humanities Research Group, 2003), 21–50.

18. R. S. Khangarot and P. S. Nathawat, *Jaigarh: The Invincible Fort of Amber* (Jaipur: RBSA Publishers, 1990), 14–15.

19. Khangarot and Nathawat, *Jaigarh*, 58.

20. G. Z. Brown, *Sun, Wind, and Light: Architectural Design Strategies* (New York: John Wiley and Sons, 1985), 72.

Chapter 8: *Landscapes within Buildings in Late Eighteenth-Century France*

1. Dora Wiebenson, *The Picturesque Garden in France* (Princeton: Princeton University Press, 1978), 104.

2. See, for example, Georges-Louis Le Rouge, *Détail des nouveaux jardins à la mode* [a.k.a., *Jardins anglo-chinois*], 21 *cahiers* (Paris: Le Rouge, [1775–1789]), *cahier* 2, plate 23 (1775); *cahier* 3, plates 1 and 2 (1776); *cahier* 20, plate 4 (1788).

3. That practice was by no means new. In chapter three, paragraph twelve, of his influential treatise, *La Théorie et la pratique du jardinage* (1st edition, 1709, with many later editions in the eighteenth century), Antoine-Joseph Dezallier d'Argenville identified the fourth of four "maximes fondamentales" (fundamental maxims) for laying out a garden well as "de le faire toujours paroître plus grand qu'il ne l'est effectivement." In paragraph sixteen of the same chapter, Dezallier listed various techniques for creating that illusion (to make it always appear larger than it really is): "soit en arrêtant le coup d'œil avec adresse par des rideaux que forment des palissades, des allées, des bois placés à propos, et contraints à une hauteur convenable à la vue, ou en pratiquant des lizieres de bois contre les murs, pour tromper agréablement par l'étendue considérable dont cela fait paroître un enclos. Il faut encore principalement s'appliquer dans un Jardin à couvrir de verdure tous les murs dont l'aspect est des plus triste."

4. The technique is similar to that used in wildlife dioramas. See, for example, Karen Wonders, *Habitat Dioramas: Illusions of Wilderness in Museums of Natural History*, Acta Universitatis Upsaliensis. Figura, nov. ser. 25 (Uppsala, Sweden: 1993).

5. As a device for producing illusions of extension beyond property limits, the picture-as-space approach was similar in purpose to the technique of appropriating adjacent terrains through visual openness, achieved through the absence or invisibility of physical boundaries (e.g., the ha-ha). See, for example, Claude-Henri Watelet, *Essay on Gardens: A Chapter in the French Picturesque*, ed. John Dixon Hunt, trans. Samuel Danon (Philadelphia: University of Pennsylvania Press, 2003), 55: "It is an important skill to be able to give the impression that the terrain occupied is continuous with the land beyond it. This is how properties are made to

look more spacious without cost, and thus the unavoidable expenses of large estates are averted. For the kind of establishment I am speaking of is not vast and must avoid great expenditures." Originally published as *Essai sur les jardins* (Paris: Prault; Saillant & Nyon; Pissot, 1774), 121: "Dans ces établissemens, le choix des situations & l'agrément des entours sont nécessaires. L'art de joindre en apparence les espaces extérieures au terrein qu'on occupe est importante. C'est ainsi qu'on agrandit sans frais les possessions, & qu'on se soustrait aux dépenses inédita- bles qu'exigent des lieux trop étendus. Car le genre d'établissement dont je parle ne comporte pas de vastes dimensions, & doit fuir les grandes dépenses." Of course, illusions of spatial ex- tension were also prized in larger gardens.

6. Most historians of Chantilly concur that the prince de Condé's walk took place in 1772 and that the *jardin anglais* was laid out by 1773. In contrast, Raoul de Broglie indicated that the walk took place in 1774 and that the garden was laid out by 1775. De Broglie appears to have confused the dates of the *jardin anglais* with those of the hamlet later built therein. According to contemporary published descriptions and guidebooks by Nicolas Le Camus de Mézières (1783), Jacques-Antoine Dulaure (1786), Luc-Vincent Thièry (1788), and J. Mérigot (1791), as well as a manuscript guide in the collection of the Musée Condé, Chantilly (MS 1365 [1116]: Garnier du Brueil, *Mes Souvenirs ou lettres à M. le comte M****, *sur un voyage à Chantilly en 1788*), work on the *jardin anglais* began in 1780, but this is plainly incorrect and is disproved by references in Jacques Toudouze's "Journal des Chasses" as well as by evidence such as the fact that Emperor Joseph II of Austria visited the hamlet in May 1777. See Nicolas Le Camus de Mézieres, *Description des eaux de Chantilly et du Hameau* (Paris: chez l'Auteur, 1783), 7, 11; Dulaure, *Nouvelle description des environs de Paris* (1787), 1:79; Luc-Vincent Thièry, *Guide des amateurs et des étrangers voyageurs dans les maisons royales, châteaux, lieux de plaisance, établissements publics, villages et séjours les plus renommés. Aux environs de Paris. Avec une in- dication des beautés de la nature & de l'art qui peuvent mériter l'attention des curieux*, 2 vols. in 1 (Paris: chez Hardouin & Gattey, 1788), 226; J. Mérigot, *Promenades ou Itinéraires des Jardins de Chantilly* (Paris: Desenne; Gattey; Guyot; Chantilly: Hédouin, 1791), 32; Gustave Macon, *Les arts dans la maison de Condé* (Paris: Librairie de l'Art Ancien et Moderne, 1903), 111, citing Jacques Toudouze, "Journal des Chasses de S. A. S. Mgr. le prince de Condé" (1748–85), 2 vols., Musée Condé Chantilly, MS 371–72, pag. non cit., for completion by May 1773; Henri Malo, *A Visit to Chantilly: An Illustrated Guide to the Museum, the Park, the Abode of Sylvia, the Hamlet, the Rackets Courts, the Stables*, trans. Mary E. Rodocanachi (Paris: Braun & Cie, 1946), 45; Raoul de Broglie, *Chantilly: Histoire du château et de ses collections* (Paris: Calmann-Lévy, 1964), 96; Eleanor P. De Lorme, *Garden Pavilions and the Eighteenth-Century French Court* (Woodbridge, Suffolk, England: Antique Collector's Club, 1996), 218–19; Jean-Pierre Babelon, *Chantilly* (Paris: Éditions Scala, 1999), 142.

7. See Toudouze, "Journal des Chasses," 404–5.

8. Images of many features within the *jardin anglais* and hamlet were published in Mérigot's *Promenades*. Disparities in the dating of the hamlet are discussed in Wiebenson, *Picturesque Garden*, 100, n99. Wiebenson suggested that the hamlet was begun in 1775.

9. Henriette-Louise de Waldner de Freundstein, baronne d'Oberkirch, *Mémoires de la*

baronne d'Oberkirch, ed. Suzanne Burkard (Paris: Mercure de France, 1970), 204: "l'extérieur est entouré de tout ce qui est nécessaire à un bon laboureur."

10. The sufficiency of the hamlet as an aristocratic pleasure suite was noted by Jean-Pierre Babelon in *Album du Comte de Nord: Recueil des plan des château, parcs, et jardins de Chantilly levé en 1784*, ed. Jean-Pierre Babelon (Saint-Rémy-en-l'Eau, France: Éditions Monelle Hayot, 2000), 54; "ces dernières [i.e., "la grange, les maisons d'habitations des fermiers"] renferment tous les espaces nécessaires aux plaisirs de la société aristocratique venue pour la collation, la conversation et le concert: la cuisine, la salle à manger, le salon, la salle de billard, le cabinet des livres." As a suite separated into freestanding components, the hamlet at Chantilly may have inspired the description of a house as a cluster of cottages included within "Mr. L. L. G. D. M.," *Lettre sur les jardins anglois, adressée aux auteurs du Jounal* [sic] *de* *** (Paris: chez Moutard, 1775), 11–13.

11. See *Jardins en France, 1760–1820: Pays d'illusion, Terre d'expériences* [exhibition: Hôtel de Sully, Paris, May 18–September 11 1977] (Paris: Caisse Nationale des Monuments Historiques et des Sites, 1977), 136. See also Raoul de Broglie, "Le Hameau et la Laiterie de Chantilly," *Gazette des Beaux-Arts*, series 6, vol. 37 (Oct.–Dec. 1950): 309–24, which includes photos of the interior with painted walls intact; Ibid., 323n15, citing Jean Étienne Guettard, Jean Benjamin de la Borde, and Edme Béguillet, *Voyage pittoresque de la France* (Paris: Lamy, 1784), in reference to the painted trees; and Nicolas Le Camus de Mézières, *Description des Eaux de Chantilly et du Hameau* (Paris: chez l'Auteur, 1783), 80, for other descriptions.

12. The *banc de gazon* at the east end of the dining hall interior, and its counterpart at the west end, appear in the *Album du comte du Nord* in the plan and section CD, but not in section AB.

13. Contemporary guidebooks described additional elements not depicted in the *Album du Comte du Nord*. See Dulaure, *Nouvelle description*, 1:81; "les siéges imitent des troncs d'arbres, des canapés de verdure; & des groupes de fleurs naissent en pleine terre: quelque ouvertures ménagées çà & là entre les branches d'arbres, laissent pénétrer la lumière"; Mérigot, *Promenades*, 36; and "Des troncs d'arbres, des tapis de verdure sont les sièges. Des groupes de fleurs naissent en pleine terre. Quelques ouvertures ménagées ça et là dans le mur et entre les branches des arbres dont cette salle est décorée, laissent pénétrer la lumière du jour"; Ibid., 36n1; "Lorsqu'on y soupe, on éclaire cette salle avec des guirlandes de lanternes qui semblent être tout autour suspendues aux arbres, ce qui produit un effet très-piquant."

14. Concerning the interiors of the theater at Chantilly, see Raoul de Broglie, "Le Théâtre de Chantilly," *Gazette des Beaux-Arts*, LVII (March 1961): 155–166, and Babelon, *Album du Comte de Nord*, 44–45.

15. Consider, for example, Gabriel-Germain Boffrand's decorations for the Salon de la Princesse in the Hôtel de Soubise (1738–40), Paris, or the costume ball held at Versailles on February 25, 1745, at which eight participants appeared dressed as clipped yews. The latter was depicted in a print by Charles-Nicolas Cochin.

16. François de Bastide, *La Petite Maison* (1758; rev. ed., 1763; Paris: Gallimard, 1995), 115; "on croit être dans un bosquet naturel éclairé par le secours de l'art."

17. Charles-François Ribart, called Ribart de Chamoust, *Architecture Singulière; l'Éléphant Triomphal, Grand Kiosque à la Gloire du Roi, par M. Ribart, Ingénieur, et Membre de l'Académie des Sciences et Belles-Lettres de Béziers* (Paris: de l'Imprimerie de Moreau [text]; Pierre Patte [plates], 1758); Ibid., "Préliminaire," plates IV and VI, with accompanying descriptions.

18. Bastide described the stream, but it was not represented in the images engraved by Patte.

19. Ibid., description of plate VI. These furnishings were not represented in the images engraved by Patte.

20. For contemporary criticism of Ribart's *Architecture Singulière*, see Élie Fréron, *L'Année littéraire* (Paris: Crapard, 1758), 2:154–60, 2:328–35. The dining room and its odd location are mentioned in 2:158–59. "Se peut-il, Monsieur, qu'il y ait un cerveau capable d'enfancer des idées aussi baroques! Quel projet de pratiquer dans un Eléphant des chambres, des antichambres, des garderobes, des bains, de placer le Parlement entre ses épaules, de faire une salle à manger de son cul, &c, &c, &c, &c, &c!" In the later entry, Fréron accused Ribart of having plagiarized the elephant from Béroalde de Verville's French edition (1600) of the *Hypnertomachia Poliphili* (Venice: Aldus Manutius, 1499).

21. Dulaure, *Nouvelle description*, 1:80–81. "Le dehors & l'intérieur semblent s'étonner de se trouver réunis, & n'étonnent pas moins les spectateurs par le contraste singulier de ce rapprochement des extrêmes." (The exterior and interior seem astonished to find themselves reunited, and they astonish no less the spectators by the singular contrast of this bringing together of extremes). In the 1795 edition of his *Coup d'œil sur Belœil*, the prince de Ligne called huts and cottages within gardens "magnifiques [. . .] à cause du contraste et de la surprise" (magnificent [. . .] because of the contrast and the surprise). See Charles-Joseph, prince de Ligne, *Coup d'œil sur Belœil et sur une grande partie des jardins de l'Europe*, ed. Ernest de Ganay (Paris: Bossard, 1922), 277, and Ernest de Ganay's reference to the hamlet at Chantilly, 277–78, note a.

22. One guidebook to Chantilly, written by the *conservateur adjoint* Henri Malo, described the exteriors of the hamlet and then declared: "But inside what a contrast" (*Visit to Chantilly*, 45). Raoul de Broglie, another important chronicler of Chantilly, wrote: "L'intérieur des maisons réservait, en général, une surprise. Leur attraction principale résidait dans la différence entre la richesse des appartements et l'aspect modeste de la demeure. [. . .] Une réelle surprise était ménagée par la grange." (A surprise was held in store [. . .] by the interior of the houses. . . . [t]he barn held in store a real surprise) (*Chantilly*, 97–98). The historian of gardens Ernest de Ganay identified the hamlet as an example of "the startling contrast between a rustic exterior and a luxurious interior in eighteenth century gardens." Quoted in Charles-Joseph, prince de Ligne, *Coup d'œil sur Belœil et sur une grande partie des jardins de l'Europe*, ed. Ernest de Ganay (Paris: Bossard, 1922), 3:32, translated by Basil Guy as *Coup d'œil at Belœil and a Great Number of European Gardens*, 118, n6. More recently, the distinguished historian Jean-Pierre Babelon has written that the interiors of the hamlet "must have aroused cries of surprise from the visitors" (*Album*, 54). Babelon suggested that those provocations "started with the barn," and "[t]here were even greater surprises in store in two peasants' cottages" (*Chantilly*, 133).

23. Oberkirch, *Mémoires*, 204: "C'était commode, gai, sans façon et parfaitement bien imaginé."

24. See Louis Carrogis, known as Carmontelle, *Jardin de Monceau, Près de Paris* (Paris: Delafosse, 1779), 8.

25. The cottage in question, fitted out with elegant furniture from Paris, was situated in the woods at Étupes, an estate belonging to the family of the baronne d'Oberkirch's childhood friend, Princess Dorothée de Wurtemberg, the future Maria Feodorovna, Empress of Russia. The baronne stayed overnight in the cottage when a teenager. See Oberkirch, *Mémoires*, 48–49.

26. Charles-Joseph, prince de Ligne, *Coup d'œil sur Belœil*, second edition (1786), 125: "Je ne lui trouve pourtant pas assez l'air d'une citation. A force d'être naturel, il fait regretter d'abord qu'on ne l'ait point abattu." The abbé de Lubersac de Livron complained, similarly, that the Ruined Castle in the Jardin de Monceau had "un peu trop l'air d'un bien depuis long-temps en décret, & dont le propriétaire fuit les Créanciers & les Sergens" (a bit too much of the air of a property renounced for a long time and the proprietor of which is fleeing creditors and police). See C.-F. de Lubersac de Livron, "Monumens qui se trouve dans les Jardins de Plaisance du Baron de Cobham, près de Londres, & ceux de M. le duc de Chartres, à la Barrière de Monceaux, près de Paris," in *Discours sur les momumens publics de tous les âges et de tous les peuples connus* (Paris: De l'Imprimerie royale, 1775), lviii–lix.

27. Carmontelle expressed a similar attitude when explaining the artificial Farm he designed for the Jardin de Monceau. See Carmontelle, *Jardin de Monceau*, 5. "Nous ne saurions nous amuser des soins d'une ferme; c'est une multiplicité d'occupations, qui ne laisse aucun loisir, & ces détails de la vie rurale s'accordent mal avec nos goûts, pour la société, les plaisirs & la dissipation; on en aime plus la description que la pratique." See also David L. Hays, "'This is not a *jardin anglais*': Carmontelle, the Jardin de Monceau, and Irregular Garden Design in Eighteenth-Century France," in *Villas and Gardens in Early Modern Italy and France*, ed. Mirka Beneš and Dianne Harris (New York: Cambridge University Press), 294–326, 408–19, 304.

28. Wiebenson, *Picturesque Garden*, 3.

29. De Lorme, *Garden Pavilions*, 222. See also Broglie, *Chantilly*, 96. "Inspiré par l'anglomanie, les descriptions de la *Nouvelle Héloïse* et les tableaux de Greuze, le prince de Condé, lassé par l'ordonnance de ses jardins et le protocole de la cour, rêvait de nature sauvage et des mœurs simples des paysans que les écrivains de son temps lui représentaient comme idylliques."

30. The reputation of Chantilly as a destination for elite travelers was noted in contemporary guidebooks. See Dulaure, *Nouvelle description*, 1:84–85. "Presque tous les Princes de l'Europe sont venus admirer Chantilly. Dans un court espace de temps, ce beau lieu a été visité par le Roi de Danemarck, le Grand Duc de Russie, le Roi de Suède, le Prince Henri de Prusse, &c. Chaque fête que le Prince de Condé a donnée à ces illustres Voyageurs, a laissé une époque de sa magnificence, comme chacun de ses voyages laisse de nouveaux témoignages de sa bienfaisance." See also Thièry, *Guide des amateurs*, 226–27.

31. Oberkirch, *Mémoires*, 209: "Il y a deux espèces de convives: ceux du dîner et ceux

du souper; ceux du dîner sont souvent, presque toujours (quand ce ne sont pas des amis), des personnes sérieuses, âgées, des obligations, des ennuyeux même; on dîne facilement en ville, pour peu qu'on ait une société un peu étendue. Mais le souper, c'est différent; il faut des qualités très-difficiles à réunir, dont la plus indispensable est l'esprit. Sans esprit, sans élégance, sans la science du monde, des anecdotes, des mille riens qui composent les nouvelles, il ne faut pas songer à être admis dans ces réunions pleins de charmes. Là seulement on cause: on cause sur les propos les plus légers, par conséquent les plus difficiles à soutenir; c'est une véritable mousse qui s'évapore et qui ne laisse rien après elle; mais dont la saveur est pleine d'agrément. Une fois qu'on en a goûté, le reste paraît fade et sans aucun goût. Madame la comtesse du Nord m'a écrit bien des fois que ce qu'elle regrettait le plus de Paris, c'était l'esprit. Tous les étrangers intelligents disent de même."

32. Louis Badré, *Histoire de la forêt française* (Paris: Arthaud, 1983), 98.

33. Ibid., 31–33, 37–99.

34. Ibid., 68.

35. Ibid., 66: Commoners also had *droits d'usage* to many woods owned by nobles and the church.

36. See Philippe Salvadori, *La chasse sous l'ancien régime* (Paris: Fayard, 1996), chap. 1: "Un privilège," 15–36; Badré, *Histoire*, 28.

37. See Jacques Hillairet, *Les villages*, vol. 3. of *Connaissance du Vieux Paris* (Paris: Éditions Gonthier, 1954), 117; Y. Cazenave de la Roche, *La Vénerie royale et le régime des capitaineries au XVIIIe siècle* (Nîmes: J. Courrouy, 1926), 127. Louis XIV lifted the death penalty in 1669, for which he was considered merciful.

38. P.-F. Pihan de la Forest, ed., *Esprit des coutumes du bailliage de Senlis; et les textes tant de la première compilation de ces coutumes & des ordonnances du bailliage de Senlis, faites en 1493; que des rédaction de 1506, & réformation de 1539, conférées ensemble; avec des notes élémentaires qui déterminent le sens des articles & des mots obscurs* (Paris: Butard, rue Saint Jacques, à la Vérité, 1771), 1: "La coutume de Senlis n'admet pas de serfs; elle ne connoît que deux classes d'hommes, les nobles & les roturiers. Elle distingue ceux-là par nombre de privileges qu'elle refuse à ceux-ci."

39. See, especially, Musée Condé, Chantilly; Musée de la vénerie, Senlis; Musée de la chasse et de la nature, Paris, *Chasse à courre, chasse de cour: Fastes de la vénerie princière à Chantilly au temps des Condés et des Orléans, 1659–1910* (Tournai, France: Renaissance du livre, 2004).

40. Salvadori, *La chasse sous l'ancien régime*, 166. Source for quote not cited: "il aimait beaucoup la chasse et se livrait fort souvent à ce genre d'exercice, mais pourtant avec modération: la chasse à courre était celle qu'il préférait, et il aimait surtout à faire jouir les dames de ce plaisir. Elles suivaient la chasse en calèche; dans la forêt de Chantilly étaient plusieurs rendez-vous de chasses où l'on déjeunait quelquefois sur des tables de pierre."

41. Jean-François Perdrix (ca. 1746–1809) was hired by the prince de Condé in 1764. According to Macon, *Arts*, 92–94, four paintings by Perdrix were among the collections at

Chantilly until the Revolution. See also Benedicte Ottinger, *Tableaux de chasse: peintures du musée de Vénerie* (Paris: Somogy; Senlis: Musées de Senlis, 2001), 88. An account of a dramatic hunt at Chantilly held during the visit of the comte du Nord, and of Le Paon's work on-site to capture the hallali in a drawing, is reported in Dulaure, *Nouvelle description*, 1:84n1. "Le Grand Duc de Russie n'avoit jamais vu de chasse au cerf dans ses voyage [*sic*]; il étoit sur le point de partir sans jouir de ce divertissement, & il ne lui restoit que peu de temps. Au bout d'une heure tous les apprêts furent faits. On ne tarda pas à rencontrer le cerf; il enfile une allée qui aboutit à la grille du vertugadin de Chantilly, de là court dans le parc: M. le Duc de Bourbon le suit & le force à se jeter dans le canal. Les chiens l'assaillent, la multitude l'effraye; le canal est bientôt entouré d'une foule de curieux de tous états, de toutes couleurs. Les eaux, réfléchissant tant d'objets mouvans & variées, offrent le plus beau cadre & le plus curieux des tableaux. Dans les transports de la joie la plus vive, on entendit le Grand Duc d'écrier à plusieurs reprises: *Ah, mon Dieu, le beau tableau!* M. *le Paon*, Peintre de bataille, saisit rapidement le bel instant de cette scène, & l'a rendu avec le plus grand succès dans un tableau destiné au Grand Duc de Russie, & qu'on a vu quelque temps au Salon de la Correspondance, exposé à l'admiration des connoisseurs." See also Babelon, *Chantilly*, 148–49. For a brief glossary of French hunting terms, see Ottinger, *Tableaux de chasse*, 106. For more substantial lexicons, see Jean Baptiste Claude Izouard, called Delisle de Sales, *Dictionnaire theorique et pratique de chasse et de pêche*, 2 vols. (Paris: J.B.G. Musier Fils, 1769); and Pierre-Louis Duchartre, *Dictionnaire analogique de la chasse historique contemporaine* (Paris: Chêne, 1973).

42. Philippe-Jacques de Loutherbourg's *Rendez-vous de chasse du cerf à la Table* (1765) was displayed on the chimneypiece in the billiards room at the château de Chantilly. See Dulaure, *Nouvelle description*, 1:65, and Mérigot, *Promenades*, 20. See also Macon, *Arts*, 92. La Table was laid out in 1669–1670 under the direction of André Le Nôtre. See Gustave Macon, *Historique du domaine forestier de Chantilly*, 2 vols. (Senlis: E. Dufresne, 1905–1906), 119; Dulaure, *Nouvelle description*, 1:62; and Mérigot, *Promenades*, 60.

43. The image commemorated a banquet hosted by the prince de Conti in honor of the prince of Brunswick-Lünebourg.

44. Le Camus de Mézieres, *Description des eaux de Chantilly*, 77: "elle forme une halte qu'on croiroit être celle de Diane, lorsqu'au rendez-vous de chasse elle rassemble les différentes Nymphes invitées à partager ses plaisirs."

45. Dulaure, *Nouvelle description*, 1:81: "halte ou rendez-vous de chasse"; Mérigot, *Promenades*, 36: "rappelle un rendez-vous de chasse." See also Macon, *Arts*, 113.

46. De Lorme, *Garden Pavilions*, 224.

47. Oberkirch, *Mémoires*, 350: "Le 19 [i.e., 19 June 1784], nous fûmes conduits, toujours en calèche, et par un temps commandé exprès, au charmant hameau; le déjeuner nous y attendait dans la grande chaumière. Jamais je n'ai mangé d'aussi bonne crème, aussi appétissante et aussi bien apprêtée."

48. Broglie, "Le Hameau," 315, citing Toudouze, "Journal des Chasses," 1:351 [N.B., in copy at the Musée Condé, Chantilly, this is II, 578]; "le 20 juillet [i.e., 1784], le roi de Suède

Gustave III arriva vers les 5 heures du soir à Chantilly; il se rendit tout de suite au Théâtre, à l'Ile d'Amour, au Hameau où il mangea de la crème [. . .]."

49. Pierre Laujon, "Fête donnée par un père à sa fille, le 3 juin 1777 / Fête villageoise donnée dans un hameau, pour la reception de Mademoiselle, à Chantilly, en 1777," in *Œuvres choisies*, 4 vols. (Paris: C.-F. Patris, 1811), 4:13–70.

50. For example, M. d'Auteuil, a *gentilhomme* and member of the prince de Condé's "chambre de noblesse," sang with the "bergers" (i.e., the garçons cabaretiers) in the scene called "Le Cabaret" in Laujon's fête. See Broglie, Chantilly, 99, citing Toudouze, "Journal des Chasses," 1:928.

51. These diversions were counterparts to performances by real locals that took place at Chantilly on festival days. See, for example, Mérigot, *Promenades*, 5: "Derrière le jeu de paume est un quinconce où, les jours de fête, la jeunesse du bourg s'assemble, forme plusieurs danses autour d'un petit orchestre, et présente, à côté de tant de monumens de l'opulence, un tableau simple, riant, et champêtre." Unlike the practices of class blurring through vestimentary exchange associated with masked balls and *fêtes champêtres* earlier in the century, the parodic performances in Laujon's "Fête Villageoise" reinforced class distinction. On the earlier practices, see, for example, Amy Wyngaard, "Switching Codes: Class, Clothing, and Cultural Change in the Works of Marivaux and Watteau," *Eighteenth-Century Studies* 33, no. 4 (2000): 523–41.

52. Laujon, *Œuvres choisies*, 4:15: "Je n'ay jamais si ben senti, qu'au moment où c'que j'ons l'honneur de voir Mamselle, le bonheur que j'ay d'être le fils de ma chère mère, madame Louvet, dont même alle est la concierge du hameau, où c'que vous v'là, et que moi qui z'ai que l'honneur de vous en ouvrir la porte"; "Je m'appelle Nicodême Louvet, ou Nicodême tout seul, parce que c'est pas asie à r'tanir."

53. Ibid., 24: "I.er Gondolier: Si Mam'selle veut nous faire l'amiquié de monter dans nos gondoles avec sa compagnie? je vous épargnerons la fatigue de chemin; je n'aurons jamais eu tant de plaisir à l'ouvrage, et je ramerons d'eune fière magnière."

54. Ibid., 28. The key to bringing Nostradamus back from the dead was the princesses's own enunciation of the command "Paraissez!"

55. Ibid., 30: "En les [i.e., the stars Castor and Pollux, where Nostradamus was then residing] quittant pour être un instant avec vous, Je n'ai pas cru changer d'asiles."

56. Laujon, *Œuvres choisies*, 4:59. In the first line, the extra "a" in *sæcula* is a rhythmic supplement. The Father and Son refer, audaciously, to the prince de Condé and his son, the duc de Bourbon.

57. Ibid., 60: "Puisse, Son Altesse Mademoiselle, agréer ces fleurs / Comme des hommages qui prouvent la satisfaction que sa vue donne à tous les cœurs! / Quel bonheur si nous pouvions lire dans ses yeux, / Qui sont si doux, si brillans et si gracieux, / Que le Dieu du plaisir qu'on voit, ici comme ailleurs, sur ses pas, / N'en brille pas moins à travers ce galimatias!"

58. Ibid., 63: "c'est la métamorphose d'une chaumière en salon."

59. Ibid., 45: "Mam'selle voit bian que v'là une chaumière? et bian, par la vartu de la sorcellerie de la bohémienne, j'allons la changer en forest."

60. Ibid.

61. Ibid., 47–48. This aria of Céphale was undoubtedly that of Act I, Scene II, André-Ernest-Modeste Grétry's *Céphale et Procris* (1773). Laujon and Grétry collaborated on *Matroco*, a "drame burlesque" staged at the French court in 1777 and in Paris in 1778. See Yves Lenoir, ed., *Documents Grétry dans les collections de la Bibliothèque Royale Albert Ier* (Bruxelles: Bibliothèque Royale Albert Ier, 1989), 87, entries 25, 26, and 27.

62. Cazenave de la Roche, *La Vénerie royale*, 25, citing Jean-Baptiste-Jacques Le Verrier de la Conterie, *Vénerie normande, ou l'École de la chasse aux chiens courants* (Rouen: L. Dumesnil, 1778), 9 et suiv.

63. Cazenave de la Roche, 25.

64. Ibid., 127.

65. See Ibid., 185–91. See also the "Carte de la Capitainerie royale d'Halatte, ses environs, et de la seigneurie de Chantilly" (18C) [Archives Nationales de France, Cartes et Plans: N III Seine 56], reprinted in Babelon, *Chantilly*, 18.

66. Ibid., 108.

67. Mérigot, *Promenades*, 3: "Enfin, en 1661, le roi donna Chantilly en toute propriété au même prince de *Condé*, et y établit, en 1675, la capitainerie des chasses de la forêt de Hallate, qui avoit été supprimée en 1645: depuis ce temps la maison de Condé en a toujours joui." See also Cazenave de la Roche, *La Vénerie royale*, 186.

68. See, for example, Cazenave de la Roche, 153.

69. Ibid., 130, with reference to Archives Nationales, Paris, O1 1035 56 to 274: "Demandes d'autorisation de construire."

70. See Y. Gaultier, *La Capitainerie royale des chasses de la Varenne du Louvre* (Paris: Grande Vénerie de France, 1959), 58.

71. Arthur Young, *Travels in France and Italy during the years 1787, 1788 and 1789* (London: 1942), sv "25 May 1787."

72. This measurement is based on the "Carte de la Capitainerie royale d'Halatte, ses environs, et de la seigneurie de Chantilly" (18C). Dulaure's *Nouvelle Description* 1:62 indicated that the forest of Chantilly covered 7,600 arpents (about ten square miles). That figure would have been available to Young, but he either ignored or misunderstood it. He may have amalgamated the forest of Chantilly with other forests in the vicinity. Mérigot repeated the 7,600-arpent figure in *Promenades*, 59.

73. See Gustave Macon's magesterial *Historique du domaine forestier de Chantilly*, 2 vols. (Senlis: Eugène Dufresne, 1905–1906), vol. 1 (1905): "Forêts de Chantilly et de Pontarmé"; vol. 2 (1906): "Forêts de Coye, Luzarches, Chaumontel et Bonés." See also Babelon, *Chantilly*, 19–20, 22, 24–25, 27, 29–30, 32, 65, 67, 72, and 150.

74. See Macon, *Historique*, 38–39, 47–62, 136, and plan "Forêt de Chantilly." Because land ownership and fiscal rights over woodland (*gruerie*) were separate legal conditions, the prince de Condé was able to exert control over some regional tracts not in his possession, including the one belonging to Saint-Nicolas d'Acy. See Macon, *Historique*, 62.

75. Robert Pogue Harrison, *Forests: The Shadow of Civilization* (Chicago: University of Chicago Press, 1992), 108.

76. See Macon, *Historique*, 123–34.

77. Badré, *Histoire*, 96. "Dans un rapport au roi en 1770, il est indiqué que 358 282 arpents ont été défrichés. Quelques années plus tard, Necker déclare que, de 1766 à 1780, il a été accordé des autorisations de déricher portant sur 950 000 arpents, plus de 476 000 hectares, chiffre qui devait être sensiblement supérieur, l'autorisation n'ayant certainement pas été sollicitée avant chaque défrichement."

78. Harrison, *Forests*, 121, 114, 121.

79. See, for example, Emmanuel, duc de Cröy, *Journal inédit du duc de Cröy 1718–1784, publié d'après le manuscrit autographe conservé à la Bibliothèque de l'Institut*, 4 vols. (Paris: Ernest Flammarion, 1906), 4:130 (June 18, 1778): "Ce hameau devenait fort fameux et tout le monde voulait le copier" (This hamlet became very famous and everybody wanted to copy it); Malo, *Visit to Chantilly*, 46: "The Hamlet of Chantilly was a precursor of the one in the *Petit Trianon*"; Wiebenson, *Picturesque Garden*, 100: "It would become, as the Prince de Cröy observed in 1778, a model for all later hamlets."

80. The buildings conformed in various ways to positive aspects of "architecture champêtre" and "architecture naïve" as defined by Jacques-François Blondel (1705–1774), professor of the French Academy of Architecture from 1762 until his death in 1774. See Jacques-François Blondel, *Cours d'architecture, ou Traité de la décoration, distribution, & construction des Bâtiments; contenant les leçons données en 1750, & les années suivantes, par J. F. Blondel, Architecte, dans son École des Arts*, 12 vols. (Paris: Desaint, 1771–1773, 1777): 1 (1771): 417–19. Nevertheless, the deliberate discontinuities between exteriors and interiors violated a principle of architecture highly prized by Blondel, who believed that classical French architecture surpassed that of the ancient Greeks and Romans specifically through a new "initimacy" between exteriors and interiors. See Werner Szambien, *Symétrie, Goût, Caractère: Théorie et terminologie de l'architecture à l'âge classique, 1550–1800* (Paris: Picard, 1986), 49, 108.

81. The association of woodland imagery and rustic cabin form in the dining hall evokes the theory of the "Primitive Hut" described by Marc-Antoine Laugier in his *Essai sur l'architecture* (1753; rev. ed. 1755).

82. This conceit is also exemplified in Vivant Denon's *Point de lendemain* (1777; 1812), the narrative of which culminates in a room decorated to appear as if a bosquet floating in a void, with a grotto on one side and a carpet plucked to resemble grass. See Gallimard "Folio Classique" edition (1995), 58–59 (1812) and 94–95 (1777).

83. See Emil Kaufmann, *Three Revolutionary Architects: Boullée, Ledoux, and Lequeu* (Philadelphia: American Philosophical Society, 1952); Emil Kaufmann, *Architecture in the Age of Reason* (New York: Dover, 1968), 160–66; Emil Kaufmann, *Visionary Architects: Boullée, Ledoux, Lequeu* (Houston: University of St. Thomas, 1968); Monique Mosser, "Le temple et la montagne: généalogie d'un décor de fête révolutionnaire," *Revue de l'Art* 1 (1989): 21–35; James A. Leith, *Space and Revolution: Projects for Monuments, Squares, and Public Buildings*

in France, 1789–1799 (Montreal: McGill-Queen's University Press, 1991), especially 22–25, 222–25. The dining hall also merits comparison with an elaborate project by the Polish architect Szymon Bogumil Zug for the basement of a palace in Warsaw (1775–1777). See Monique Mosser, "Paradox in the Garden: A Brief Account of *Fabriques*," in *The Architecture of Western Gardens: A Design History from the Renaissance to the Present Day*, ed. Monique Mosser and Georges Teyssot (Cambridge, Mass.: The MIT Press, 1990), 262–80, especially 269–73.

84. Concerning the conception of space in modern architecture and its debt to French garden design, see Silvia Lavin, "Sacrifice and the Garden: Watelet's *Essai sur les jardins* and the Space of the Picturesque," *Assemblage* 28 (1996): 16–33, especially 19: "while the invention of the idea of space as a fundamental element of design is often credited to and claimed by modern architecture, it may well have its sources in the French picturesque garden"; and 28, where Lavin describes Le Corbusier's desire to control exterior space in terms that strongly evoke the specific picture-as-space strategy employed in the dining hall at Chantilly: "When Le Corbusier maintains that the horizon defines a penetrable space of sensual pleasure he directly recalls the French eighteenth-century garden. But more significant is his belief that the extensive fluidity of this exterior constitutes a danger that must be brought under control. This control is asserted precisely by bringing the outside to the inside, by locating the space of the picturesque in a domestic interior."

Chapter 9: Sites of Power and the Power of Sight

The research presented here was made possible by the generous support of a Huntington Library Fellowship and research support from the Center for Advanced Study in the Visual Arts, National Gallery of Art. I have also benefited greatly from the expertise and helpful assistance of librarians and archivists at repositories throughout California including The Huntington Library, Mission San Juan Capistrano, Santa Barbara Mission Archives, the Southwest Museum, California State Library, the Bancroft Library at University of California, Berkeley, California Historical Society, Historic American Buildings Survey, the National Gallery of Art, the Smithsonian Library, and the Library of Congress.

1. "Mission Construction Described by Father O'Sullivan: Priest Gives Life to Work at Capistrano," *Santa Ana Register*, June 13, 1929.

2. Barbara Bender, "Introduction," in *Contested Landscapes: Movement, Exile, Place*, ed. Barbara Bender and Margot Winder (Oxford: Berg, 2001), 4.

3. For example, phenomenological approaches such as Christopher Tilley, *A Phenomenology of Landscape: Places, Paths and Monuments* (Oxford: Berg, 1994) or structuralist approaches such as André Leroi-Gourhan, *Préhistoire de l'Art Occidental* (Paris: Éditions d'art L. Mazenod, 1965), translated as *Treasures of Prehistoric Art* (New York: H. N. Abrams, 1967); and J. David Lewis-Williams, *Believing and Seeing: Symbolic Meanings in Southern San Rock Paintings* (London: Academic Press, 1981).

4. More generally this model draws on structural linguistics and notions of *langue* and

parole. Ferdinand de Saussure, *Course in General Linguistics,* ed. Charles Bally and Albert Sechehaye, trans. Wade Baskin (New York: The Philosophical Library, 1959). The debates about the broad applicability of the Sapir-Whorf hypothesis, specifically its notion of Linguistic Determinism (language determines thought) and Linguistic Relativity (difference in language equals difference in thought), constitute a literature in themselves, but the parallel with the cultural construction of vision is a cogent theoretical model, I argue, for understanding past landscapes. See Benjamin Lee Worf, "Science and Linguistics," *Technology Review* 42, no. 6 (1940): 229–31, 247–48; Edward Sapir, "The Status of Linguistics as a Science" (1929), in *Culture, Language and Personality,* ed. D. G. Mandelbaum (Berkeley: University of California Press, 1958).

5. William F. Shipley, "Native Languages of California," in *California: Handbook of North American Indians,* vol. 8, vol. ed. Robert F. Heizer, gen. ed. William C. Sturtevant (Washington, D.C.: Smithsonian Institution, 1978), 80.

6. For an overview of California archaeology and prehistory see Joseph L. Chartkoff and Kerry Kona Chartkoff, *The Archaeology of California* (Stanford: Stanford University Press, 1984); and *California: Handbook of North American Indians,* vol. 8, vol. ed. Robert F. Heizer, gen. ed. William C. Sturtevant (Washington, D.C.: Smithsonian Institution, 1978).

7. Mary Forsell, "Gardens of the Spirit," *Garden Design* 11, no. 4 (July–August, 1991): 29–31; Nancy Powers, *The Gardens of California: Four Centuries of Design from Mission to Modern* (Santa Monica: Hennessey and Ingalls, 2001); David Streatfield, *California Gardens: Creating a New Eden* (New York: Abbeville Press, 1994).

8. Technically, San Antonio de Pala is an *asistencia* or sub-mission, but is included here because it is located on a current Native American Indian reservation and presents a unique and valuable expression of the ongoing multivalence of the missions.

9. Thomas C. Blackburn, ed., *December's Child: A Book of Chumash Oral Narratives, Collected by J. P. Harrington* (Berkeley: University of California Press, 1975), 91.

10. Father Juan Crespi, translated by Alan Brown and quoted in Jan Timbrook, John R. Johnson, and David D. Earle, "Vegetation Burning by the Chumash," *Journal of California and Great Basin Anthropology* 4, no.2 (1982): 166.

11. Blackburn, 72, quote 66.

12. For a review of Franciscan thought informing the California missionaries, see Michael J. González, "'The Child of the Wilderness Weeps for the Father of Our Country': The Indian and the Politics of Church and State in Provincial California," in *Contested Eden: California Before the Gold Rush,* ed. Ramón A. Gutiérrez and Richard J. Orsi (Berkeley: University of California Press, 1998), 147–72, esp. 153–59.

13. Historian David J. Weber has characterized these celebratory accounts as "Christophalic Triumphalism," in "Blood of Martyrs, Blood of Indians: Toward a More Balanced View of Spanish Missions in Seventeenth Century North America," in *Columbian Consequences,* vol. 2, *Archaeological and Historical Perspectives on the Spanish Borderlands East,* ed. David Hurst Thomas (Washington D.C.: Smithsonian Institution Press, 1990), 428–48.

14. The terms Native American and Indian are used interchangeably and, where relevant, historical terms such as neophyte are also referenced with the acknowledgment of the constructions and problematics implied by each term.

15. Marking property lines and establishing of dedicated use areas (pasturage or agricultural) has long been an aspect of colonizing new territory. For a detailed study of practices in southern New England see William Cronon, *Changes in the Land: Indians, Colonists, and the Ecology of New England* (New York: Hill and Wang, 1983). For a more in-depth view of the missions' place in the mercantile economy of Alta California see Steven W. Hackel, "Land, Labor, and Production: The Colonial Economy of Spanish and Mexican California," in *Contested Eden: California Before the Gold Rush*, ed. Ramón A. Gutiérrez and Richard J. Orsi (Berkeley: University of California Press, 1998), 111–46.

16. The active management of the environment has been richly documented in numerous recent studies. See T. C. Blackburn and K. Anderson, eds., *Before the Wilderness: Environmental Management by Native Californians* (Menlo Park, Calif.: Ballena Press, 1993); M. Kat Anderson, Michael G. Barbour, and Valerie Whitworth, "A World of Balance and Plenty: Land, Plants, Animals, and Humans in a Pre-European California," in *Contested Eden: California Before the Gold Rush*, ed. Ramón A. Gutiérrez and Richard J. Orsi (Berkeley: University of California Press, 1998), 12–47.

17. James A. Sandos, "Music and Conversion," in *Converting California: Indians and Franciscans in the Missions* (New Haven: Yale University Press, 2004), 128–53.

18. Michel Foucault, *Discipline and Punish: The Birth of the Prison*, trans. Alan Sheridan (New York: Vintage Books, 1979), 135–230.

19. Jean François de Galaup, Comte de la Pérouse, "A Visit to Monterey in 1786, and a Description of the Indians of California," *California Historical Society Quarterly* 15, no. 3 (1936): 220.

20. John R. Stilgoe, *Common Landscape of America, 1580 to 1845* (New Haven: Yale University Press, 1982), 12–21.

21. Robert F. Heizer and Albert B. Elsasser, "World View of California Indians," in *The Natural World of the California Indians* (Berkeley: University of California Press, 1980), 202–20.

22. Alfred Robinson, *Life in California During a Residence of Several Years in that Territory . . .* (New York: Wiley and Putnam, 1846; repr., New York: Da Capo Press, 1969), 59 (description from visit in 1829).

23. Mark P. Leone, "Rule by Ostentation: the Relationship between Space and Sight in Eighteenth-Century Landscape Architecture in the Chesapeake Region of Maryland," in *Method and Theory for Activity Area Research: An Ethnoarchaeological Approach*, ed. Susan Kent (New York: Columbia University Press, 1987), 604–33.

24. Julia G. Costello, *Santa Inés Excavations: 1986–1988* (Salinas, Calif.: Coyote Press, 1989), 89.

25. James C. Scott, *Domination and the Arts of Resistance: Hidden Transcripts* (New

Haven: Yale University Press, 1990). James Sandos also draws on Scott's model to assess Indian resistance to missionization, although he does not explore the significance of landscape in that contest of power. See James A. Sandos, "Indian Resistance to Missionization," in *Converting California: Indians and Franciscans in the Missions* (New Haven: Yale University Press, 2004), 154–73.

26. Foucault, *Discipline and Punish*, 219.

27. Timbrook, Johnson, and Earle, "Vegetation Burning by the Chumash," 163–186.

28. Hackel, "Land, Labor, and Production," 124–28; Edward D. Castillo, "Neophyte Resistance and Accommodation in the Missions of California," in *The Spanish Missionary Heritage of the United States: Selected Papers and Commentaries from the November 1990 Quincentenary Symposium*, ed. Howard Benoist and Sr. María Carolina Flores (San Antonio: National Parks Service, 1993), 60–75; James A. Sandos, "Neophyte Resistance in the Alta California Missions," in *Columbus, Confrontation, Christianity: The European-American Encounter Revisited*, ed. Timothy J. O'Keefe (Palo Alto: Forbes Mill Press, 1994), 170–78.

29. "Diseño for Rancho San Miguelito," in Julia G. Costello, *The Ranches and Ranchos of Mission San Antonio de Padua* (California Mission Studies Association, Keepsake Volume, December 1994), 9.

30. For example, deer and marine resources (fish and shellfish) have been excavated at Santa Inés. Phillip L. Walker and Katherine D. Davidson, "Analysis of Faunal Remains from Santa Inés Mission," in *Santa Inés Excavations: 1986–1988* (Salinas, Calif.: Coyote Press, 1989), 162–76.

31. Julia G. Costello and David Hornbeck, "Alta California: an Overview" in *Columbian Consequences, Vol. 1, Archaeological and Historical Perspectives on the Spanish Borderlands West*, ed. David Hurst Thomas (Washington, D.C.: Smithsonian Institution Press, 1989), 303–31; Daniel O. Larson, John R. Johnson, and Joel C. Michaelsen, "Missionization Among the Coastal Chumash of Central California: A Study in Risk Minimization Strategies," *American Anthropologist* 96, no.2 (1994): 263–99.

32. Georgia Lee and Norman Neuerburg, "The Alta California Indians as Artists Before and After Contact," in *Columbian Consequences, vol. 1: Archaeological and Historical Perspectives on the Spanish Borderlands West*, ed. David Hurst Thomas (Washington, D.C.: Smithsonian Institution Press, 1991), 467–80; Norman Neuerburg, "Indian Pictographs at Mission San Juan Capistrano," *Masterkey* 56, no.2 (1982):55–58; Norman Neuerburg, *The Decoration of the California Missions* (Santa Barbara: Bellerophon Books, 1991).

33. For a review of resistance manifested in the decorative programs of the missions churches, see James A. Sandos, "Between Crucifix and Lance: Indian-White Relations in California, 1769–1848," in *Contested Eden: California Before the Gold Rush*, ed. Ramón A. Gutiérrez and Richard J. Orsi (Berkeley: University of California Press, 1998), 207–9.

34. Foucault, *Discipline and Punish*, 215–22.

35. Jean François de Galaup, Comte de la Pérouse, *The First French Expedition to California: Laperouse in 1786*, trans. Charles N. Rudkin (Los Angeles: G. Dawson, 1959), reprinted

in Francis J. Weber, *Prominent Visitors to the California Missions, 1786–1842* (Los Angeles: Dawson's Book Shop, 1991), 15.

36. Hackel argues that the appointment of *alcaldes* paralleled and built on the traditional leadership structure of the chiefdom ("Land, Labor, and Production," 211), but the context of mission leadership roles was divorced from other essential aspects of indigenous governance and social organization to the extent that I would argue the parallel is more a formal similarity than an expression of traditional power relations.

37. Antonia I. Casteñeda, "Engendering the History of Alta California, 1769–1848: Gender, Sexuality, and the Family," in *Contested Eden: California Before the Gold Rush*, ed. Ramón A. Gutiérrez and Richard J. Orsi (Berkeley: University of California Press, 1998), 232.

38. Casteñeda, "Engendering the History," 230–59.

39. Anna Caroline Field, "A Southwest Sleepy Hollow," *Land of Sunshine* 15 (1901): 126–38; Eleanor Gates, "Motoring Among the Missions: A Real Joy Ride Through the Cathedral Towns of California," *Sunset* 28, no. 3 (1912): 305–14.

40. Charles Irwin Douglas Moore, *In the Footsteps of the Padres* (Los Angeles: The Pacific Mutual Life Insurance Company of California, 1930), 6.

41. Maude Robson Gunthorp, *With a Sketch Book Along the Old Mission Trail* (Caldwell, Idaho: The Caxton Printers, 1940), 34.

42. Gunthorp, *With a Sketch Book*, 13.

43. Henry Oak, *A Visit to the Missions of Southern California in February and March, 1874*, ed. Ruth Frey Axe, Edwin H. Carpenter, and Norman Neuerburg (Los Angeles: Southwest Museum, 1981), 21.

44. William Henry Hudson, *The Famous Missions of California with Sketches in Color* (New York: Dodge Publishing Co., 1901), quoted in Mary Pius Carroll, "The Influence of the Missions on Present-day California" (Newman Prize essay, University of California, Berkeley, 1915, mss. on file, Bancroft Library), 11–12.

45. For a comprehensive treatment of Watkins, see Peter E. Palmquist, *Carleton E. Watkins: Photographer of the American West* (Albuquerque: University of New Mexico Press for the Amon Carter Museum, 1983).

46. Enola Flower, *A Child's History of California* (Sacramento: California State Department of Education, 1949), 55.

47. Tim Edensor, *Tourists at the Taj: Performance and Meaning at a Symbolic Site* (London: Routledge, 1998).

48. Other representations are even more marginalized. Visiting Mission San Juan Capistrano in 1993 I encountered a diorama tucked into a small passageway off the main corridor of the courtyard with no labels or explanation. The scene inside the glass vitrine had all the inviting detail of a miniaturized world, with scale plants and trees evoking a lush, green forest (not a terribly accurate rendering of southern California hills), but even more striking was the pose of the inhabitants in this Edenic world—the native peoples with arms outstretched were clearly welcoming the arriving padres. The obscure location of the diorama was as intriguing

as the message was troubling—whether it was moved because of protests or whether it had stood there for years, I do not know, but it seems a telling symbol of the challenge of reinterpreting the romanticized spaces of the mission gardens, beloved and iconic spaces that cannot be just parked in a side hallway.

49. These observations were made during site visits in 1993–1997.

50. Arthur Byne and Mildred Stapley Byne, *Spanish Gardens and Patios* (New York: The Architectural Record, 1924).

51. These connections are touched on in Elizabeth de Forest, "Old Santa Barbara Gardens," in *The Pacific Horticulture Book of Western Gardens*, eds. George Walters and Nora Harlow (Boston: David R. Goodwin, in association with the Pacific Horticulture Foundation, 1990), 77–83.

52. The polemics of the contested histories are evident in titles such as Rupert Costo and Jeanette Henry Costo, eds., *The Missions of California: A Legacy of Genocide* (San Francisco: Indian History Press, 1987) and Daniel Fogel, *Junípero Serra, the Vatican, and Enslavement Theology* (San Francisco: ISM Press, 1988).

Chapter 10: Four Views, Three of Them through Glass

1. John Ruskin, *Sesame and Lilies* (New York: Wiley and Sons, 1866), 91, discussed in Clifford Edward Clark, *The American Family Home, 1800–1960* (Chapel Hill: University of North Carolina Press, 1986), 116; Herman Melville, "The Piazza," *The Piazza Tales* (New York: Dix, Edwards, and Co., 1856), 8; Reverend William G. Eliot Jr., *Lectures to Young Women* (Boston: Crosby, Nichols, 1854), cited in Kenneth Jackson, *Crabgrass Frontier: The Suburbanization of the United States* (New York: Oxford University Press, 1985), 48.

2. Andrew Jackson Downing, *Cottage Residences* (New York: Wiley and Sons, 1842), 56.

3. Henry Hudson Holly, *Holly's Picturesque Country Seats* (New York: Dover, 1993), 91–92, originally published as *Holly's Country Seats* (New York: D. Appleton and Co., 1863).

4. See "Plate-Glass Making," *American Architect and Building News*, September 17, 1887, 137; and Frank Handler, "History and Facts about the Development of the Sheet Glass Business," *Glass Digest* (September 1955).

5. Henry Hudson Holly, *Modern Dwellings in Town and Country* (New York: Harper and Bros., 1878), 22, 66–67, 204.

6. "Why architects object" is from Walter Shaw Sparrow, *Our Homes and How to Make the Best of Them* (London: Hodder and Stoughton, 1909), 70. Mr. Rogers's health is discussed in "Interesting Items," *Harpers' Weekly*, September 10, 1864, 579. On the "sense of coolness," see Edith Wharton and Ogden Codman Jr., *Decoration of Houses* (New York: Scribner's Sons, 1897), 66–67.

7. Ruby Ross Goodnow, *The Honest House* (New York: Century, 1914), 84, 89.

8. Russell Sturgis, *Dictionary of Architecture and Building* (New York: Macmillan, 1901–2), 1066. The English travel writer's comment is from James John Hissey, *The Charm of the*

Road (London, Macmillan, 1910), and cited in Robert Alexander Briggs, *The Essentials of a Country House* (London, New York: B. T. Batsford; Scribner's Sons, 1911), 54.

9. Caroline Klingensmith, "Seeing Out," *House Beautiful* 33 (April 1913): 158.

10. Briggs, *Essentials of a Country House*, 54.

11. Thorstein Veblen, *Theory of the Leisure Class* (New York: Augustus Kelley, 1970), 33–37.

12. See Sandy Isenstadt, "The Visual Commodification of Landscape in the Real Estate Appraisal Industry, 1900–1992," *Business and Economic History* 45 (Winter 1999): 60–69.

13. Frank Jessup Scott, *The Art of Beautifying Suburban Home Grounds of Small Extent* (New York: Appleton, 1870), 26–27, 214–17.

14. John Taylor Boyd Jr., "Some Principles of Small House Design. Part VII. Interiors," *Architectural Record* 47 (May 1920): 455.

15. See "House and Site United," *Construction Aid* 3, Housing and Home Finance Agency (1952), 20–22, and "The Emerging American Style," *House Beautiful* 92 (May 1950): 121–53.

16. "Marcel Breuer, Teacher and Architect," *House and Home* 1 (May 1952): 104; William Wilson Wurster, "When is a Small House Large?" *House and Garden* 92 (August 1947): 72–75.

17. The "large window" as "modern architecture's most important contribution to house design" is from George Nelson and Henry Wright, *Tomorrow's House: A Complete Guide for the Home-builder* (New York: Simon and Schuster, 1946), 34. "Dear to the heart" is from "The New House 194X . . ." *Architectural Forum* 77 (September 1942): 69. "Freed from the vertical" is from "Houses," *Architectural Forum* 89 (November 1948): 144.

18. "A Little House with a Western Look," *Architectural Record* 104 (September 1948): 104.

19. "40 Houses," *Architectural Forum* 88 (April 1948): 113.

20. Marcel Breuer quoted in "Houses," *Architectural Forum* 89 (November 1948): 147.

21. Marcel Breuer, *Sun and Shadow: The Philosophy of an Architect*, ed. Peter Blake (New York: Dodd, Mead, 1955), 113.

22. Compare modernism's rejection of character as described in Colin Rowe, "Character and Composition; or Some Vicissitudes of Architectural Vocabulary in the Nineteenth Century," in *The Mathematics of the Ideal Villa and Other Essays* (Cambridge, Mass.: MIT Press, 1976), 59–88.

23. Elizabeth Mack, *Tomorrow's Small House* (New York: Museum of Modern Art, 1945), 42.

24. Isenstadt, "Visual Commodification," 60–69.

25. See Isenstadt, "Visual Commodification."

26. Thomas Church, *Gardens Are for People* (New York: Reinhold Publishing Corp., 1955), 28; Thomas Hutchinson, *Here Is Television, Your Window on the World* (New York: Hastings House, 1946); Ray Faulkner, *Inside Today's Home* (New York: Henry Holt, 1954), 314.

27. "Television: Its Hypnotic Screen Will Change Our Approach to Designing Living

Rooms and Making Love," *Architectural Forum* 89 (September 1948): 118–20; Bruno Funaro, "Windows in Modern Architecture," *Windows and Glass in the Exterior of Buildings* (Washington, D.C.: National Research Council, 1957), 63–66; "Expanding the World of Your Living Room," *House Beautiful* (January 1953). See also See Cecelia Tichi, *Electronic Hearth: Creating an American Television Culture* (New York, 1991); Lynn Spigel, "Installing the Television Set: Popular Discourses on Television and Domestic Space, 1948–1955," in *Private Screenings. Television and the Female Consumer*, ed. Lynn Spigel and Denise Mann (Minneapolis: University of Minnesota Press, 1992), 3–38.

28. "Good Design for Production," *House and Home* 6 (September 1954): 104–42. "Visual recreation" is discussed in Samuel Paul, *The Complete Book of Home Modernizing* (New York: H. S. Stuttman, Co., 1953), 53. Paul suggests that, for convenience, the television may be placed inside the hearth, since the functions of the two devices had become one. On shifting focus, see Raymond McGrath and A. C. Frost, *Glass in Architecture and Decoration* (London: The Architectural Press, 1937), 154. Similarly, Colin Rowe observed a "peripheric principle" in modern architecture that replaced an inward focus with a centrifugal orientation, in Colin Rowe, "Neo-'Classicism' and Modern Architecture I" and "Neo-'Classicism' and Modern Architecture II," in *Mathematics of the Ideal Villa* (Cambridge, Mass.: MIT Press, 1976), 127–30, 143–44.

29. Richard Payne Knight, quoted in Gina Crandell, *Nature Pictorialized: "The View" in Landscape History* (Baltimore: The Johns Hopkins University Press, 1993), 136. See also Walter Hipple, *Beautiful, The Sublime, and The Picturesque in Eighteenth–Century British Aesthetic Theory* (Carbondale: Southern Illinois University Press, 1957), 232; Stephen Daniels "Humphry Repton and the Morality of Landscape," in *Valued Environments*, ed. John R. Gold and Jacqueline Burgess (London: Allen and Unwin, 1982), 124–44; Grant Kester, "The Faculty of Possession: Property and the Aesthetic in English Culture, 1730–1850" (PhD diss., University of Rochester, 1997), 248; and Humphry Repton, *Fragments on the Theory and Practice of Landscape Gardening* (London: J. Taylor, 1816), 154.

30. Sargent is cited in "Landscape Gardening," *North American Review* 91 (July 1860),

31. Burroughs is cited in Peter Schmitt, *Back to Nature* (Baltimore: The Johns Hopkins University Press, 1969), 25. Hooper's quote is from Charles Edward Hooper, *The Country House. A Practical Manual of the Planning and Construction of the American Country Home and its Surroundings* (Garden City, N.Y.: Doubleday, 1913), 104. Hooper appears to have taken this statement verbatim from an article by the similarly initialed E. C. Holtzoper, in *Country Life in America* 6 (October 1904): 511. Hopkins's quote is from Alfred Hopkins, *Planning for Sunshine and Fresh Air* (New York: Architectural Book Publishing, 1931), 36–39.

31. Asylum windows are discussed in Kenneth Blair Hawkins, "The Therapeutic Landscape: Nature, Architecture, and Mind in Nineteenth-Century America" (PhD dissertation, University of Rochester, 1991), 2, 103. Johanson's clients are cited in "New York House," *Architectural Record* 119 (May 1956): 111. "Restful comfort" is from "Glass Designed for Happiness," Libbey-Owens-Ford promotional brochure (1940).

32. Charles Greene is cited in "A New Appreciation of 'Greene and Greene,'" *Architec-

tural Record 103 (May 1948): 138. Compare Sigfried Giedion's linking of architectural motives and driving in *Space, Time, and Architecture* (Cambridge, Mass.: Harvard University Press, 1967), 826; Repton, *Fragments*, 107; Florence Taft Eaton, "Natural Environment in Landscape-Gardening," *House Beautiful* 49 (June 1921): 478–80, 512.

33. Carol Aronovici, *Housing the Masses* (New York: Wiley and Sons, 1939), 4; Carl Biemiller, "Garden Homes in the Golden Land," *Holiday* (September 1951): 104; "Nine Hillside Houses," *House and Home* 1 (April 1952): 82.

34. On the relation of suburbs to refrigerators, see Arthur Johnson, "Economy Since 1914," *Encyclopedia of American Economic History*, vol. 1 (New York: Scribner's Sons, 1980), 113; and Sandy Isenstadt, "Visions of Plenty: Refrigerator Design in America around 1950," *Journal of Design History* 11 (Autumn 1998): 311–21.

Chapter 11: Clean and Bright and Everyone White

I would like to thank Mirka Beneš, David Hays, D. Fairchild Ruggles, Sharon Irish, and David Roediger for their comments on early drafts of this chapter.

1. In my book on eighteenth-century Lombard villa culture, I discuss a "habit of perception" linked to the culture of the theater and its relationship to landscape reception and construction. See Dianne Harris, *The Nature of Authority: Villa Culture, Landscape, and Representation in 18th-Century Lombardy* (University Park: Pennsylvania State University Press, 2003). On the concept of a "period eye," see Michael Baxandall, *Painting and Experience in Fifteenth-Century Italy* (New York: Oxford University Press, 1972), sec. II.

2. Karen Brodkin, *How Jews Became White Folks and What That Says About Race in America* (New Jersey: Rutgers University Press, 2000), 21, and chap. 5.

3. "Florida Sheriff Calls White Family Black," *Ebony*, March 1955, 37; "Where Mixed Couples Live," *Ebony*, May 1955, 61.

4. Brodkin, *How Jews Became White Folks*, 50. For an excellent analysis of the federal government's role in the construction of racist housing and lending policies, see George Lipsitz, *The Possessive Investment in Whiteness: How White People Profit from Identity Politics* (Philadelphia: Temple University Press, 1998). See also Arnold R. Hirsch, "Containment on the Home Front: Race and Federal Housing Policy from the New Deal to the Cold War," *Journal of Urban History* 26 (January 2000): 158–89.

5. Arnold R. Hirsch, *Making the Second Ghetto: Race and Housing in Chicago, 1940–1960* (New York: Cambridge University Press, 1983), 55–60.

6. For a more complete bibliography on this topic, see Dianne Harris, "Race and Space," in *Towards a Discipline-Specific Bibliography of Critical Whiteness Studies*, ed. Tim Engles and David Roediger (Champaign, Illinois: Occasional Paper Series, Center on Democracy in a Multiracial Society, University of Illinois, 2004). Geographers, sociologists, and urban historians have made the greatest contributions so far to our understanding of the spatial dimensions of racism in the United States. Architectural and landscape historians are only be-

ginning to ask questions about the relationship between the construction of racial identities and the construction of the built environment.

7. In 1955 *House and Home*, a magazine that targeted builders, developers, and architects, began a monthly series of articles surveying the latest trends in a range of consumer and shelter magazines. As one author wrote, "*House and Home* feels that the consumer magazines are such an important barometer of what the home-buying public is going to want—and going to get—that we will, henceforth, publish a monthly pictorial review of what consumers are finding on their newsstands. We hope that this feature will help builders to gauge accurately the demand for better design that is being created throughout the U.S." See "Better Keep Your Eye on the Newsstands. . . Because Your Customers Do," *House and Home* (May 1955): 175. In addition to the forecasted 50 million monthly readers, the magazine noted that circulation figures represented a fraction of the actual readership since they estimated that each copy was read by five or six people (169). *House Beautiful* records provide some indication of the breadth of circulation, with 628,942 subscribers in 1955. By 1965, the number was close to one million subscribers annually. My thanks to Steve Chiarello at *House Beautiful* for furnishing this information.

8. Richard Dyer, *White* (London: Routledge, 1997), xiii.

9. See, for example, J. B. Harley, "Silences and Secrecy: The Hidden Agenda of Cartography in Early Modern Europe," *Imago Mundi* 40 (1988): 57–56; and Harris, *Nature of Authority*.

10. In fact, the architect's drawing has become a symbol of spatial exclusion. See David Sibley's description of a British documentary on a shopping mall in which he describes the consumers as "all apparently white, middle-class nuclear families, the kind of public which populates architects' sketches." David Sibley, *Geographies of Exclusion: Society and Difference in the West* (London: Routledge, 1995), xi. On the crafting of white settings, see Annie Gilbert Coleman, "The Unbearable Whiteness of Skiing," *Pacific Historical Review* 65 (November 1996): 584.

11. Coleman, "Unbearable Whiteness," 586.

12. Ibid., 589, 592.

13. On white dominance of the architectural profession, see Kathryn Anthony, *Designing for Diversity: Gender, Race, and Ethnicity in the Architecture Profession* (Urbana: University of Illinois Press, 2001).

14. "Push Button Home: Michigan Physician's Plush Estate Almost Runs by Itself," *Ebony*, November 1954, 42–48. By 1965, as Lynn Spigel has noted, *Ebony* addressed the housing segregation issue head-on with a feature that focused on a black military officer who could not obtain housing close to his work at a key missile site in the Midwest, forcing him to commute vast distances. According to Spigel, the article used "the example of the officer at the missile site to suggest that even if blacks could buy homes in suburbia they often did not want to live in the 'monotonous' white neighborhoods with 'look-a-like' houses and shopping malls." Spigel, *Welcome to the Dreamhouse: Popular Media and Postwar Suburbs* (Durham: Duke University Press, 2001), 156–57. See also Hamilton J. Bims, "Housing—the Hottest Issue in the

North," *Ebony*, August 1965, 93–100 (issue entitled "The White Problem in America"). Although Andrew Wiese contends that *Ebony* "ran regular features publicizing the housing and domestic lifestyles of the nation's black elite," he also notes that these features focused primarily on celebrities rather than housing for ordinary, middle class people. See Wiese, *Places of Their Own: African American Suburbanization in the Twentieth Century* (Chicago: University of Chicago Press, 2004), 148–49.

15. "A Message from the Publisher," *Ebony*, November 1945, 121.

16. See, for example, Wiese, *Places of Their Own*.

17. Recognizing the difficulty faced by laymen when confronted with architectural plans, *Popular Mechanics* published an article titled "How to Read a Blueprint," *Popular Mechanics*, October 1953, 154.

18. On the iconography of the bird's-eye view or aerial perspective, and on the relationship between perspective and aerial views and scopic knowledge, see David Harvey, *The Condition of Postmodernity* (Cambridge, Mass.: Blackwell, 1990); Michel de Certeau, *The Practice of Everyday Life*, trans. Steve Randall (Berkeley: University of California Press, 1984), 92–93; Louis Marin, *Portrait of the King*, trans. Martha M. Houle (Minneapolis: University of Minnesota Press, 1988); Lucia Nuti, "The Perspective Plan in the Sixteenth Century: The Invention of a Representational Language," *Art Bulletin* 76, no. 1 (March 1994): 128.

19. On "soft modernism" or "everyday modernism" see Marc Treib, ed., *An Everyday Modernism: The Houses of William Wurster* (Berkeley: University of California Press, 1995). That the FHA made it difficult or impossible to obtain their mortgages for nontraditional house forms is not a widely known fact. But architects' files clarify the point. For example, although the Los Angeles architect A. Quincy Jones published and sold designs for a modern house that could be affordably built, many of those who purchased his plans were unable to obtain FHA loans because the plans were considered too modern, untested, and therefore, a poor lending risk. A. Quincy Jones papers, "San Diego House" Files, courtesy Elaine Sewell Jones. Some of the documents pertaining to this project are in the correspondence file for Huistendahl. See, for example, Hiustendahl, X060.0 482, letter to Henry F. LaVoie, February 4, 1954.

20. Yves-Alain Bois, "Metamorphosis of Axonometry," *Daidalos* 1 (September 1981): 45, 48.

21. On the problem of noise from neighbors and lack of privacy in prewar housing conditions, and on fears about a return to those conditions, see Alan Ehrenhalt, *The Lost City: The Forgotten Virtues of Community in America* (New York: Basic Books/Harper Collins, 1995).

22. On the importance of privacy from neighbors in the postwar period, see Dianne Harris, "Making Your Private World: Modern Landscape Architecture and the *House Beautiful*, 1945–1965," in *The Architecture of Landscape, 1940–1960*, ed. Marc Treib (Philadelphia: University of Pennsylvania Press, 2002), 180–205. On the postwar cult of family togetherness, see Laura J. Miller, "Family Togetherness and the Suburban Ideal," *Sociological Forum* 10, no. 3 (1995): 393–418.

23. Sibley, *Geographies of Exclusion*, 14, 24. Undoubtedly derived, at least in part, from

European modernism of the 1920s and 1930s which showcased domestic interiors that were characterized by a sterile, white, laboratory aesthetic, postwar houses were similarly modeled on a European social reality that was largely divested of non-whites. Although this precedent deserves consideration, its complexity demands a separate essay. I thank Mirka Beneš for bringing this question to my attention.

24. Jenna Weissman Joselit, "A Set Table: Jewish Domestic Culture in the New World, 1880–1950," in *Getting Comfortable in New York: The American Jewish Home, 1880–1950*, ed. Susan L. Braunstein and Jenna Weissman Joselit (New York: Jewish Museum, 1990), 25, 27, 31. Joselit contends, however, that immigrants seldom acted on the expert's advice, preferring instead of clean lines and Mission furniture, the more ornate, heavy, and colorful aspects provided by traditional styles.

25. James A. Davis, "Cultural Factors in the Perception of Status Symbols," *Midwest Sociologist* 21, no. 1 (December 1958): 5–10. My thanks to Harvey Choldin for bringing this article to my attention.

26. From *Better Homes and Gardens Gardening Guide*, "Ever Really Look at Your Place? Sure you have—but lately? Have things gotten a bit out of line? Take an appraising look as you swing into your drive tomorrow" (6–7), Doug Baylis Collection [1999–4], Office Records/Clippings, Environmental Design Archives, University of California, Berkeley.

27. "Andrew Means: Steel City Builder," *Ebony*, January 1956, 52.

28. Kevin Fox Gotham, *Race, Real Estate, and Uneven Development: The Kansas City Experience, 1900–2000* (Albany: State University of New York Press, 2002).

29. Leon Paul, "I Live in a Negro Neighborhood," *Ebony*, June 1956, 47.

30. Mary Wright and Russel Wright, *Guide to Easier Living* (New York: Simon and Schuster, 1950; repr., 1951, 1954, 2003). Valerie Babb, *Whiteness Visible: The Meaning of Whiteness in American Literature and Culture* (New York: New York University Press, 1998), 160. On household advice manuals, see for example, Dena Attar, *A Bibliography of Household Books Published in Britain, 1800–1914* (London: Prospect Books, 1987); Caroline Davidson, *A Woman's Work is Never Done: A History of Housework in the British Isles, 1650–1950* (London: Chatto and Windus, 1986); Barbara Ehrenreich and Deirdre English, *For Her Own Good: 150 Years of the Expert's Advice to Women* (New York: Anchor/Doubleday, 1978).

31. Wright and Wright, *Guide to Easier Living*, 1954, 50.

32. On the desire to escape an "Okie" past, see also D. J. Waldie, *Holy Land: A Suburban Memoir* (New York: Norton and Company, 1996), 172–73.

33. See Matt Wrayle and Annalee Newitz, eds., *White Trash: Race and Class in America* (New York: Routledge, 1997). On "trailer trash" see also Andrew Hurley, *Diners, Bowling Alleys, and Trailer Parks: Chasing the American Dream in the Postwar Consumer Culture* (New York: Basic Books, 2001), 251–53.

34. Wright and Wright, *Guide to Easier Living*, 1954, 135, 154, 160.

35. Virginia Scott Jenkins, *The Lawn: A History of an American Obsession* (Washington, D.C.: Smithsonian Insitution Press, 1994), 128.

36. See M. Manring, *Slave in a Box: The Strange Career of Aunt Jemima* (Charlottesville: University of Virginia Press, 1998), 111–12.

37. Suellen Hoy, *Chasing Dirt: The American Pursuit of Cleanliness* (New York: Oxford University Press, 1995), chap. 6.

38. Wright and Wright, *Guide to Easier Living*, 1954, 106, 108, 111, 113.

39. "Washable Rooms," *Life*, May 18, 1953, 76.

40. Joseph Howland, *House Beautiful*, September 1950, 108, with quote from Thomas Church.

41. Elizabeth Mock, *If You Want to Build a House* (New York: Simon and Schuster, 1946), 17.

42. American Trust Company, San Francisco, *Things to Know About Buying or Building a Home* (San Francisco: American Trust Company, 1946).

43. Laura Lawson, *City Bountiful: Urban Garden Programs in American Cities, 1890s to Present* (Berkeley: University of California Press, 2005).

44. See Harris, "Making Your Private World."

45. On sociologists' fears of societal overconformity, see William H. Whyte, *The Organization Man* (New York: Doubleday, 1956); David Reisman, *The Lonely Crowd* (New Haven: Yale University Press, 1950); John Seeley, *Crestwood Heights: A Study of the Culture of Suburban Life* (New York: Basic Books, 1956); and John Keats, *The Crack in the Picture Window* (Boston: Houghton Mifflin, 1956).

46. "Five Ground Rules for Playing the National Pastime: The Most Beautiful Garden for the Least Work," *House Beautiful*, April 1958, 101; "Do You Know These 26 Time-Tested Work-Savers?" *House Beautiful*, April 1958, 230; "If You Pave it, You Don't Have to Mow It," *House Beautiful*, April 1959, 118–19; Thomas Church, "How Lazy You Are Should Dictate Your Garden Design," *House Beautiful*, June 1948, 112.

47. Wayne C. Lecky, "Unusual and Modern Ideas for Living Outdoors," *Popular Mechanics*, April 1959, 176.

48. Stuart Hall, Chas Critcher, Tony Jefferson, John Clarke, and Brian Roberts, *Policing the Crisis: Mugging, the State, and Law and Order* (New York: Holmes and Meir, 1978), 394; Paul Gilroy, *The Black Atlantic: Modernity and Double Consciousness* (Cambridge, Mass.: Harvard University Press, 1993), 85.

49. Brodkin, *How Jews Became White Folks*, 11.

50. Babb, *Whiteness Visible*, 199.

CONTRIBUTORS

DENIS COSGROVE is Alexander von Humboldt Professor of Geography at UCLA. His books include *Social Formation and Symbolic Landscape* (1984/1998), *The Palladian Landscape* (1993), *Apollo's Eye* (2003), and *Mappings* (1999). A collection of essays on *Geography and Vision* will appear in 2007.

DIANE FAVRO is professor and acting chair of the Department of Architecture and Urban Design at UCLA. Her work focuses on Roman urban environments and experiences, as well as on the research and educational applications of digital technology for architectural history. She is the author of *The Urban Image of Augustan Rome* (1984), and the director of the UCLA Experiential Technologies Center and former president of the Society of Architectural Historians.

DIANNE HARRIS is professor of landscape architecture, architecture, art history, and history at the University of Illinois, Urbana-Champaign. She is the author of *The Nature of Authority: Villa Culture, Landscape, and Representation in Eighteenth-Century Lombardy* (2003), and *Maybeck's Landscapes: Drawing in Nature* (2005). She is coeditor of *Villas and Gardens in Early Modern Italy and France* (2001), and editor of a forthcoming volume on the Pennsylvania Levittown. She is currently working on a book about race, class, and ordinary postwar houses in the United States.

DAVID L. HAYS is assistant professor of landscape architecture at the University of Illinois at Urbana-Champaign. His research concerns gardens of late-eighteenth century France as well as contemporary theory and practice of landscape architecture. In fall 2004, he was the guest editor of *306090 07: Landscape within Architecture*.

SANDY ISENSTADT teaches the history of modern architecture in Yale University's Department of the History of Art. His book, *The Modern American House: Spaciousness and Middle-Class Identity*, a study of visual space in the architectural, interior, and landscape design of American houses, was published in 2006.

MARTIN JAY is Sidney Hellman Ehrman Professor of History at the University of California, Berkeley. Among his works are *The Dialectical Imagination* (1973 and 1996), *Marxism and Totality* (1984), *Adorno* (1984), *Permanent Exiles* (1985); *Fin-de-Siècle Socialism* (1989), *Force Fields* (1993), *Downcast Eyes* (1993), *Cultural Semantics* (1998), *Refractions of Violence* (2003), and *Songs of Experience* (2004). He is currently working on a book on lying in politics.

ELIZABETH KRYDER-REID is associate professor of anthropology and director of the Museum Studies Program, Indiana University School of Liberal Arts, IUPUI. Dr. Kryder-Reid has published on landscape archaeology and historic gardens in the Chesapeake. Her current work is on California mission landscapes.

W. J. T. MITCHELL is professor of English and art history at the University of Chicago, and editor of *Critical Inquiry*. His books include *Iconology* (1986), *Picture Theory* (1994), *The Last Dinosaur Book* (1998), and *What Do Pictures Want?* (2005). He is working on a new book entitled *Cloning Terror*.

D. FAIRCHILD RUGGLES is an associate professor in the Department of Landscape Architecture at the University of Illinois, Urbana-Champaign. In addition to several edited works, she is the author of the award-winning *Gardens, Landscape, and Vision in the Palaces of Islamic Spain* (2000) and a new comprehensive volume on Islamic gardens, *Islamic Gardens and Landscapes*, forthcoming in 2007.

MARC TREIB is professor of architecture at the University of California, Berkeley, and a practicing designer. He is the editor of *Thomas Church, Landscape Architect* (2004) and author of *The Donnell and Eckbo Gardens: Modern Californian Masterworks* (2005), *Settings and Stray Paths: Writings on Landscape Architecture* (2005), and other works.

INDEX